Restorative Justice in Legal Systems,
Education, and the Community

of related interest

Becoming a Trauma-informed Restorative Educator
Practical Skills to Change Culture and Behavior
Joe Brummer and Marg Thorsborne
Foreword by Dr. Lori L. Desautels
ISBN 978 1 83997 568 4
eISBN 978 1 83997 569 1

Violence, Restorative Justice and Forgiveness
Dyadic Forgiveness and Energy Shifts in Restorative Justice Dialogue
Marilyn Armour and Mark Umbreit
ISBN 978 1 78592 795 9
eISBN 978 1 78450 795 4

A Real-World Guide to Restorative Justice in Schools
Practical Philosophy, Useful Tools, and True Stories
Nicholas Bradford and David Lesal
ISBN 978 1 78775 571 0
eISBN 978 1 78775 572 7

Restorative Justice in Legal Systems, Education, and the Community

Reflections On What Works,
Where We Can Grow, and What's Next

Edited by
Dr. SANDRA PAVELKA and ANNE SEYMOUR

Foreword by
Dr. Mark Umbreit

Jessica Kingsley Publishers
London and Philadelphia

First published in Great Britain in 2024 by Jessica Kingsley Publishers
An imprint of John Murray Press

1

Copyright © Jessica Kingsley Publishers 2024

The right of Sandra Pavelka and Anne Seymour to be identified as the Author of the Work has been asserted by them in accordance with the Copyright, Designs and Patents Act 1988.

Foreword © Mark Umbreit 2024, Restorative Justice: From a Maximalist to a Consequential Vision © Lode Walgrave 2024, Restorative Justice Law and Policy © Sandra Pavelka and Carsten Erbe 2024, Community Justice © Dale Landry 2024, Mirror, Mirror, on the Wall… © Kay Pranis 2024, Balanced and Restorative Justice © Susan Blackburn 2024, School-Justice Partnerships © Steven Teske 2024, Mitigating Harm and Restoring Trust © Sydney Pidgeon and David Karp 2024, Readiness Assessments Matter © Martha Brown 2024, Measuring What Really Matters in Juvenile Justice © Douglas Thomas 2024, Guiding Principles and Restorative Practices for Crime Victims and Survivors © Sandra Pavelka and Anne Seymour 2024, Are We Serving Harmed People Well? © Ted Lewis 2024, The Evolution of a Brief Restorative Justice Intervention © Dennis E. McChargue, Sandra Pavelka and James Jones 2024, Dialogue Among Those Committing and Harmed by Crime © Jacob Otis and Mark Umbreit 2024, Restorative Justice and Gender Responsive Programming © Aggie Pappas 2024

Guiding Principles and Restorative Practices for Crime Victims and Survivors reprinted with kind permission from Pavelka, S. and Seymour, A. (2019) "Guiding principles and restorative practices for crime victims and survivors," *Corrections Today*, American Correctional Association.

All rights reserved. No part of this publication may be reproduced, stored in a retrieval system, or transmitted, in any form or by any means without the prior written permission of the publisher, nor be otherwise circulated in any form of binding or cover other than that in which it is published and without a similar condition being imposed on the subsequent purchaser.

A CIP catalogue record for this title is available from the British Library and the Library of Congress

ISBN 978 1 80501 251 1
eISBN 978 1 80501 252 8

Printed and bound in the United States by Integrated Books International

Jessica Kingsley Publishers' policy is to use papers that are natural, renewable and recyclable products and made from wood grown in sustainable forests. The logging and manufacturing processes are expected to conform to the environmental regulations of the country of origin.

Jessica Kingsley Publishers
Carmelite House
50 Victoria Embankment
London EC4Y 0DZ

www.jkp.com

John Murray Press
Part of Hodder & Stoughton Ltd
An Hachette Company

Contents

   Preface 7
   Dr. Sandra Pavelka and Anne Seymour

   Foreword 9
   Dr. Mark Umbreit

   Introduction 13

1. Restorative Justice: From a Maximalist to a
   Consequential Vision. 17
   Lode Walgrave

2. Restorative Justice Law and Policy: A Comparative Analysis
   of the United States and Canada 33
   Sandra Pavelka, PhD and Carsten Erbe

3. Community Justice: The Village Model, a Definitive
   Restorative Community Justice Model 51
   Dale Landry

4. Mirror, Mirror, on the Wall.... 63
   Kay Pranis

5. Balanced and Restorative Justice: Not Simply a Buzzword in
   Pennsylvania. 73
   Susan Blackburn

6. School-Justice Partnerships: Building a Safe and Healthy
   Community through Restorative Justice 95
   Judge Steven Teske (Ret.)

7. Mitigating Harm and Restoring Trust: A Restorative Justice
   Approach to Campus Policing 121
   Sydney Pidgeon and David Karp

8. Readiness Assessments Matter: A Case Study of Two US Middle Schools' Organizational Capacity to Implement Restorative Justice in Education 141
   Martha Brown, PhD

9. Measuring What Really Matters in Juvenile Justice: An American Case Study. 175
   Douglas Thomas

10. Guiding Principles and Restorative Practices for Crime Victims and Survivors 199
    Sandra Pavelka, PhD and Anne Seymour

11. Are We Serving Harmed People Well? Assessing Challenges and Opportunities in Restorative Work Regarding Criminal Victimization. 219
    Ted Lewis

12. The Evolution of a Brief Restorative Justice Intervention 239
    Dennis E. McChargue, PhD, Sandra Pavelka, PhD and James Jones

13. Dialogue Among Those Committing and Harmed by Crime: Five Decades of Practice and Research 251
    Jacob Otis and Mark Umbreit, PhD

14. Restorative Justice and Gender-Responsive Programming: A Blended Approach for Girls and Young Women in Diversion . . 271
    Aggie Pappas

    Reflections 295

    Subject Index 297

    Author Index 302

Preface

DR. SANDRA PAVELKA AND ANNE SEYMOUR

Our individual and collective road to restorative justice in America has been bumpy, beautiful, and filled with chances to pave over existing roads of justice, and in some cases injustice, with hope and healing, and bridge timely and critical new roads.

To us, restorative justice is about options and opportunities. The traditional systems of criminal justice and juvenile justice have often been rigid and restrictive in terms of allowing justice-involved individuals, victims and survivors, and community members to have a voice and choice in ways to strengthen community safety and, at the same time, address the myriad root causes of crime and delinquency.

Dr. Gordon Bazemore was a true visionary and trailblazer in the restorative justice movement. His insightful and eloquent writings in restorative justice, youth development, and justice reform are known worldwide. Academics, researchers, practitioners, advocates, and believers of restorative justice have all been influenced, knowingly and unknowingly, by Gordon's writings and work. Gordon was beloved by all of those who were truly blessed to connect with him and work in his universe, just knowing that our collective journey would be a true adventure with amazing, evidence-based outcomes and lasting friendships.

The Balanced and Restorative Justice (BARJ) Project, funded by the Office of Juvenile Justice and Delinquency Prevention, US Department of Justice, in the 1990s and early 2000s was instrumental in the development and implementation of restorative justice in a number of dedicated, special emphasis states. The emergence of restorative justice offered an alternative to simply building more prisons, juvenile residential facilities, and juvenile detention centers, and lingering at the "tail-end" of justice processes to act. Gordon helped us realize that, together – judges, victim/survivor advocates, prosecutors, defense attorneys, probation, law enforcement, and others – we could be proactive in seriously addressing crime and delinquency with a more holistic and preventative approach that is personal, and that reflects and respects each person involved in justice processes: those who cause harm; those who are harmed; and members of the community. The journey of restorative justice has since expanded and evolved to the current day, with a highly positive future enhanced by those who have the most to gain from restorative justice practices, policies, and laws.

When our beloved dear friend and colleague, the late Dennis Maloney, former Director of the Community Justice Department of Deschutes County, Oregon, trained across our Nation, he had an overhead transparency—long before the days of PowerPoints—that showed the image below, with this important message:

The true beauty of restorative justice is its grass roots impetus, trusting in the "roots" of individual and community-based responses to crime, in a respectful manner embedded in dedicated partnerships that commit to effectively prevent, respond to, and address the impact of crime and delinquency in a more holistic manner than that offered by traditional justice systems.

Nothing grows from the top down.

Our special thanks are extended to our Research Assistant, Devor Rodabaugh, whose careful and concise assistance with editing and reference formatting was truly masterful.

We are grateful to the trailblazing authors who contributed their research and experiences to this book, and who paved the path for our continuing journey to restorative justice.

Much love and peace,
Dr. Sandra Pavelka and Anne Seymour

Foreword

DR. MARK UMBREIT

Dr. Gordon Bazemore embodied passion for juvenile justice reform in his broader commitment to restorative justice for all those who have been harmed by criminal behavior and those causing the harm and the communities affected. While Dr. Bazemore was a distinguished professor, researcher, and author of many publications, some of which I co-authored, it is important to first acknowledge the kind, gentle, creative, and humorous spirit of his presence among friends and colleagues.

The authors of each chapter in this book bear witness to the legacy and impact of his life's work in truly promoting a more balanced and restorative approach to serving those most directly affected by crime (victims/survivors, offenders, families, and communities) and inviting their participation in the process of holding offenders accountable but also fostering healing among all involved in the wake of crime and its many impacts. Some authored or contributed to monographs published and distributed by the Balanced and Restorative Justice (BARJ) Project. Many of us contributed to or led training seminars or presentations at regional and national BARJ conferences across the country.

I first met Gordon in the late 1980s when he invited me to be a partner with several other colleagues in designing a whole new approach to doing justice, building upon the pioneering work of our late friend and colleague Dennis Maloney, in advocating the balanced approach to juvenile justice, focusing on accountability, competency development, and community safety. From our first phone conversation to our first meeting with the Office of Juvenile Justice and

Delinquency Prevention (OJJDP) in Washington, DC years later, I advocated the importance of adding the principles and practices of restorative justice, based on my many years of involvement in the restorative justice movement. I will never forget our initial meeting with a Program Officer at OJJDP.

Humor is part of my earliest fond memories of Gordon, who I did not yet know well. Sitting in a conference room at the US Department of Justice, OJJDP in Washington, DC, Gordon, two other colleagues, and I were a bit anxious, having never met in person or worked together as a team. We began with introductions and discussing the broad hopes and objectives for this entirely new approach to justice with an OJJDP official who was considering generous multi-year funding for this new nationwide initiative. We then had a discussion of what should be the title for this new initiative as required on the grant application. How could we blend the names of "the balanced approach" (already quite well known among juvenile justice practitioners) and "Restorative Justice?"

Each of us offered thoughts about a possible name. None fitted well. As we sat back, a bit frustrated, a moment of quiet came upon us and Gordon, in a very serious tone, offered a solution: the BARF Project, Balanced and Restorative Forever. What an ice breaker! After many laughs and some further consideration, we came up with the name for the project, BARJ, Balanced and Restorative Justice. BARJ later connected well with policymakers and practitioners and the project was funded for nearly 10 years, an exceptionally long funding period for OJJDP. Many states today have reference to BARJ in state legislation, and programs in many cities still bear the legacy of Gordon's BARF.

Gordon was not just the wit but also the brains behind the development of BARJ, with a great deal of savvy in working with federal funding sources. His passion for BARJ principles and practices was evident any time he gave presentations or lectures in classes or conferences. I was honored to be asked to serve as a co-principal investigator with him on the OJJDP grant that launched the BARJ Project, with us representing both Florida Atlantic University and the University of Minnesota. Together we co-authored numerous monographs and journal articles. We also collaborated on numerous regional and national conferences and seminars.

Working with Gordon was a joy. I miss the presence of my dear friend and colleague. The nationwide BARJ movement involving many thousands of practitioners and policymakers has lost a founding pioneer of the movement and a tremendously influential mentor and friend.

Mark Umbreit, PhD
Professor Emeritus
School of Social Work
University of Minnesota,
Founding Director Emeritus
Center for Restorative Justice & Peacemaking
University of Minnesota

Introduction

This edited collection of internationally distinguished contributors reflects on the wealth of research that has been accumulated in the restorative justice field, along with their perspectives and experiences, and the overall evolution of restorative justice. These authors were all, at one point, colleagues of the late Dr. Gordon Bazemore, to whom this book is dedicated, and a significant part of the restorative justice journey.

The book chapters are sequenced from a macro-level to a micro-level perspective, addressing matters in the legal system, education, and the community, beginning with "Restorative Justice: From a Maximalist to a Consequential Vision," in which Dr. Lode Walgrave offers a maximalist agenda for restorative justice, rooted in his work with the late Dr. Gordon Bazemore. Dr. Sandra Pavelka and Carsten Erbe, in "Restorative Justice Law and Policy: A Comparative Analysis of the United States and Canada," conduct a comparative analysis of the international legal systems and analyze restorative justice law and policy specifically relating to legislative mandate, mechanism, machinery, mode, and multiculturalism. "Community Justice: The Village Model, a Definitive Restorative Community Justice Model" by Dale Landry offers the community justice model, first outlined in "Bringing Justice Back to the Community" by O'Brien et al. (2003). This model emphasizes how involving community residents as mutual collaborative partners in developing a restorative community response to crime provides a means for the community to take an active role in identifying the issues contributing to criminal and harmful behaviors, community involvement in response to criminal and other harmful behaviors, and providing the necessary community resources to help those impacted by crime and harmful behavior.

Following, "Mirror, Mirror, on the Wall..." by Kay Pranis explores an aspect of restorative justice with young people in trouble with the law, whether incarcerated or in the community, and the question "Who needs to change for the wellbeing of us all?" is posed. Pranis supports the circle process, a space for practicing community, based on universal human dignity, human worth, and voice. Susan Blackburn then reviews the implementation of Balanced and Restorative Justice in Pennsylvania's statutory mission, the related operational goals through policy, practice, and programmatic enhancements that transformed the state's juvenile justice systems, and the ongoing efforts to sustain its mission in "Balanced and Restorative Justice: Not Simply a Buzzword in Pennsylvania."

Judge Steven Teske (Ret.) reflects on his impactful work in "School-Justice Partnerships: Building a Safe and Healthy Community through Restorative Justice." Further, Sydney Pidgeon and Dr. David Karp, in "Mitigating Harm and Restoring Trust: A Restorative Justice Approach to Campus Policing," provide a case study of restorative policing on a university campus, offering a new vision for policing and safety on college and university campuses. Following along the education track, Dr. Martha Brown, in "Readiness Assessments Matter: A Case Study of Two US Middle Schools' Organizational Capacity to Implement Restorative Justice in Education," discusses the importance of readiness assessments, allowing schools and other organizations to determine their capacity and motivation for change and to decide whether they have the structure and strengths needed to successfully implement a complex initiative like restorative justice in education. In "Measuring What Really Matters in Juvenile Justice: An American Case Study," Douglas Thomas describes the legacy of *Measuring What Really Matters in Juvenile Justice* (Bazemore 2006), which exceeded its original purpose and provided a defensible basis for a unique approach to measuring performance in juvenile justice.

Dr. Sandra Pavelka and Anne Seymour, in "Guiding Principles and Restorative Practices for Crime Victims and Survivors," offer a historical perspective of the United States' crime victim and survivor assistance field and its role in restorative justice as well as six guiding principles for victim- and survivor-focused restorative justice. Ted Lewis presents recent changes in our understanding of victimhood as not only a set of challenges to restorative dialogue work but also as opportunities for growth and holistic services within the North American context in "Are We Serving Harmed People Well? Assessing Challenges and Opportunities in Restorative Work Regarding Criminal Victimization."

Dr. Dennis McChargue, Dr. Sandra Pavelka, and James Jones discuss their research in "The Evolution of a Brief Restorative Justice Intervention," which has shown effectiveness in studies on restorative justice interventions with meta-analytic data in both youth and adult offenders indicating, on average, a reduction in repeat offending, and victim and offender satisfaction. Jacob Otis and Dr. Mark Umbreit offer a summary of 50 years of research on the most empirically substantiated form of restorative justice—victim offender mediation. Our last chapter, "Restorative Justice and Gender-Responsive Programming: A Blended Approach for Girls and Young Women in Diversion," by Aggie Pappas, describes how the Pace Center for Girls has blended restorative justice and gender-responsive approaches by developing a girl-focused, gender-specific juvenile diversion and civil citation program in Broward County, Florida, and explores the connections between restorative justice practices and gender-responsive programming to reduce recidivism while improving girls' lives, supporting long-term positive outcomes and a healing experience benefiting the community.

References

Bazemore, G. (2006) "Measuring What Really Matters in Juvenile Justice," Alexandria, VA: American Prosecutors Research Institute.

O'Brien, S., Maloney, D., Landry, D., and Costello, D. (2003) "Bringing Justice Back to the Community," *Juvenile and Family Court Journal*, 54, no. 3.

— Chapter 1 —

Restorative Justice

From a Maximalist to a Consequential Vision

LODE WALGRAVE, PHD

A "Maximalist Agenda"

In 1999, Gordon Bazemore and I proposed a "maximalist agenda for restorative justice" (Bazemore and Walgrave 1999, p.7). Our objective was to divert the system from its retributive and/or treatment focus towards a steadfast priority for restorative responses. Our ideal was a "fully-fledged, systemic alternative to both the retributive and the social welfare responses to crime" which would offer:

> as many legal safeguards as the traditional criminal justice system. But it should be socially more constructive, provide more standing and support for crime victims, and offer (at a minimum) no fewer opportunities for offender reintegration and rehabilitation than systems grounded in individual treatment assumptions. (Bazemore and Walgrave 1999, pp.363-4)

We defined restorative justice as "every action that is primarily oriented towards doing justice by repairing the harm that has been caused by a crime" (Bazemore and Walgrave 1999, p.48). This definition is clearly outcome-focused and also includes the possibility of reparative judicial sanctions under the restorative justice umbrella.

The reception of this maximalist version of restorative justice was not enthusiastic, to say the least. On the contrary, it was subjected to severe criticisms. The main fear was that including coercive sanctions would betray the initial restorative approach and open the floor for—possibly alternative—new types of punishments. The original purpose of imposing sanctions with a view on reparation would soon fade away to become punishments *tout court* (McCold 2000), landing restorative justice in the trap of an imitator paradox (Pavlich 2005).

Bifurcation

Since its reappearance at the end of the twentieth century, restorative justice developed in different versions or trends. One of the most salient dividing lines is its relationship with the justice system. A very strong driver for the emergence of restorative justice is deep dissatisfaction with the criminal justice system as it functions nowadays. Therefore, several scholars emphasize a clear distinction between restorative justice and criminal justice. Christie (1977, 2013), McCold (2000), Pavlich (2005), Schiff and Hooker (2019), Llewellyn (2021), and other prominent scholars reject criminal justice's coercive potentials, its rigid (ab)use of power, making it distant from "real life," and they try to loosen as much as possible the connection with the criminal justice system.

To underline the contrast, the focus is pointed to the quality of the encounter between the direct stakeholders. For many, the respectful, inclusive dialogue is the key to characterize restorative justice, excluding the use of coercion from any restorative justice approach (Hoyle 2010; Marshall 1996; McCold 2000). It may still be the current mainstream vision on restorative justice.

The rejection of the top-down approach in criminal justice and the option for the dialogic encounter model is grounded in values. Braithwaite (2002), Van Ness and Heetderks Strong (2006), Pranis (2007), Kirkwood (2022), and others pay extensive attention to the values underlying the option for restorative justice.

It is of course important to be more explicit about the underlying values, the social ethical roots of restorative justice. But identifying restorative justice with these values is problematic. It leads to a one-sided view of restorative justice through the inclusive processes only and to the link with justice being played down. A few publications even reject the notion "justice" (as in Christie 2013; Schiff and Hooker 2019).

Where do these lists of values come from? Why do we value, for example, respect, individual dignity, inclusion, or making amends? Because we have a certain image, an ideal of how humans should relate to each other and how our living together should be governed. It is this ideal we must search after. We must explore the binding ideology or ethical belief, the underlying reason why we find these values important.

We will see then that respect, individual dignity, inclusion, and the other often-quoted values are also extremely desirable to steer social relations and institutions in general. They are not the monopoly of restorative justice. It is not these values that make the particularity of restorative justice. It is the fact that these values converge on the pursuit of an outcome: doing justice through restoration, as Gordon and I argued in 1999 (Bazemore and Walgrave 1999).

Hence, we should not be too perseverant in an exclusive attachment to the process and focus more on the objectives. For several reasons, a purely process-based view of restorative justice cannot hold out.

First, valorizing a process without knowing the objective it seeks to achieve is like pedaling in the air. Respectful inclusive processes after an injustice are not good on their own. For example, we cannot rely on "inclusive respectful dialogue" to stop a shoot-out in a school or a terrorist attack. Sometimes, a prompt and strong reaction is necessary. However, the dialogue is preferable, if possible, because it may yield more socially constructive outcomes. It facilitates (expressions of) respect and support, mutual understanding, regret, willingness to make up, and willingness to accept it. These are restorative outcomes. If the process does not facilitate these attitudes and emotions, it has failed to be a restorative process.

Second, much of the reticence towards restorative justice among victims' advocates is based on the purely process-based view. Characterizing restorative justice only through the process, without a clear reference to the objective to repair, may deviate. Prominent victimologists express their fear that de-emphasizing the restorative objective and emphasizing unilaterally the process may lead to subordinating the victims' needs and interests to the needs for rehabilitation of the offender (Pemberton 2019; Wemmers 2020). The victim's story may be used as a "pedagogical tool" to confront the offender, not to genuinely understand the victim's suffering and needs and to determine appropriate restorative actions.

Third, the process-focused view keeps restorative justice interventions at the margins. Unless one believes that we shall soon live in a natural park with good-willed people only, the possibility of coercion remains indispensable in the response to many offenses. No society can do without the possibility of using coercion, if necessary. Instead of leaving this issue to the existing criminal justice system, restorative justice scholars must seek a balanced relation with this unavoidable system. They must make "their hands dirty" and include the judicial responses in the restorative reflection. The aim is curbing the judicial coercion also in a more constructive restorative/reparative orientation, through responses which maximize their possible reparative/restorative impact, while safeguarding the rights of the stakeholders.

Not facing this difficult but unavoidable relationship with the justice system is much like an escapist attitude, avoiding the most difficult aspect of developing restorative justice in society. Restorative justice scholars must not behave like ostriches. When the good intentions confront the thorny aspects of reality, the challenge is to find out how to achieve as much as possible of the good intentions while living with the thorns.

Taking the Fork

The discussion described briefly above has been characterized as the purist approach to restorative justice versus the maximalist approach (McCold 2000). One could say that, confronted with this bifurcation in the restorative justice road, Gordon Bazemore and I took the fork. On the one hand, our "maximalist" vision of restorative justice aimed at transforming the criminal justice system. The currently evident orientation to inflicting an appropriate proportionate punishment on the offender must be changed into a systematic priority for seeking reparative/restorative outcomes. But on the other hand, we also understand that respectful, inclusive encounters among the direct stakeholders represent the most appropriate tool for achieving the fullest possible restoration. Like the mainstream conception, we promote restorative processes as much as possible. Unlike the mainstream conception, we push the restorative/reparative philosophy through in the judicial system, if such processes are not possible.

An Espresso-Definition

The maximalist option of restorative justice has remained the guideline for my own pathway through restorative justice. I fine-tuned our earlier definition and specified it as "an option for doing justice after the occurrence of an offence that is primarily oriented towards repairing the individual, relational and social harm caused by that offence" (Walgrave 2008, p.21).

I have called it an "espresso-definition." Like an espresso, it is strong, because it penetrates the judicial response to crime, but also short, because it is limited to doing justice after an offense. Obviously, this is an atypical approach compared to the mainstream vision. It deviates on two issues. First, it characterizes restorative justice by the outcome it pursues, and not by the process that is used to achieve restoration. The arguments for this outcome-focused approach have been briefly developed in a previous section.

Second, the option to keep restorative justice within the limits of responding to offending is opposite to a currently strong movement to extend the notion to other social fields and even as a philosophy to transform the way social life is governed (as for example in Llewellyn 2021; Sullivan and Tifft 2006). While I am a dedicated partner with the many social movements aiming for more just, more respectful, and more solidary social relations and institutions, I prefer to avoid stretching the concept restorative justice too much (Walgrave 2023). I shall develop my arguments for this later in this chapter.

From "Maximalist" to "Consequential"

For Gordon Bazemore and me, the addition "maximalist" would indicate that restorative justice does not stop when dialogic processes cannot be achieved and a referral to judicial coercion is considered. In our maximalist view, also the judicial system itself should be penetrated by restorative justice principles.

However, it appeared through the years that the label "maximalist" was often misunderstood. It sounds very ambitious, suggesting that we claimed a monopoly, whereas we wanted to emphasize the priority of the option. Priority does not equal monopoly. Our maximalist approach did not push forward restorative responses to all cases in all situations, without exceptions. What we wanted to express is that the potentials of restorative justice must always be considered and always be given priority if possible. The addition "if possible" includes that it may also be not possible. Limits to the reach of restorative justice are accepted and explored.

Another misunderstanding is that "maximalist" was seen as a complete reparation, erasing all negative consequences of the offense. That is of course impossible. Some crimes leave indelible harm and suffering. A murdered person cannot return. Some events leave ineffaceable traumas. We pursue reparation that goes as far as possible while recognizing that wounds can leave scars. Restorative justice then helps victims who are suffering from such losses to live a meaningful and satisfying life despite the remaining consequences of the crime.

It brought me to look for another label than "maximalist" (Walgrave 2021). In my understanding (as a non-native speaker), "consequential" is more nuanced. It indicates more accurately what is meant: consequentially giving priority to restorative responses wherever and whenever it is possible, also if (relatively) free deliberation among the main stakeholders appears not to be possible for one reason or another. Indeed, the arguments for the principled option for restorative justice do not fade away if a crime is very serious. On the contrary, the suffering and commotion may be higher after serious crimes, so that the need for reparation is higher as well. Also, if a restorative dialogue appears to be impossible or undesirable, the need for reparation in the victim may persist, or the willingness in the offender to make amends may remain. But instead of a direct dialogue, other methods may be used, including the judicial imposition of obligations with reparative purposes.

"Consequential" also includes the acceptance of limits that are intrinsically linked to the conceptualization of restorative justice, just like the punitive and the rehabilitative responses also have their limits. Restorative justice is not the panacea against all social evils. At least two limits are recognized: (1) imminent threats to public safety can overrule the wish to give priority to restorative responses; and (2) the reduced mental capacity or a particular mental disposition of (one of the) stakeholders may limit or exclude the possibilities to straightforwardly go for a restorative process.

Consequential Restorative Justice Includes Reparative Sanctions

The priority for inclusive, respectful dialogue among the direct stakeholders also applies to consequential restorative justice. Well-conducted encounters may indeed open the pathway toward a powerful sequence of moral emotions and exchanges, leading to a common understanding of the harm and suffering caused and to an agreement on how to make amends (Harris, Walgrave and Braithwaite 2004; Suzuki and Yuan 2021). In both victim and offender, the chances for a sense of procedural justice (Tyler 2006), satisfaction, and compliance with the agreements are significantly higher than after a traditional judicial procedure.

However, consequential restorative justice goes beyond the process. If a direct dialogue cannot happen, the reparative orientation is consequentially pursued in the coercive criminal justice intervention, which must also prioritize the possible reparative effects of its action. The consequential option tries to curb the current punitive premise toward a priority for reparative interventions, including reparative sanctions. That requires a "new architecture" of the system (Mazzucato 2017). How that would look is a matter of ongoing reflection (Braithwaite 2002; Claessen 2020; Dignan 2002; Mazzucato 2017; Rossner 2019; Walgrave 2021).

Many questions remain. In earlier publications, I have discussed two of the most crucial ones (Walgrave 2021 and 2022). (1) Are these reparative sanctions alternatives to punishment, or are they alternative punishments, as Duff (1992) or Daly (2002) assume and McCold (2000) fears? (2) How does a restorative criminal justice system relate to conventional criminal justice?

Punishment?

Calling reparative sanctions punishments rests upon a double confusion.

First, all important definitions of criminal punishment (as in Hart 1960 or von Hirsch 1993) include the intentional infliction of pain as one of the key characteristics. Reparative sanctions do not intentionally inflict pain. The reparative obligation is not imposed to make the actor suffer, but because it is a logical and social consequence of the harmful act, they are accountable. There is an essential difference between obliging someone to repair or compensate for the damage caused, which may be painful, and intentionally imposing pain as a kind of streamlined revenge. This difference is even recognized in conventional criminal justice where civil compensations may be added to punishments.

Second, punishment and restoration are at different levels. Punishment is a means, while restoration/reparation is a goal. Punishment in conventional criminal justice is an act of power chosen *a priori* to express disapproval, possibly to enforce compliance. In contrast, restoration/reparation is not a tool, but a pursued outcome. To restore a broad range of harm, suffering, and commotion a variety of social and legal tools may be chosen, such as dialogue, persuasion, social pressure, and reparative sanctions. Theoretically, punishment could also be a tool for reparation, but ample research has made clear that it is not an effective tool for it.

The clear distinction between reparative sanctions and punishment is necessary for socio-ethical considerations. Having to comply with painful social obligations is part of life. But all ethical systems reject intentionally inflicting pain on another person unless it is necessary for some higher purpose. The "golden rule" not to do to others what you would not want others to do to you (Claessen 2010; London 2011) is applicable also in judging how to respond to criminal behavior. Psychologically, anger and revenge are understandable emotions, but the inclination to inflict pain on the offender is ineffective and unethical (Nussbaum 2016), certainly if it is inflicted rationally by state institutions.

Consequential Restorative Justice and the Law

While consequential restorative justice opts for the least possible coercion, and for the most possible inclusive dialogue among the direct stakeholders, it also examines what to do if such a process cannot take place, and the option arises to activate the coercive institutional power to enforce a response that should be as reparative as possible.

Current criminal justice is guided by a series of principles such as equality, presumption of innocence, due process, proportionality, and others. They are meant to safeguard the rights of defendants and other players in a procedure that usually ends in the infliction of punishment. But restorative justice conceptualizes the essentials of crime differently, aims at different goals, involves other key actors, uses dissimilar means, and operates in a distinct social and juridical context. Consequently, the current principles of the punitive system need to be reconsidered and possibly revised. One cannot play American football with the rules of soccer. The principles must be focused at safeguarding the rights of the participants in a procedure with ample space for restorative deliberation among the stakeholders and pursuing reparative outcomes.

Basically, two axioms must be respected in both conventional criminal justice and restorative criminal justice: (1) equivalence of all citizens before the law and (2) protection of all citizens against abuse of power by social institutions and by co-citizens.

The platform on which to erect the legal construct for restorative justice is seeing restorative justice as a kind of inversed constructive retributivism (Baehler 2007; Walgrave 2008; Zehr 2002). Retribution is based on three components: the rejection of the act, the indication of a responsible actor and the attempt to re-install a balance. Both punitive and restorative responses to law-breaking hold these components, but in a different inversed way.

Restorative justice unambiguously disapproves of the criminal act. But contrary to conventional criminal justice, restorative justice includes the reasons for the disapproval in its intervention, confronting the offender with the harm their conduct has caused. Restorative censuring thus refers to the obligation to respect the quality of social life, rather than making the simple observation that a punishable offense has been committed.

Conventional justice submits the offender to the punitive consequences imposed by the system. Their responsibility is passive. Restorative justice relies on active responsibility. The offender is invited (under pressure) to take active responsibility by making gestures of restoration. Eventually, an imposed sanction may require an active contribution to (symbolic) reparation. The active responsibility is retrospectively invoked because of the act committed in the past, but the response is prospectively taken with a view on the quality of social relations in the future.

Punitive retributivism is supposed to take away the illegitimate advantages by inflicting on the offender a proportionate amount of suffering. As a result, the amount of suffering is doubled, but equally spread. Restorative justice, on the contrary, aims to reduce or compensate for the suffering and damage: "Because crime hurts, justice should heal" (Braithwaite 2005, p.296). Hence, the idea of restorative justice as reversed retribution. Instead of "just desserts," one could speak now of "just due." Restorative justice asks what debt the offender has taken on by the criminal act and what they can reasonably do to redeem it.

In sum, restorative justice is clear in its censuring and in the indication of the offender's responsibility. But its objective is to reduce the amount of suffering instead of increasing it. Recognizing restorative justice as inversed retributivism connects it to its retrospective dimension. It is the ground on which judicial guarantees can be constructed.

Consequential Restorative Justice and the Transformative Agenda

Several colleagues involve the innovative potentials of restorative justice as a drive for "transformative justice" aiming at the transformation of social relations and structures (Braithwaite 2022; Llewellyn 2021; Sullivan and Tifft 2006). Their argument is that restorative justice addressing only individual cases fails to include the structural injustices grounding the current criminal justice system and the social-structural dimensions of individual criminalized problems. They seek a coalition with emancipation movements to remove the consequences of structural injustices, based on racism, gender or socio-economic inequalities, and colonialism.

Different Endeavors

However, repairing the consequences of structural inequality is not the same as repairing the harms caused by an offense. These injustices go back in socio-cultural history; the kind of harm is broader and more difficult to assess. Repairing structural injustices requires a broad, more fundamental investment in the longer term, a sustainable shift in social institutions and relations. Such emancipatory movements wage a long-lasting socio-cultural and political struggle, penetrating all aspects of social life. I consider myself a dedicated partner in this movement.

However, I find it difficult to grasp, in one "restorative justice" notion, restorative policy regarding structural inequalities together with systematic restorative responses to crime (Walgrave 2023). I do not see the advantage of joining them under one conceptual umbrella. On the one hand, emancipatory movements do not lose power if they are not included in "restorative justice." On the other, crime-focused restorative justice risks paying a high price if it were to be drowned in a very broad and vague movement. It would be strategically detrimental because it would lose its sharp focus and innovative appeal. And scientifically, vague notions cannot be researched accurately. Even theoretical constructions based on vague notions risk remaining shaky. Putting too much in a concept makes it empty of meaning.

Shared Values

That said, I strongly believe that restorative justice, even when it is focused only on responding to criminalizable matters, shares the social-ethical roots with these movements and that has great potentials for constructive partnerships.

First, together with other trends in criminology, restorative justice composes a "criminology of trust," underlining the crucial significance of respect, solidarity, equity, and active participation as fundamentals of all policy regarding crime, justice, and (un)safety, and by extension of the governance of social life in general (Walgrave 2021).

Second, restorative justice addresses one of the most delicate moments in societal life, when the potentials for deliberation are played out and coercion is to be considered. Restorative justice seeks to extend the approaches to crime and injustice that minimize the use of coercion and, if necessary, to keep it as socially constructive as possible. Restorative justice is an example of how a top-down sentencing machine can be reconceived as a bottom-up problem-solving system.

Third, restorative justice offers a constructive and inclusive response to individual expressions of structural injustices such as racist incidents, gender-related abuses, environmental crime, or massive tax fraud. In doing so, it illustrates the power of such attitude and approach.

Fourth, restorative justice encounters represent very powerful experiences for the participating stakeholders. The emotional process attempts to transform seemingly opposite interests into a ground of common interest. Participants learn that blaming the act is not the same as blaming the actor. They experience the strength of respectful dialogue, leading to more satisfying outcomes. Restorative justice experiences help to promote the values of respectful and solidary co-citizenship.

Restorative justice and social transformation are mutually reinforcing. A more strictly circumscribed restorative justice offers precise contributions to the wider social movements, while the transformative agenda remains a normative and motivational beacon for restorative justice advocates and practitioners. "The (restorative justice) brand is useful, but it is more powerful interconnected in a respectful way with the brands of other social movements" (Dzur 2020, p.145).

Epilogue

The option for a strictly focused but consequential approach to restorative justice is rooted in my earlier work with Gordon

Bazemore. If I remember well, Gordon and I met for the first time in Vienna, at the occasion of the World Congress of Criminology in 1996. We clicked personally, and we discovered common opinions on youth justice and on the then emerging interest in restorative justice. Our exchanges resulted in a project to compose a reader on restorative justice for juveniles. Several years ago, we had intensive written exchanges and we met regularly in person in Fort Lauderdale, in Leuven, or at the occasion of other conferences in San Diego, Dubrovnik, and more. Our long and deep discussions were also fuelled by the input of the chapters written by other authors such as John Braithwaite, Barry Feld, Susan Guarino, Curt Taylor Griffiths, Russ Immarigeon, Klaus Sessar, Dan Van Ness, Mark Umbreit, and Elmar Weitekamp. Looking back at this period, I think that our discussions fed by these contributions (and by the contacts with the authors) had a decisive impact on our development as restorative justice scholars.

But most essential was the personal climate between Gordon and me. I appreciated Gordon very much as a highly intelligent, insightful, and wise soulmate. Our talks were lubricated with friendship and respect and seasoned with great humor. I shall never forget the friendly (and even a bit shy) smile with which he sometimes confronted me with the inconsistency or the incompleteness of my ideas, and brought, in his deep and wide insights, his sensitivity.

The most important result was the volume *Restorative Juvenile Justice: Repairing the Harm of Youth Crime* (1999). The option for a maximalist approach to restorative justice we presented was certainly not mainstream at that time. I am fully aware that my tenacity to continue that track towards a consequential vision still deviates from the option taken by most of the restorative justice advocates, maybe especially in the US.

How would Gordon have reflected on it? He was sympathetic to my continuation of the maximalist track as elaborated in 2008, but the consequential vision of restorative justice goes further. I think that he would go a long way with my reasoning, but that he would be hesitating here and there. But what is sure is that Gordon would always be constructive and supportive in his critical approach. I miss the reflections of this wonderful man.

References

Baehler, K. (2007) "Justifying Restorative Justice." In G. Maxwell and J. Liu (eds) *Restorative Justice and Practices in New Zealand: Towards a Restorative Society*. Wellington: Institute of Policy Studies, Victoria University.

Bazemore, G. and Walgrave, L. (1999) "Restorative Juvenile Justice: In Search of Fundamentals and an Outline for Systemic Reform." In G. Bazemore and L. Walgrave (eds) *Restorative Justice for Juveniles: Repairing the Harm of Youth Crime*. Monsey, NY: Criminal Justice Press.

Braithwaite, J. (2002) *Restorative Justice and Responsive Regulation*. Oxford: Oxford University Press.

Braithwaite, J. (2005) "Between proportionality & impunity: confrontation => truth => prevention". *Criminology* 43 (2): 283-306. doi.org/10.1111/j.0011-1348.2005.00009.x

Braithwaite, J. (2022) *Macrocriminology and Freedom*. Canberra: ANU Press.

Christie, N. (1977) "Conflicts as property." *British Journal of Criminology 17*, 1, 1-15. doi.org/10.1093/oxfordjournals.bjc.a046783

Christie, N. (2013) "Words on words." *Restorative Justice: An International Journal 1*, 1, 15-19. doi.org/10.5235/20504721.1.1.15

Claessen, J. (2010) *Misdaad en straf: Een herbezinning op het strafrecht van mystiek perspectief*. Nijmegen: Wolf Legal Publishers.

Claessen, J. (2020) "Pleidooi voor en uitwerking van een maximalistisch herstelrecht." *Tijdschrift voor Herstelrecht 20*, 4, 18-30.

Daly, K. (2002) "Restorative justice: The real story." *Punishment & Society 4*, 1, 55-79. doi.org/10.1177/14624740222228464

Dignan, J. (2002) "Restorative Justice and the Law: The Case for an Integrated, Systemic Approach." In L. Walgrave (ed.) *Restorative Justice and the Law*. London: Willan Publishing.

Duff, A. (1992) "Alternatives to Punishment—or Alternative Punishments?" In W. Cragg (ed.) *Retributivism and its Critics*. Stuttgart: Franz Steiner Verlag.

Dzur, A. (2020) "A talk with John Braithwaite." *The International Journal of Restorative Justice 3*, 1, 132-146. doi.org/10.5553/TIJRJ/258908912020003001015

Harris, N., Walgrave, L., and Braithwaite, J. (2004) "Emotional dynamics in restorative conferences." *Theoretical Criminology 8*, 2, 191-210. doi.org/10.1177/1362480604042243

Hart, H.L.A. (1960) "Prolegomenon to the principles of punishment." *Proceedings of the Aristotelian Society 60*, 1, 1-26.

Hoyle, C. (2010) "The Case for Restorative Justice." In C. Cunneen and C. Hoyle (eds) *Debating Restorative Justice*. Oxford: Hart Publishing.

Kirkwood, S. (2022) "A practice framework for restorative justice." *Aggression and Violent Behaviour 63*. doi.org/10.1016/j.avb.2021.101688

Llewellyn, J. (2021) "Transforming restorative justice." *The International Journal of Restorative Justice 4*, 3, 374-395. doi.org/10.5553/TIJRJ.000096

London, R. (2011) *Crime, Punishment, and Restorative Justice: From the Margins to the Mainstream*. Boulder, CO: Lynne Rienner Publishers.

Marshall, T. (1996) "The Evolution of Restorative Justice in Britain." *European Journal of Criminal Policy and Research 4*, 4, 21-43. doi.org/10.1007/BF02736712

Mazzucato, C. (2017) "Restorative Justice and the Potential of 'Exemplarity': In Search of a 'Persuasive' Coherence Within Criminal Justice." In I. Aertsen and B. Pali (eds) *Critical Restorative Justice*. Oxford: Hart Publishing.

McCold, P. (2000) "Towards a holistic vision of restorative juvenile justice: A reply to the maximalist model." *Contemporary Justice Review 3*, 4, 357-414. www.researchgate.net/publication/292733753_Toward_a_holistic_vision_of_restorative_juvenile_justice_A_reply_to_the_maximalist_model

Nussbaum, M. (2016) *Anger and Forgiveness: Resentment, Generosity, Justice*. Oxford: Oxford University Press.

Pavlich, G. (2005) *Governing Paradoxes of Restorative Justice*. London: Glasshouse Press.

Pemberton, A. (2019) "Time for a rethink: Victims and restorative justice." *The International Journal of Restorative Justice 2*, 1, 13-33. doi.org/10.5553/IJRJ/258908912019002001002

Pranis, K. (2007) "Restorative Values." In G. Johnstone and D. Van Ness (eds) *Handbook of Restorative Justice*. London: Willan.

Rossner, M. (2019) "Restorative justice, anger, and the transformative energy of forgiveness." *International Journal of Restorative Justice 2*, 3, 368-384. doi.org/10.5553/IJRJ.000005

Schiff, M. and Anderson Hooker, D. (2019) "Neither boat nor barbeque: In search of new language to unleash the transformative possibility of restorative justice." *Contemporary Justice Review 22*, 3, 219-241. doi.org/10.1080/10282580.2019.1644624

Sullivan, D. and Tifft, L. (2006) "Introduction: The Healing Dimension of Restorative Justice: A One-world Body." In D. Sullivan and L. Tifft (eds) *Handbook of Restorative Justice*. London: Routledge.

Suzuki, M. and Xiaoyu, Y. (2021) "How does restorative justice work? A qualitative metasynthesis." *Criminal Justice and Behaviour 48*, 10, 1347-1365. http://dx.doi.org/10.1177/0093854821994622

Tyler, T. (2006) "Restorative justice and procedural justice: Dealing with rule breaking." *Journal of Social Issues 62*, 2, 307-326. doi.org/10.1111/j.1540-4560.2006.00452.x

Van Ness, D. and Heetderks Strong, K. (2006) *Restoring Justice: An Introduction to Restorative Justice*. Cincinnati, OH: Anderson Publishing.

von Hirsch, A. (1993) *Censure and Sanctions*. Oxford: Clarendon Press.

Walgrave, L. (2008) *Restorative Justice, Self-Interest and Responsible Citizenship*. Cullompton: Willan Publishing.

Walgrave, L. (2021) *Being Consequential About Restorative Justice*. The Hague: Eleven Publishing.

Walgrave, L. (2022) "Restorative Justice, Punishment, and the Law." In M. Altman (ed.) *The Palgrave Handbook on the Philosophy of Punishment*. Cham (CH): Springer (Palgrave-Macmillan Publishing).

Walgrave, L. (2023) "Concerns about the meaning of restorative justice: Time for a rethink." *The International Journal of Restorative Justice 6*, 3, 353-369.

Wemmers, J. (2020) "Restorative justice: How responsive to the victim is it?" *The International Journal of Restorative Justice 3*, 1 (April), 30-37. DOI:10.5553/TIJRJ/258908912020003001004

Zehr, H. (2002) *The Little Book of Restorative Justice*. Intercourse, PA: Good Books.

— Chapter 2 —

Restorative Justice Law and Policy

A Comparative Analysis of the United States and Canada

SANDRA PAVELKA, PHD and CARSTEN ERBE

To those who weren't lucky enough to know Gordon, there was always a slow and methodical approach to his mannerisms and thought. These were highly veiled in his presentation, but it was clear that there was larger processing afoot that would only reveal itself deeper into play. Tactically brilliant, presented in an offbeat manner, those who encountered him did not always know what they were being drawn into, but they knew a larger objective was in mind.

Working for the BARJ Project and for Gordon, we experienced this process firsthand. Despite his day-to-day challenges of work and the personal juggling of his life, he was always set on the larger objectives and the contributions he could make to it. His professional focus on evaluating for improvement, legislation for convening, practice from theory, and policy to action was seemingly entangled with his love of Elvis, enjoyment of basketball, and devoted attention to his wife and daughters. While his daily life was always a challenge, the slow and methodical person that was Gordon eventually won praise as an astute academic, prolific writer, and champion of restorative justice nationally and abroad. His loving family, strong friendships, and humble presence are what he, more importantly, left behind.

Gordon was a one-of-a-kind individual who could mix with any group, talk to any audience, and present long-standing words and guidance that people could take forward into their lives or work. His was a unique gift and one that warrants respect and legacy of inspiration as this book hopefully presents. A seminal figure, a gracious soul, and monumental contributor to restorative justice, "El Gordo" will always be.

Emergence of Restorative Justice in Law and Policy

Restorative justice has emerged as a standard in law and policy, while being considered a contemporary justice solution. Laws and policies incorporating restorative principles and practices have been developed and implemented, formally and informally, to varying degrees by countries internationally. As the shared political and cultural histories of the United States (US) and Canada are intertwined, so are their modern-day development of restorative justice law and policy. The authors will provide a comparative analysis of the legal systems in these two countries and analyze restorative justice law and policy specifically relating to "the 5 M's": legislative mandate, mechanism, machinery, mode, and multiculturalism.

The manifestation of restorative justice practices appears to have paradoxically developed against the main political and cultural forces in each country. Canada, with a formal policy of multiculturalism and pluralism, has embraced a more unicultural perspective of restorative justice, recognizing it almost exclusively as the domain of Indigenous people, despite the recognition that restorative justice is based on principles and values which are not exclusive to any particular worldview or culture. The American development of restorative justice appears to be rooted in pluralist cultures, reflected under the more dominant centralized state. Restorative justice models in the US have tailored their perspectives to consider Hispanic, Black, Mennonite, and other migrant origins. A comparison of these developments is warranted to assure that the core tenets of restorative justice are being respected and that outside factors are not subverting the restorative justice ethos and brand.

Within the context of the criminal justice system, restorative justice remains on the periphery of each country's operation. Nevertheless, there have been periodic breakthroughs of its place with both systems and its place within or parallel to the more dominant adversarial system. The mainstay of these opportunities exists within the juvenile justice systems and opportunities for diversion from the mainstream criminal justice structure. Notwithstanding the diversity and complexities of each system of justice and exploration of the models of restorative justice, development is necessary to understand the future opportunities that exist in the field and where the likely advancements are to occur.

Against the backdrop of this model development are two fundamentally diverse systems which impact the transformation on justice alternatives in different ways. Within the Canadian context, justice is highly uniform with a more centralized model with a sub-delegation of administrative authorities to the provinces and the territories, and where law and policy are positioned (Pavelka forthcoming). Within the US context, more autonomy and authority are delegated to the state and local levels, whereas the federal government plays a more functionally secondary level. This factor has impacted community-focused interventions in different ways, primarily by increasing opportunities for experimentation in more fragmented models but impinging on the capacity to implement where uniformity does not exist. Further, there is no federal law relating to restorative justice in the US, but rather, restorative justice and its concepts are cited in state laws or codes. In fact, the majority of states have referenced restorative justice language in statutes of code (Pavelka 2008, 2016). The comparisons of the US and Canadian dynamics are interesting in this domain in that they provide stark contrasts in justice models, despite their proximity and shared restorative justice origins.

Restorative Practices and Implementation

As the shared political and cultural histories of the US and Canada are intertwined, so is the modern-day development of restorative justice practices and implementation. From the earliest iterations of justice practiced by Native American and First Nation populations to the shared 1970s development of victim offender mediation practices, the US and Canada have had parallel visions practiced and implemented in different ways. Politically, Canada has had a strong colonial influence that has focused its government on peace, order, and good government with America based in the rejection of colonialism and with more focus on life, liberty, and the pursuit of happiness. Framed by their cultures, shared geography, and common cultural influences, restorative justice is both a microcosm and portal of the larger societal influences at play.

The modern iteration of restorative justice in many respects was grounded in Canada and exported to the US. Circle sentencing, for example, was rediscovered and reinvigorated in the Yukon (Stuart 1996) and exported to the US via Minnesota and later Hawaii. Victim offender mediation had its first iteration among the Mennonite culture in Kitchener/Waterloo and expanded to Elkhart, Indiana and even further expanded by the seminal work of Howard Zehr (1990). American development and implementation of restorative justice such as reparative boards have remained primarily within the domain of the US, but the shared exchange of ideas, struggles, practices, and legislative frameworks has proliferated in both countries and set and established restorative justice development on a shared path to its implementation and acceptance among institutional practitioners.

As a larger, more dominant, and risk-averse culture, American restorative justice has greater permission to experiment than the more structurally uniform Canadian justice context. In Canada, until the development of the Youth Crime Justice Act of 2002, community justice was in its infancy and only existed within small pockets of the country, marginalized by the institutional parameters established by the Criminal Code of Canada. In the US, a number of state governments exercised a vastly expansive vision of restorative justice, facilitated by more fragmented powers of legislative authority locally (Pavelka 2016). In contrast, provinces were tasked with the more tepid responsibility of being the administrators of federal Canadian justice (Pavelka forthcoming).

Weighed by the historical legacies of slavery and colonialism on its Native and First Nation populations, restorative justice has been inserted as a tool to discuss and to focus on means of addressing historical wrongs and movements towards broader societal ends of reconciliation and amends. Focus within the context of the US has been on overrepresentation of black populations within the justice system (Valandra and Hokšíla 2020). Contrary to this, indigenous issues in Canada have been more focused on inherent rights of self-governance, treaty rights, and self-autonomy of native populations and the historical destruction of language, culture, and customs of First Nation people. Restorative justice, in many respects, has been positioned as a tool to reclaim some of those cultural components back and to move the larger society towards better recognition, understanding, and shared peace.

At the intersection of the two countries are parallel paths of restorative justice, which can facilitate better experimentation, learning, and implementation of service delivery, policy, and legislative frameworks. Further, these paths better correspond to the shared principles of restorative justice and the better client-centric needs of the victim, offender, and community of the two countries.

The seminal research of Bazemore and Schiff (2005) captures the dynamic and provides a snapshot of restorative justice practice in the US, while establishing a benchmark of the theoretical understandings of the foundations of restorative justice in the country. Research by Hansen and Umbreit (2018) and others (Ernest 2019; Piggott and Wood 2018) contribute additional insight into the implications of the practice and the future dynamics of restorative justice practices. In the Canadian context, an inventory and analysis of restorative justice has not been developed in the same fashion. That is, there has been some cataloging of restorative justice practices (Federal-Provincial-Territorial Working Group on Restorative Justice 2016) but little accompanying analysis of the components and thematic undercurrents that universally run through the real-life practice. The work in this area has been more administrative and often consumed by definitional debates of the term's use and the parameters in which it exists. Namely, is it a worldview, a practice particular to cultures (as indigenous populations), age cohorts (youth or adult), or a legally defined organization (i.e., youth justice committee) tasked with administrative justice functions? To a large measure, however, the stewards of this information have been the federal and the provincial and territorial governments themselves. Analysis of their released information—the policy work that they have developed—gives a good indication on the state of restorative justice and the thematic drivers of the practice across the land.

In the Canadian context, Manitoba is the only known jurisdiction in North America to have created the Restorative Justice Act of 2014, which defines the use and provides guidance as to its leadership and form within the province. Symbolic in nature, the legislation demarks the place of restorative justice within the system and provides stewardship over the model in the province. Restorative justice features prominently in the province's Criminal Justice Modernization Strategy, which is the vanguard of justice reforms in the country. Restorative justice has also featured prominently in many Senate reports, and public commissions, as the country seeks a new relationship with its indigenous populations and to address the large and complex operational issues within its justice system.

To better understand, the dynamics of the development and divergence of restorative justice in both countries must be further explored. While there are numerous points of comparison, there is increasing evidence that the evolution of restorative justice is not the same. The dynamics of this evolution speak to both strengths and weaknesses in both jurisdictions and to the more enhanced understanding of restorative justice in alignment with its core values and principles. This chapter will employ a cross-comparative analysis of the legislative mandate, mechanism, machinery, mode, and multiculturalism of restorative justice, which will comprehensively detail the development of restorative justice and speak to the leveraging components that expedite and enhance restorative justice implementation and adoption.

Legislative Mandate

The mandate or legislative authority of restorative justice is vastly different between the two countries. The US reflects a more fragmented but creative legislative framework among its states, while Canada is more uniform but further removed from the more directive processes and clarity of roles among institutional actors. Both legislative approaches reflect the larger constitutional and administrative roles of their governments, which is not easily teased from their institutional policies and cultural institutional practices. Nevertheless, as a foundational component to the administration of justice and the engagement of institutional partners in addressing the harm caused to victim, offender, and community, it is no surprise that this has shaped the robustness and innovation of restorative justice in each jurisdiction. Without the context for restorative justice to function and integrate with the traditional administration of justice, restorative justice practice will remain ostracized from its true capacity to establish a more satisfactory option for the resolution of harm and accountability (Pavelka forthcoming).

Over the last decade, there has been the development of various legislative schemes in the US directed to support the development and use of restorative justice. Thirty-eight American states have referenced restorative justice language in statute or code primarily authorized since the 1980s. However, there are currently no federal laws specific to restorative justice. The degree to which the state policy and legislation is explicitly or implicitly applied varies. Common language, however, is pervasive cross-jurisdictions. These states have incorporated restorative justice statutory language that includes general provisions and intent, restorative practices, funding, and evaluation. However, few directives and structures are included to support systemic implementation with adequate funding required for successful implementation of the stated policy goals (Pavelka 2008, 2016).

Legislative developments and mandates in Canada have been incremental and slow moving in supporting the expansion and use of restorative justice practice. Despite this, the political will to support this has been strong with endorsements from every Minister of Justice within the nation. Canada has embraced restorative justice with its rich history and demographics of indigenous and Aboriginal cultures and allows them to adapt to every unique community's needs. Restorative justice is enforced through the Youth Criminal Justice Act, which includes special provisions at the youth court level, recognizing the harm done to victims and the communities while encouraging the victim, their families, and their community's involvement in the individual's rehabilitation and reintegration. In *R. v Gladue* (1999), the Supreme Court of Canada rejected the view that a restorative approach is a more lenient approach to crime or that a sentence focusing on restorative justice is a lighter sentence.

Restoring harmony involves determining sentences that respond to the needs of the victim, the community, and the offender (Correctional Services Canada 2017).

Restorative justice practices, such as family group conferencing, peacemaking circles, circles of support and accountability, healing circles, sentencing circles, community-assisted hearings, and releasing circles, have been an integral part of Canada's criminal justice system since the 1970s. Legislation has permitted restorative justice to be implemented in every federal, provincial, and territory government. Entry points for a referral to a restorative justice process can enter in stages within the criminal justice system from pre-charge (referral by police), post-charge (Crown), pre-sentence (courts), post-sentence (corrections), or pre-revocation (parole). The Canadian Victim Bill of Rights information pertaining to services and programs is available to all victims upon request (section 6b). This is also granted in Canada's Corrections and Conditional Release Act (Subsection 26.1(1)), which also includes information on restorative practices. In 1996, the Canadian Criminal Code's sentencing principles were revised to reflect the restorative and community-based sentencing approach. Section 717 of the current criminal code suggests "alternative measures" when referring to sentencing (Pavelka forthcoming).

Mechanism

There has been a long-held contention among many scholars and practitioners that restorative justice is more than its models, and that it is rooted in values and principles for those it serves and to the objectives it seeks to achieve. While there is great debate as to the precise nature of these values and principles, the consensus of these larger values is clear, in that it represents a grassroots democratization of justice that focuses on the needs of those most impacted by crime and on the needs of those to repair the harm caused by the crime or wrongful occurrence. As a response to matters which, in the collective, harm that of the state, the mechanism by which restorative justice manifests in many ways reflects the core difference among the American and Canadian legal and state cultures, and the perspectives of sanctioned citizen engagement. It also represents the ways in which the cultures primarily recognize the harm and the main actors in the redress of harm.

The US, with its more individualist and self-deterministic culture, tends to gravitate towards restorative justice practice that is more individual in nature and addresses harm as more personal responsibility and that more directly engages the individual actors in dialogue about the resolution of wrongs and the personal culpability that actions entail. While this is not reflective in all areas of the country, victim offender mediation (VOM) and Victim Offender Reconciliation Program (VORP) models of restorative justice are vastly more prominent than those models of restorative justice which incorporate a multitude of stakeholder perspectives and adopt a more universalist narrative. Ironically, this model was primarily a Canadian Mennonite invention which quickly bridged to Indiana but has seen strong footholds in Texas, California, and Minnesota. While other models of restorative justice exist and are embraced by Americans, VOMs and VORPs are wholly dominant in many jurisdictions (Umbreit 1994).

Canadian mechanisms of restorative justice better reflect a more collectivist approach towards conflict and a more multi-stakeholder approach to examining the harms caused by crime. Committee approaches and circle sentencing which incorporate perspective into the resolution of matters are primarily seen as the preferred practice in the execution of restorative justice. Youth Justice Committees which are sanctioned by the Youth Criminal Justice Act and have stated objectives like "communities and families should work in partnership with others to prevent crime" and "providing the opportunity for the broader community to play an important role in developing a community-based response" reflect this broader collectivist ethos. Furthermore, circles which are much broader in scope and an engaging restorative justice practice are more widely adopted in Canada and are seen in many respects as the ideal for restorative justice practice.

The differences in the mechanisms of restorative justice are challenging to tease out as there is regional variation and implementation of restorative justice in various jurisdictions. However, it is clear that restorative justice models are pragmatically related to the perspective of conflict and responsibility and the legal and cultural perspectives on its resolution and focus of community engagement.

Machinery

The integration of community participation into the traditionally state-operated domains of justice requires not only legislative parameters but also the willingness of citizen participation in these systems. This is often an overlooked consideration of jurisdictions looking to advance restorative justice practice and to increase options for its larger legal justice system to adapt. In many instances, these state-driven considerations seek to improve the quality, saliency, and potency of resolution-focused interventions. While it remains a challenge to improve long-standing systems and their institutional apparatus, citizen participation exists where populations perceive the efforts are warranted and where the largest yields are gained.

The prominence of crime- and state-oriented systems looms vastly larger in the context of American life and its communities. With one of the largest incarcerated criminal populations in the world and the industrial complex to match, it is no surprise that innovations are sought along the entire continuum of the criminal justice system. This is not only a reflection of need, but the realization of the failure of the adversarial justice system, and the wake of human tragedies related to its function. Further, with the rise of behavioral psychology and activist populism, the opportunities for restorative justice grow and intrude in more diverse aspects of criminal justice reform. Orchestrated from the ground, and the growing frustration over the futility of traditional approaches, American communities are rising above and taking justice matters into their own hands and implementing change where the opportunities best present.

The work of justice reform and the inclusion of restorative justice practice has been dramatically wider in scope and focused on all aspects and populations within the legal system in the US. This has been reflective of the introduction of restorative practice in policing, courts, probation, and corrections and even into systems peripheral to the criminal justice apparatus, such as family group conferencing and school dispute resolutions (NACRJ 2022). Additionally, these measures have been more balanced with the considerations of both adult and youth justice populations, and the mixture and blending of restorative justice practice which was reflective of the work of Bazemore and Schiff (2005) in the cataloging of restorative justice practices throughout the US. The US appears more open and accepting of the introduction of restorative justice practice, likely as a counter-narrative to the law-and-order and adversarial approaches advocated by many political leaders, and the overwhelming evidence that these approaches have considerable return in regards to public safety, behavioral change, and victim and community satisfaction.

Canada's approach towards the use and application within its justice machinery has been more pedestrian and conservative in its nature. Overwhelmingly focused on youth interventions and diversionary approaches, there has been dramatically less innovation and licence to explore the use of restorative justice within its systems. Since the introduction of the Youth Criminal Justice Act, innovation has stagnated and been primarily a consideration of implementation within the young offender context, with limited consideration as to its possible expanded application. Recently this has been changing, but the absence of restorative justice in areas like community corrections reflect that the country has more opportunity to develop and to expand its scope of service.

Federalism in the Canadian context appears to be a challenge in developing innovative approaches in Canada. Additionally, the less combative and more rule-orientated culture invites less exploration of the possible uses of restorative justice practice, especially highlighted in the conservative domains of justice and the courts. This is not to say that no innovation or exploration occurs, as there are many localized instances of this taking place. However, scaling these interventions to a level that requires federal-provincial agreement, and the balancing of constitutional considerations in its function, appears to enforce the status-quo biases that exist within the system.

Mode

Within the context of more fragmented justice administration and operation, there is greater diversity in the adoption of restorative justice practice throughout the US. This diversity is highlighted through the concentration of restorative justice legislation and state-supported practices throughout the country. However, it has not dramatically changed throughout the past decades, with states such as Colorado, California, Illinois, Minnesota, and Pennsylvania leading the way. The disparity and polarization of restorative justice along political lines threatens a more expansive adoption of restorative justice approaches beyond the communities in which it currently exists.

Even in states that have the legislative and administrative capacity to support restorative justice, efforts in expanding its use in a statewide fashion seem limited and narrow to selective jurisdictions within the state. In many instances this seems to be driven by local leadership and not broader system considerations and functioning of systematic approaches. Canada is more uniform in the adoption of restorative justice practice. From the largest of jurisdictions of Ontario to the smallest of the Prince Edward Islands, restorative justice is a practice of consideration among all provinces and territories. In fact, as previously cited, all Ministers of Justice committed to increasing referrals to restorative justice practices by five percent year over year and have invested in tracking and reporting on their progress to this commitment. This has created heightened commitment to promote the use of restorative justice throughout the country and to advocate better referral mechanisms and trainings on the utility of restorative justice practice.

Another component which has facilitated the broader use of restorative justice is its connection to indigenous self-determination and to reconciliation efforts among governments across the country. While restorative justice is reflective of multiple cultures and societies, the close associations to indigenous Canadian practices and worldviews provides a tangible touchstone to redress the historical wrongs committed against indigenous Canadians. Furthermore, with vast over representation of indigenous Canadian populations in both provincial and federal prisons, restorative justice provides an alternative approach to address this dynamic.

The political and cultural aspects that are assigned to restorative justice practices have created a more uniform appetite for the increased use of restorative justice. Much work, nevertheless, remains to gain broader understanding of the practice and in building the larger communities' demand as this is a first measure of the justice system response.

Multiculturalism

The US and Canada have strong immigration influences that have developed and shaped each respective country. These influences have resulted in the development of separate legal systems, institutions, and cultural norms and assumptions that have guided the criminal justice system and its administration. As the demographic, social structures, and cultures shift in each nation, so should the criminal justice system change to reflect these needs. Restorative justice is no different with cultural factors shaping the operations and dynamics of restorative justice within both countries. These changes have been more dramatic given the ever-shrinking world in which we now exist and the diversity of populations that make up both nations. In the face of these dynamics, restorative justice has developed in a divergent path within the US and Canada, which requires further examination and exploration.

The US has long been a beacon to immigrant populations who wish to pursue freedoms and enhance their economic position in life. America's prominence and place in the world are even more important as new geopolitical shifts occur with nations that do not overtly share the key tenets of democracy and the freedoms Western democracies enjoy. Additionally, immigration from non-western nations and the rise and reinvigoration of marginalized and minority populations have pressured the majority culture to become more understanding and reflect a diversity of cultural perspectives to which it has not been previously compelled. As an economic and geopolitical leader, these immigrant pressures and the changing face of America seem to become more pronounced and potentially more needed and essential.

Overall, the US seems less willing to embrace multiculturalism as a concept and rebukes the efforts to make its culture more representative beyond the inclusion of minority populations into the larger cultural domain. This is both a strength and a weakness in that it develops a common narrative but stagnates potential adaptation, innovation, and societal growth. This is reflected in many political contexts, especially of the adaptation to improve the administration of justice, and to deal with the increasing costs and failed outcomes of the dominant criminal justice system.

Similarly, as a nation, Canada has been shaped by immigration and the prominence of the two dominant cultures of French and English. However, since the adoption of the official policy of multiculturalism in the 1970s, and significant changes in the Immigration Act during that time (1979), Canada has become more demographically diverse and accepting of different cultures and perspectives. Recent census data reveals this diversity, with 25 percent of surveyed participants being foreign born (Statistics Canada 2021). Canada has informally adopted a globalist culture in which diversity is not only celebrated but advanced within the context of the official state. Recent government policy even seeks to exacerbate this trend by seeking a half million new immigrants per year into the country, as a function of skill shortages, aging demographics, and economic stimulus.

As the demographic and cultural faces of both countries change, it is important to examine what this means for restorative justice and the acceptance of the practice as a legitimate means with which to deal with conflict and social disorder in the criminal justice context. While restorative justice is strongly rooted in indigenous and pacifist cultures, there are aspects of the practice that speak to all cultures with traditional means of resolving disputes and addressing issues of crime.

While the US is overall more reluctant to adopt cultural diversity and a more globalist perspective in its culture—and for the purposes of this discussion, crime—this does not appear true with the practice of restorative justice within its various states and jurisdictions. There have been multilinguistic accommodations to the application of the practice and the recognition of its uses and applicability to a diversity of cultures or historical contexts. Whether this is to the increasingly dominant Hispanic cultures, Hmong of Minnesota, the Mennonites of Pennsylvania, or Black populations addressing the legacy of slavery, restorative justice in the US encourages diversity and the broader engagement of populations that have been marginalized or devoid of a voice. In its truest form, restorative justice in the US is reflective of the overarching community justice ethos that justice must be contextualized to those impacted by the harm and accountability of crime and that the situational, historical, and cultural contexts enrich the content of the discussion (Pavelka and Thomas 2019).

Canada, on the other hand, despite its formal multicultural policy and broader accommodation of diversity, primarily treats restorative justice as an indigenous Canadian practice that is grounded solely in their cultural beliefs and ethos. While other cultures have had influence on restorative justice's foundation and practice in Canada (i.e., Mennonites), restorative justice in Canada has shown little accommodation to new Canadian cultures other than participation in the indigenous-led process. Additionally, an adaptation of the practice without engagement of indigenous populations has been co-option of the process from that of those populations and people.

In the Canadian context, and the historical foundation of colonization and the mistreatment and appropriation of indigenous peoples and artifacts, the resistance to allow for the sharing is understandable. Nevertheless, the failure to have the diversity of voices shape and engage in the practice stunts the practice's ability to develop and to reflect the people who are impacted by crime. Further, other cultural perspectives are relegated into a supportive but not leading role, despite the relevance to the community and local issues. Unfortunately, the rhetoric of pluralism does not resonate in this domain and will likely thwart the expansion of restorative justice as a mechanism and process for broader adaptation and appeal.

Concluding Thoughts

As the practice of restorative justice incrementally advances and learnings are gained, it is important to take stock of the evolution of restorative justice in both countries. Both countries remain vibrant and imaginative locations that share the ability to enhance the workings of their justice systems and administrative capacity to better serve victims, offenders, and communities. The parallel paths of this modern intervention which borrows heavily from traditional cultures and interfaces with increasing complex criminal justice matters are stark. Nevertheless, this comparative analysis provides insight into the different challenges and opportunities that exist and the communal challenges to overcome.

It is clear that additional research is needed in comparing and learning from the development and evolution of restorative justice in both countries. This work is non-existent in the literature, and the function of this chapter is to introduce its value and to build a foundation in which this research may occur. It is our hope that through the development of this framework advancements can be sought and potential obstacles can be overcome, while both jurisdictions seek to enhance the inner capacity to improve its systems and to develop a more robust restorative justice process continuum. This research is in its infancy. It is presented to advance this analysis and build a better understanding of how and what works within the real-world context. The authors are encouraged by the possibilities of this dialogue to build learnings and construct foundations for the implementation of this work.

References

Bazemore, G. and Schiff, M. (2005) *Juvenile Justice Reform and Restorative Justice: Building Theory and Policy from Practice*. New York: Willan Publishing.

Correctional Services Canada (2017) Restorative opportunities—Victim-Offender Mediation services 2016–2017, correctional results for face-to-face meetings. www.csc-scc.gc.ca/restorative-justice/003005-1002-en.shtml

Ernest, K. (2019) "Is Restorative Justice Effective in the U.S.? Evaluating Program Methods and Findings Using Meta-analysis." Doctoral dissertation, Arizona State University. https://keep.lib.asu.edu/items/157635

Federal-Provincial-Territorial Working Group on Restorative Justice (2016) "Restorative Justice in the Canadian Criminal Justice Sector." www.csc-scc.gc.ca/restorative-justice/092/003005-4012-en.pdf

Hansen, T. and Umbreit, M.S. (2018) "State of knowledge: Four decades of victim-offender mediation research and practice: The evidence." *Conflict Resolution Quarterly 36*, 2, 99–113. doi.org/10.1002/crq.21234

NACRJ (National Association of Community and Restorative Justice) (2022) NACRJ Policy Statement on Community and Restorative Justice in Criminal and Juvenile Legal Systems. https://growthzonesitesprod.azureedge.net/wp-content/uploads/sites/3964/2023/03/NACRJ-Policy-Statement-on-Community-and-Restorative-Justice-in-Criminal-and-Juvenile-Legal-Systems.pdf

Pavelka, S. (forthcoming) "Public Policy and Legislation: International Comparisons." *Encyclopedia of Social Justice in Education.*

Pavelka, S. (2008) "Restorative juvenile justice legislation and policy: A national assessment." *International Journal of Restorative Justice 4*, 2, 100-118. www.researchgate.net/publication/237118300_Restorative_juvenile_justice_legislation_and_policy_A_national_assessment

Pavelka, S. (2016) "Restorative justice in the States: A national assessment of legislation and policy." *Justice Policy Journal 13*, 2, 1-23. www.researchgate.net/publication/317007535_Restorative_Justice_in_the_States_An_Analysis_of_Statutory_Legislation_and_Policy

Pavelka, S. and Thomas, D. (2019) "The evolution of balanced and restorative justice." *Juvenile and Family Court Journal 70*, 1, 37-58. www.researchgate.net/publication/331878046_The_Evolution_of_Balanced_and_Restorative_Justice

Piggot, E. and Wood, W. (2018) "Does Restorative Justice Reduce Recidivism? Assessing Evidence and Claims about Restorative Justice and Reoffending." In T. Gavrielides (ed.) *International Handbook on Restorative Justice.* London: Routledge.

Statistics Canada (2021) Census Profile, 2021 Census of Population. www12.statcan.gc.ca/census-recensement/2021/dp-pd/prof/index.cfm?Lang=E

Stuart, B. (1996) "Circle sentencing in Canada: A partnership of the community and the criminal justice system." *International Journal of Comparative and Applied Criminal Justice 20*, 2, 291-309.

Umbreit, M.S. (1994) *Victim Meets Offender: The Impact of Restorative Justice and Mediation.* Monsey, NY: Criminal Justice Press.

Valandra, E.C. and Hokšíla, W. (2020) *Colorizing Restorative Justice: Voicing Our Realities.* St. Paul, MN: Living Justice Press.

Zehr, H. (1990) *Changing Lenses: A New Focus for Crime and Justice.* Scottsdale, PA: Herald Press.

— Chapter 3 —

Community Justice

The Village Model, a Definitive Restorative Community Justice Model

DALE LANDRY

During the early 2000s, Dennis Maloney and I traveled to New York to conduct workshops as a part of the federally funded US Department of Justice Office of Juvenile Justice and Delinquency Prevention (OJJDP) Balanced and Restorative Justice (BARJ) Project administered out of Florida Atlantic University. Maloney and I traveled to numerous sites across the nation providing technical assistance support to designated "special emphasis" states and specific locales, directly supported for implementing the BARJ model of restorative justice. As we often did during these trips, we discussed issues and gaps with the BARJ model we encountered on each trip. This information was often captured in outgoing surveys, but more importantly, from discussions with individuals, groups, agencies, and communities. What was missing? As our discussion continued, we began to look at the focus areas of the restorative justice movement, including the BARJ model, and they were either *victim-focused* or *offender-focused.* Emphasis on achieving justice within a restorative justice effort included these two "customers or parties," the victim and the offender. Distinctly absent was a focus on the third party, a *community-focused* area. It became clear that though *community* was included as a customer and party to any restorative justice process, it was often viewed in the abstract (as community as a whole). However, when we narrow our focus on community, we soon realize that the strength of a community lies in its members themselves, the residents. When viewed from that perspective, we realized that everyone—including elected officials; government officials; the criminal and juvenile justice system administrators and practitioners; business, faith, and educational institutions; victims and their families; offenders and their families—regardless of titles or positions, are all equals as members within the community. Collectively, if they could *all* come together as equals, they could effectively address crime and its impact within the community and, overall, restore individuals and the community, as a whole, in the aftermath of a crime or harmful behavior. More importantly, when residents come together to strategically plan to address how to react to crime and harmful behavior, this group can also plan how to work at removing opportunity to crime and move from being reactionary into a proactive response by focusing resources to eliminate the causative factors conducive to criminal and harmful behaviors and criminal opportunity. This led to Maloney and me, working with Dr. Sandra (O'Brien) Pavelka and Judge Don Owen Costello, authoring "Bringing justice back to the community," the basis for this chapter.

"Bringing justice back to the community," published in 2003, focused on developing a community justice model that would assist the court in addressing juvenile crime. A primary motivation for its use was in addressing the rising economic cost of the criminal and juvenile justice systems in processing and punishing offenders. The article emphasizes how involving community residents as mutual collaborative partners in developing a restorative community response to crime provides a means for the community to take an active role in identifying the issues contributing to criminal and harmful behaviors, community involvement in response to criminal and other harmful behaviors, and providing the necessary community resources to help those impacted by crime and harmful behavior. Over 20 years later, the situation in communities nationwide has worsened. Today, there is even more distrust of our criminal and juvenile systems. This is evidenced by numerous injustices of police misconduct, continued calls for criminal justice reforms of our prisons and jails, courts backlogged because of the COVID pandemic, and the high costs of criminal prosecution and jailing of offenders.

Case in point is the criminal processing and jailing of misdemeanor offenders. Here in Florida where I reside, misdemeanor crimes are mostly property crimes. Simple battery is the only violent misdemeanor crime in Florida's criminal statutes, all others are felonies. Further, misdemeanor property crimes are capped at approximately $1,000. I approached a local Sheriff and asked him how much it costs to house a misdemeanor prisoner in his jail. He gave me $80 per day (when he was asking for monies from the local county government) and $50 per day (if the same entities were asking him to cut his budget). Using the $50 a day costs and generally a sentence for a misdemeanor in jail cannot exceed a year or 364 days, the cost for someone sentenced to the maximum 364 days would be $18,200. At that cost, minus the maximum cost ($1,000) for a misdemeanor, the Florida taxpayer is paying $17,200 to punish that offender. At these same costs, a 20-day sentence equals the value of the harm done. How much more are we spending when we figure in the cost of police, prosecutors and public defenders, the court, and corrections? (The cost quoted above was only for housing; add in medical costs and this becomes substantial.) Today, as many communities across the nation work at their respective criminal justice reforms, I have worked at creating a model community justice initiative that will assist communities in strategically developing a program that captures the essence of "Bringing justice back to the community."

The Village Model of community justice evolved from my 25-year journey in restorative justice. Beginning with my hiring as the restorative justice coordinator for a local neighborhood justice center, through being a consultant with the BARJ Project and providing consulting services in establishing restorative justice initiatives nationwide, this journey has grounded me in the philosophy, principles, and practices of restorative, community, and restorative community justice and the foundations for this community justice model. Interactions with fellow restorative justice practitioners, agencies/organizations, and programmatic sites coupled with designing, developing, and implementing programs at various sites provided the framework for the design of the model. Finally, the interactions with diverse community members nationwide through training and working with them in implementing their respective community justice models provided the impetus to create the Village Model. This community empowerment model provides a systemic process that helps the community develop the capacity to effectively improve its quality-of-life issues through resident-led, mutually collaborative efforts inclusive of all community resources.

Community Justice Village Model

Restorative justice and community justice are two distinct concepts that have emerged in response to community collaborations with criminal justice systems; however, they are often viewed as being the same. Bazemore and Schiff (2001) differentiate the two as follows: restorative justice is practiced at the individual (micro) levels and emphasizes repairing harm in the wake of crime and being informal, community-based, and often operating outside of and distrustful of the traditional justice system; community justice is focused on systems-level intervention with shared outcomes and is oriented towards crime prevention and, more importantly, a creation of the criminal justice system evolving from community policing efforts.

In 2001, this author along with two other leaders in the field of restorative justice, Dr. Sandra Pavelka O'Brien (Florida Gulf Coast University) and Dennis Maloney (co-author of the balanced approach), began conceptualizing a new program model. Paramount to the model is a foundation built on (or evolved from) the concept and principles of restorative justice coupled with the core principles of community justice. The model would need to: address gaps (actual or perceived) in restorative justice practices; address systemic outcome failures of the traditional criminal and juvenile justice systems; and consolidate, refocus, and reinforce local criminal justice outreach efforts into a collaborative community coalition led by community residents. Collectively, this would result in an empowered community capable of overcoming crime and its impact on the community and its quality of life. In 2003, along with Judge Don Owen Costello, we outlined the framework of this community justice model (O'Brien et al. 2003).

Restorative Justice Defined

Though there are numerous models of restorative justice and, likewise, differing definitions, for the purpose of this model we use the premise that: *Crime and harmful behaviors harm individuals and the community as a whole and create an obligation to repair the harm that was done to those that were specifically harmed and the community.*

This is supported by principles developed by Van Ness and Strong (1997):

- Justice requires repair.

- Victim, offender, and community are the justice system customers, and are provided maximum opportunity for input and participation in the justice process (determining how to repair the harm).

- Government assumes a supportive role through maintaining order, while empowering the community to focus on peacemaking (offender accountability and offender reintegration) and problem solving.

Also embedded in the restorative response is the balanced approach, co-authored by Maloney, which provides for equal emphasis on community protection, accountability, and competency development in the aftermath of and response to a criminal act or other harmful behavior in the community. These three are further defined as:

- Accountability: Provides for the offender to take responsibility for their harmful behavior by participating in the process that defines the harm that was done, determine what needs to be done to repair the harm, and take action to repair the harm done.

- Competency Development: Provides resources that assist the offender in developing needed skills that deter further involvement in harmful behaviors (vocational, education, reasoning, personal/social, conflict management, communications, decision-making, problem solving, etc.).

- Community Safety: Provides both immediate and long-term

safety. Achieving this requires practices that reduce risk and promote the community's capacity to manage behavior.

Community Justice Defined

Within the context of this new model, community justice is defined as "a community-led collaborative process that systemically repairs harm, reduces risk and revitalizes community in addressing and overcoming problems that impact the community's quality of life" (O'Brien et al. 2003, p.37). Crime is viewed as dynamic and impacting a community "along a continuum, which includes causative factors, the occurrence and consequences of crime" (O'Brien et al. 2003, p.37). Correspondingly, community justice provides a community with the means to diametrically respond to this threat through a systemic, coordinated and collaborative, community-led interdiction along the continuum, using crime prevention strategies (causation), restorative justice practices (occurrence), and concentration of community resources (especially human service providers) to meet "both the short-term and long-term needs of community members impacted by crime (consequences)" (O'Brien et al. 2003, p.37).

Village Model Goal and Objectives

Building on this definition and principles, the goal is to empower community with the ability to effectively overcome crime through a community-led collaboration that develops and implements a strategic community justice plan focusing resources and efforts on interdicting crime along the crime continuum. To attain this goal, the following objectives must be achieved:

- A coalition of community systems, resources, and individual community members who mutually adopt the mission of confronting and overcoming crime within the community is developed.

- The coalition collectively develops and implements a strategic community justice plan that includes the following elements:

    - Community Justice Vision—clear, precise, and definitive

statement that reflects the community's vision of justice that *repairs harm, reduces risks and builds community.*

- Community Justice Values—a written series of statements reflecting community values that support the Vision.

- Community Justice Strategies—milieu of programmatic practices that reflect and reinforce the community's values and vision.

- Community Justice Implementation Plan—time-phased action plan that outlines the steps to achieve the Community Justice Vision.

Village Model Strategic Planning Process

The focus of all community justice efforts lies in the community itself: more specifically, comm*unity*. It is led by active participation of community residents; representatives from the business, faith, and education communities; the criminal and juvenile justice systems; and other local government resources and multi-discipline human service providers. Collectively they unite into a mutual collaboration that forms the core of the community justice effort. This core group forms the community's initial Community Justice Council that develops the community's strategic community justice plan. Utilizing a series of workshops, forums, and focus groups (ideally a three-day retreat), the Council, using a systemic process, completes the strategic plan. The steps in the systemic process are:

- analysis: defining the existing system, collaborative partners, problems, and establishing the evaluation baseline data

- design: conceptualizing and defining the new community justice system around the definitions and principles of this model and designing the new community justice system framework using the goal and objectives as the guide

- development: building the community's community justice program around the new community justice framework including program components that specifically address crime prevention—*causation*; restorative justice practices—*occurrence*; and community support services—*consequences*

- implementation: action steps transitioning from the current system into the new community justice system including outlining administrative operations.

Village Model Operations

The Council would identify a location within the community that would serve as the hub and nerve center for daily community justice operations. Daily operations would focus on *reducing risks* through the crime prevention component; *repairing harm* through the restorative justice component; and *building community* through the community services component. Although seemingly independent activities, they are inclusive and interdependent, while collectively and visibly improving the community's quality of life as community members actively and simultaneously interdict the crime continuum through each of the components. Site, staffing, and programmatic processes should build on existing resources, policies, and procedures (redefining and/or realigning) and the creation of new additions or changes *only* as gaps in services, problems, or obstacles require it. The most critical aspect and key to the success of the Village Model is its emphasis on giving leadership in addressing public safety to "the one entity with the greatest stake in safety—the community" (O'Brien et al. 2003, p.36).

Village Model Programmatic Components

The Village Model has a number of programmatic components which include the following:

- Crime Prevention (Causation): community-oriented policing component providing education programs, citizen ride-along, Crime Prevention Through Environmental Design (CPTED), crime monitoring and analysis (COMPstats), and the Criminal Justice Advisory Group.

- Restorative Justice Practices (Occurrence): restorative conferencing, circles, victim offender mediation/dialogue, reparative boards, and circle sentencing.

- Community Support Services (Consequences): multidiscipline health, mental health, and human service providers; administrative, educational, faith, and business institutions; service projects; volunteer coordination; mediation services; mentoring services; and communications.

Village Model Roles
The Village Model has distinct roles that are integral in its implementation.

Community
Community members are actively involved in all aspects of the Village Model operations, prevention, intervention, and reintegration activities. The community is involved in identifying factors in the community that provide opportunities for crime and other harmful behaviors. The community also assists in identifying at-risk individuals who are exhibiting behaviors that indicate potential involvement in criminal or other harmful behaviors. Further, community members provide ongoing monitoring and encouragement for offenders who are actively engaged in repairing the harm they have done in the community and celebrating the reintegration of those who have completed repairing the harm done to both their victims and the community. At-risk behaviors for referral include:

- attention deficit/hyperactivity disorders
- aggressive conduct
- anger management
- running away or persistent staying out late
- alcohol/tobacco/drug abuse behaviors
- domestic violence.

Schools

Schools are actively involved in prevention, intervention, and reintegration activities. Schools assist in identifying both at-risk youth and youth who have violated the school code of conduct rules. In lieu of out-of-school suspensions, youth are referred to the community's community justice programs that provide for the youth to remain in a learning environment and allow for them to be accountable for their behavior. Types of referrals include:

- at-risk behaviors
- zero tolerance behaviors (non-statutory violations)
- truancy
- poor school attendance
- bullying.

Law Enforcement

Law enforcement agencies are actively involved in prevention, intervention, and reintegration activities through their *community policing* efforts. Law enforcement assists in identifying both at-risk individuals and those who have committed non-violent crimes for diversion (in lieu of formal reporting) to community justice programs. Law enforcement actively promote referral of individuals and families to the community justice program for complaints and/or disputes that fall short of criminal violations but which, however, have the potential of escalation if no intervention is provided. The types of referrals include:

- at-risk behaviors
- property crimes
- traffic offenses
- public disorders (trespassing, prowling, disorderly conduct, etc.)
- other non-violent misdemeanor offenses.

Prosecutor/State Attorney

Prosecutors/state attorneys actively participate in prevention, intervention, and reintegration activities through their *community prosecution* efforts. Prosecutors are actively involved in identifying cases that can be diverted to a community justice initiative that allows offenders to be held accountable without incarceration. The types of referrals are the same as indicated above under law enforcement.

Courts

The court is actively involved in prevention, intervention, and reintegration activities through their *community court* efforts. Community courts are held to review the restorative agreements that have been voluntarily agreed upon in order for the offender to be held accountable for their respective behavior and to repair the harm as outlined in the agreement. The court should be held in the local neighborhood. The court can also impose increased sanctions for those in violation of the provision of their restorative contract to include secure detention. Finally, the court has the power to remand the offender back to the criminal justice system should they fail to comply and with the recommendation of a follow-up restorative practice that determines if the offender is complying with the agreement and is a threat to the community's safety. The types of referrals include community prosecution referrals.

Corrections

Corrections officials are actively involved in prevention, intervention, and reintegration activities through their *community corrections* efforts. Corrections assist in reintegrating offenders back into the community. Ideally, local jails should not be used to house nonviolent misdemeanor offenders, who should be completing their restorative sanctions in the community and from home. Local jails should be used to house inmates returning from state correctional facilities in preparation for their being reintegrated back into the community. This allows for the community to interact with them through a variety of restorative practices, to determine if they have learned the necessary competencies and skills that will allow them to remain crime free and not a threat to the community. While in the secure detention at the jail, they should be provided with vocational, medical, and educational skills while doing restorative work from the local secure detention facility. This allows the offender to demonstrate their willingness to be accountable and, through restorative service, work their way back into the community.

Final Words

In summarizing, the Village Model of restorative community justice provides a process that provides for the community to take an active role in designing, developing, and implementing a community response to interdict crime along its continuum: causation, occurrence, and consequences. Named after the African phraseology "It takes a village to raise a child," we must be cognizant that our villages have been damaged and need to be repaired. The Village Model provides for this. In these times—with our country divided, mistrust in our criminal and juvenile justice agencies, daily ongoing gun violence, our communities and residents undergoing an onslaught of trauma—restorative community justice provides the opportunity to rebuild relationships. I am reminded of Dan Van Ness's third principle of restorative justice which identifies government in a supportive role while empowering community to ensure peace and problem solving (Van Ness and Strong 1997). The Village Model provides the means for the community to restore peace and address problems impacting the community.

References

Bazemore, G. and Schiff, M. (2001) "Understanding Restorative Community Justice: What and Why Now?" In *Restorative Community Justice: Repairing Harm and Transforming Communities*. New York: Anderson Publishing.

O'Brien, S., Maloney, D., Landry, D., and Costello, D. (2003) "Bringing justice back to the community." *Juvenile and Family Court Journal 54*, 3, 35–46. doi.org/10.1111/j.1755-6988.2003.tb00079.x

Van Ness, D. and Strong, K.H. (1997) *Restorative Justice*. Cincinnati, OH: Anderson Publishing.

— Chapter 4 —

Mirror, Mirror, on the Wall...

KAY PRANIS

This chapter is an adaptation of a webinar I delivered to restorative justice practitioners in Petropolis, Brazil in November 2021. I dedicate this version to Gordon Bazemore who shaped my understanding of the relationship between youth development and the principles of restorative justice. Gordon influenced my thinking and opened doors for my voice to be heard in the nascent modern restorative justice movement in the early 1990s. I feel Gordon's spirit in the theme of this chapter. I am deeply grateful to have known Gordon!

The perspective of any writer is shaped by the particularities of the lens of the writer. I wish to identify key elements of my lens. I am a cis-gendered, middle-class, White woman over 70 years of age. I came to the work of restorative justice accidentally and have no formal training in any related field. Key influences on my thinking, in addition to Gordon Bazemore, are John McKnight, Virginia Mackey, M. Kay Harris, Barry Stuart, Mark Wedge, Tahnahga Yako, and Fania Davis. I am neither clearly a practitioner nor clearly an academic but, rather, fall between. In my work, I have focused primarily on the peacemaking circle process. My work in circle exposed me to multiple dimensions of an Indigenous worldview that have become central organizing principles of my work.

    I want to begin by acknowledging the land where we each—myself and you, the reader—are: the rocks and waters of the land we are on, the plants and animals, the shared air around our planet Earth. I acknowledge the earlier caretakers of the land—the Indigenous people who lived here, those who walked these lands before us, and our own ancestors—that we remember ourselves in a web that is connected to everything that is, and everything that ever was, and everything that will be. We are part of a vast interconnectedness. For me, there are two important implications of this interconnectedness. We are never alone. We bear responsibility for our impact on that web.

In keeping with Gordon's passion, this chapter will explore an often-unexamined aspect of restorative justice with young people in trouble with the law, whether incarcerated or in community. Mirror, mirror, on the wall: who needs to change for the wellbeing of us all?

Who Needs to Change?

When youth exhibit harmful, disruptive, or self-destructive behavior it tells us as much about ourselves as it tells us about them! Behavior is largely learned in the environment in which a young person is developing. The young person has little control over that environment. Adults are mostly responsible for the quality of that environment. As a child and as an adolescent most of our behavior patterns are learned by mimicking the adults in our lives. Looking at youth is looking into a mirror showing us what we look like to youth. They are mirroring the world they have experienced. What does the mirror of their behavior tell us about the world young people see and feel? Do we like what we see about us that they reflect through that mirror—that they reflect through their behavior?

If we want to change youth behavior, we must change adult behavior. We cannot control the behavior of other adults. So, we must begin with ourselves. We have significant control over our behavior, and we have an impressive capacity for change when we are not satisfied with our behavior. And we do not need to change the behavior of all of the adults in a youth's life. We can look into the mirror of our personal behavior and begin there.

Exposure to even a small number of adults modeling caring, respectful behavior can touch the deep well of desire in a youth for a world in which everyone is treated with dignity. Young people know that if everyone is treated with dignity then they can trust that they will be treated with dignity. As professionals working with young people in juvenile justice or schools, we can give young people a glimpse of a world where dignity is a basic practice, even if we cannot change the larger context of their lives in their family or community. In that glimpse of a different way of being together lies hope: a belief that it is possible to live well together attending to our needs while also attending to the needs of others.

We can create spaces for them to practice being together in mutual respect, non-domination, care, and truth telling. Even if they cannot transfer those behaviors immediately to their home or neighborhood environment, the seed is planted. Their hearts know it is possible to be in relationships that honor the dignity of everyone. The more places we offer to practice being together with a commitment to mutual wellbeing, the stronger the neural pathways will be for being part of a healthy community.

Checking Our Alignment

On that journey with young people, we need to watch carefully for alignment between what we, as adults, say and what we do. Adults often tell young people they care about them, but then treat them disrespectfully or engage in punishment that belies the adult claim of caring about youth. Much of the adult behavior is automatic, unconscious. We are often not really thinking about whether our actions are consistent with our underlying values and our aspirational goals for the work we do. Looking into the mirror can help us identify whether and where we are out of alignment between our professed intentions and the actual impact of our actions.

Most adults who work with youth care about youth and want good outcomes for youth. However, the socialization of these adults has taught them that control and punishment will change negative behaviors of youth. External controls, threats of punishment, disrespectful treatment, and humiliation do not produce better behavior. These strategies simply model more of the bad behavior youth have been observing in the adults around them their entire lives, reinforcing the lessons youth have learned from adults about controlling others, using coercion to get their needs met, saying one thing but doing another. Their behavior then mirrors what they have been learning from the behavior of adults.

What are we teaching youth with the ways we use our power? Methods of coercion and control model the use of power to force others to our will. Adults hold a great deal of power over youth even when the adults are feeling helpless about the behavior of youth. Harmful youth behavior often mirrors what the adult world looks like to them regarding power. The more power we hold, the more important it is to look into the mirror to see what that power looks and feels like from the other side.

Acknowledging the role of adult behavior in the behavior of young people does not excuse young people from taking responsibility when they cause harm. Restorative justice calls for both individual and collective accountability. Individual young people are responsible for repairing harm they caused and making change so it does not happen again. The adults and the community around young people are responsible for conditions that may contribute to the behavior problems of youth. Those adults and the community are called to repair the harm they may be causing to youth and to make changes so it will not happen again. Restorative justice asks the question: How do each of us need to change for the wellbeing of everyone?

If Control and Punishment Do Not Create Positive Behavior Change, What Can We Do?

Adults design and implement responses to harmful behavior by youth. Most of these responses currently rely on control and punishment. But control and punishment are not effective strategies, so adults need to change the strategies they are using. A simple idea that I learned from someone in a circle can guide our response to harmful behavior by youth. This is the idea: *It is only in an uncondemned space that anyone can change.* This idea is worth repeating: It is only in an uncondemned space that anyone can change.

If we want youth to change their behavior, we must create "uncondemned spaces"—spaces in which the basic human dignity of every youth is honored, spaces in which every youth is deemed worthy of respect, spaces where youth are seen and heard, spaces where youth can trust that they will belong even if they have made a mistake. An uncondemned space is a space of love.

If we want adults to change their behavior so that they are not modeling controlling behaviors and disrespectful treatment of youth, we need to create uncondemned spaces for the adults as well.

We live in a cultural paradigm that relies heavily on condemnation to get people to do the right thing. We criticize people, we tell them they are bad, we ridicule them, we threaten harmful consequences, we tell them they are failures, we tell them they are not worthy of our respect, we humiliate them. Those are strategies of condemnation, and they are not effective strategies for changing behavior in a positive direction. Those strategies are rooted in negative energy and a negative view of human potential. They are, however, the predominant form of response to behavior problems in our society.

Making changes in behavior entails hard work. It requires energy, persistence, practice, supportive feedback, inspiration, attention, awareness, confidence that we have the capacity, more energy, and more practice, and on and on! We cannot generate the positive energy needed for positive change through condemnation. We cannot generate positive energy through a negative strategy. We can only generate the positive energy we need to change our behaviors through caring about one another, through love.

Healthy love does not condone harmful behavior. Healthy love promotes genuine accountability. If we love someone, we care about their inner wellbeing, and we know that when we cause harm, we damage our inner wellbeing. Consequently, we want those we love to be accountable, to acknowledge if they cause harm and to repair that harm, because we know it will be healing for them. When we love someone, we encourage them to be accountable as long as we know that they will be treated with dignity and not be diminished as a human being.

How Do We Practice Loving One Another?

How do we practice loving the adults who work with youth to help them change and loving youth in trouble with the law to help them change? Communities must create uncondemned spaces for the adults who work with youth and for youth themselves. We are all responsible for what is happening in the lives of youth in trouble with the law. So, we all need to change.

The community needs to love those who work with youth—teachers, social workers, counselors, youth workers, coaches, parents—so those adults can love youth! It is often not easy to love a youth who is acting out. Therefore, adults who work with youth need support; they need a space where they feel loved and appreciated for their efforts.

How can we practice supporting each other, taking care of each other—so that we can show up in a different way with youth based on affirmation, not condemnation? In my experience, a powerful way to practice loving one another at a community level is the circle process. The circle is a space for practicing community, based on universal human dignity, human worth, and voice.

The circle, conducted properly, is an uncondemned space. It is a space where everyone's dignity is upheld; it is a space where every voice is honored and valued. It is a space that seeks to uncover the gifts of every person present. We need opportunities to practice what it is like to be together in an uncondemned space; we need to practice how to consciously construct an uncondemned space. We need to know what an uncondemned space feels like so we will know when we are not creating an uncondemned space. If we practice consistently in circle, we will build the skills to create uncondemned spaces outside of circle.

The circle process offers many gifts in our work with youth:

- The circle is a place to be more mindful and intentional about the values we want to bring to our work with youth. Values conversations are a regular part of circle practice.

- The circle strengthens our listening muscles which are needed to really hear youth—what they are saying and what they are not saying.

- The circle opens more space for the voice of youth, giving us insight into their perspective and the wisdom of their lived experience.

- The circle slows down the pace of interaction so we can be more reflective and less reactive, allowing us to break cycles of impulsive reactions among youth or between adults and youth.

- The circle provides young people with an experience of positive personal power giving them an opportunity to practice constructive use of power.

- The circle increases the emotional intelligence of both youth and the adults in the circle, building skills for healthy community.

- The circle increases commitment to the common good, clarifying individual and collective needs and making it easier to find a healthy balance between individual and collective needs.

- The circle is a place of respite from the unrelenting pressures of our daily lives that is accessible to anyone once they are familiar with it.

- The circle helps us remember the best of our potential as human beings.

Changing the Image in the Mirror

And we start with the adults. We need to have conversations among ourselves about the values that we want to guide our work with youth. Then we need to ask ourselves whether the behaviors we exhibit with youth are consistent with those values we said should guide our work with youth. We need to ask youth whether they observe those values in our behaviors toward them.

We need to listen and listen and listen. Most people working with youth have good intentions. However, the overall impact of the interventions of these systems is often not positive in the lives of the young people and their families. It is imperative that we grapple with the gap between intentions and impact. We cannot escape responsibility for impact by pleading that we had good intentions. We are obligated to go back and seek an understanding about what went wrong between intention and impact and take steps to bridge the gap between them. We have to change our actions to get intention and impact into alignment.

To do that, we must open our hearts and minds to feedback that can be very painful. We do have good intentions, so it will hurt deeply to hear that our actions harmed a youth. And yet we must know if that is the case, otherwise we will be likely to cause more harm. Shame comes up and washes over me when I get feedback that something I did felt disrespectful to someone. I never want to be disrespectful. I feel like a bad person if someone tells me they felt disrespected or hurt by my actions.

So, I must hold still when I get painful feedback. I notice the shame that comes up for me—I try to suppress my desire to immediately defend myself by saying that my intentions were good. Before telling someone my intentions were good, I must listen to how they were impacted by what I did. Later, I can talk about how I felt. First, I must understand how the other person felt when I did something that did not feel good to them. For me this is an ongoing practice. Listening, breathing deeply, not speaking while the heat of shame runs through my body—giving myself empathy for how bad it feels to cause harm. When the shame calms down, I can then say I am sorry and identify what I will do differently. I can eventually say that I did not intend to cause harm, but that comes after listening to the experience of harm and after saying I am sorry. I must practice self-talk, reminding myself that it is a gift for someone to tell me that something I did was hurtful. I must remind myself that it is better to know—otherwise, I get no opportunity to achieve my intentions. I have to look in the mirror!

All restorative processes are designed to maximize our ability to identify and correct gaps between intention and impact. The emphasis on truth telling in a respectful way supports the possibility of feedback without condemnation. We are familiar with the feedback loop between victims and wrongdoers. Now we need to think about using that feedback loop between youth and the adults who work with them. Many youth and their families are harmed by our well-intended interventions. There is a very large gap between our intentions and the impact of our work. We need truth telling to get clarity about that gap so that we can eliminate the gap, otherwise our work never succeeds in the way we intended.

Looking into the mirror is an important part of recognizing the gap between intention and impact. What does the mirror tell us about how it looks from someone else's perspective?

So, we are back to listen, listen, and listen. And I return to circle as a strategy. One of the most consistent things I hear from people who participate in circles is that they become better listeners. The discipline of the talking piece changes the way people listen and builds the muscles for listening better in conversations outside of circle.

Adults need spaces to listen to themselves, to connect with their deepest values regarding how they want to be present in the lives of young people. Adults need spaces to talk to each other about the pain they witness in youth, about the challenges they face in their work with youth. Adults need healing spaces to process their own unhealed wounds from their childhood and adolescence. We need to start with ourselves. If we are doing our own healing work, youth will benefit.

— Chapter 5 —

Balanced and Restorative Justice

Not Simply a Buzzword in Pennsylvania

SUSAN BLACKBURN

Dr. Gordon Bazemore will long be remembered and revered in the history of Pennsylvania's juvenile justice system. When Pennsylvania's juvenile justice system made the commitment to the Balanced and Restorative Justice (BARJ) model, it changed its course entirely. Pennsylvania's juvenile justice system did not implement a new program, it changed its course.

Close to three decades have passed since Balanced and Restorative Justice (BARJ) became the driving force behind system reform and improvement efforts for Pennsylvania's juvenile justice system. Pennsylvania's strong and steady progress towards advancing this statutory mission and the related operational goals through policy, practice, and programmatic enhancements dramatically and clearly transformed the Pennsylvania juvenile justice system: its response to youthful offenders, the restoration of those victimized by juvenile crime, and the safety of the communities in which we live.

The enthusiastic adoption of BARJ in Pennsylvania was fueled by Dr. Gordon Bazemore, Director of the National BARJ Project. Along with Dr. Bazemore were his colleagues, Dennis Maloney, co-author of "the balanced approach" (Maloney, Romeg and Armstrong 1988; Office of Juvenile Justice and Delinquency Prevention 1994); Mark

Carey of the Carey Group; Anne Seymour, National Crime Victim Advocate; and Dr. Sandra Pavelka, Project Administrator of the BARJ Project. The BARJ Project provided the knowledge and guidance to Pennsylvania's juvenile justice leadership that was necessary to understand and implement the foundational values and principles underlining the BARJ model.

Pennsylvania was one of eight special emphasis states initially invited to participate in the National BARJ Project, a national demonstration project funded by the Office of Juvenile Justice and Delinquency Prevention, US Department of Justice. The other states in this initiative included: California, Colorado, Florida, Illinois, Michigan, New York, and Texas. Under the leadership of Dr. Bazemore, the project laid the foundation for Pennsylvania's conversion to BARJ through education, training, and technical assistance as well as involvement in front-line activities occurring at the national level. The time and resources devoted to Pennsylvania key leaders allowed the state to participate in the national dialogue, gain and share insights with key juvenile justice leaders from co-participating states, and avail themselves of the numerous research studies and publications offered through the Project. Pennsylvania's implementation planning efforts were also greatly aided by other initiatives sponsored through the BARJ Project such as the BARJ Technical Assistance and Training Consultant Network, the Juvenile Justice Performance Measures Project, and the Special Emphasis States key leader meetings.

Pittsburgh, Pennsylvania was the site of one of the original BARJ Project's pilot programs: the Community Intensive Supervision Project (CISP). CISP has been a true community-based initiative targeting juveniles from selected neighborhoods for intensive supervision in their own communities. The program is operated by the Juvenile Section of the Court of Common Pleas of Allegheny County, and nurtures community support and incorporates community safety, competency development activities, and youth accountability approaches. This chapter will review the implementation of BARJ in Pennsylvania and the ongoing efforts to sustain the mission.

How It All Started

In the late 1990s, many juvenile justice professionals, scholars, and policymakers recognized an existential threat to the juvenile justice system. There was a strong feeling that juvenile justice was under attack. Nearly every state in the nation enacted harsh measures against juvenile crime (Snyder and Sickmund 1999; Torbet et al. 1996). Faced with an apparent epidemic of serious and violent offending, most states responded by limiting juvenile court jurisdiction over serious crimes, sweeping younger and younger offenders into adult criminal courts and adult prisons, and dismantling protections traditionally afforded to young people in trouble with the law. At the same time, an alternative model for responding to youth crime was gaining national attention in juvenile justice circles. This new approach was based on "the balanced approach" (Maloney et al. 1988; Office of Juvenile Justice and Delinquency Prevention 1994), the work of Dr. Bazemore, and the staff of the BARJ Project. Pennsylvania juvenile justice leaders and practitioners took notice of this work and began discussions on the merits of the values and principles endorsed through it. With a newly elected governor steps were taken to address youth crime by strengthening and getting smart on crime, victimization, and delinquency prevention by embracing BARJ.

Pennsylvania was one of the first states to enact the BARJ principles in their judicial code. In 1995, Pennsylvania's General Assembly was called into a special session by this newly elected governor to focus exclusively on the issue of crime. This special session dramatically influenced Pennsylvania's juvenile justice system with the passage of Act 33 of 1995, which redefined the very mission of juvenile justice as:

> to provide for children committing delinquent acts programs of supervision, care and rehabilitation which provide balanced attention to the protection of the community, the imposition of accountability for offenses committed and the development of competencies to enable children to become responsible and productive members of the community.

These goals are embedded in the Pennsylvania Juvenile Act (42 PaCS Section 6301) and guide the daily activities of juvenile justice practitioners from the judiciary to those that provide community and residential services to our youth.

The legislation was rooted in the philosophy of restorative justice, which gives priority to repairing the harm done to crime victims and communities, and which defines accountability in terms of assuming responsibility and taking action to repair harm. The "balanced attention" mandate in the Juvenile Act provided the framework for implementing restorative justice in Pennsylvania's juvenile justice system. Also, at the foundation of this mandate is the concept that crime victims and the community, as well as the offenders, should gain tangible benefits from their interactions with the system.

The principles which served as the foundation for the 1995 amendments to the purpose clause of the Juvenile Act (42 PaCS Section 6301) and redefined the overarching goals for Pennsylvania juvenile justice are laid out as follows:

- *Community Protection:* The citizens of Pennsylvania have a right to safe and secure communities. It is the process of contributing to safe communities—with particular emphasis on known delinquent youth—through prevention, supervision, and control.

- *Accountability:* In Pennsylvania, when a crime is committed by a juvenile, an obligation to the victim and the community is incurred. Accountability requires purposeful attention to participation in process(es) whereby youth understand and acknowledge: the wrongfulness of their actions; the impact of the illegal behavior on the victim and community; and their responsibility for causing harm and the need to take action towards repairing that harm.

- *Competency Development:* Juvenile offenders who come within the jurisdiction of Pennsylvania's juvenile justice system should leave the system more capable of being productive members of their community. It is the process by which delinquent youth acquire the skills that make it possible for them to become productive, connected, and law-abiding members of their communities.

- *Individualization:* Each case referred to Pennsylvania's juvenile justice system presents unique circumstances, and the response of the system must therefore be individualized and based on an assessment of all relevant information and factors.

- *Balance:* As appropriate to the individual circumstances of each case, Pennsylvania's juvenile justice system should provide balanced attention to the protection of the community, the imposition of accountability for offenses committed, and the development of competencies to enable children to become responsible and productive members of their communities. Victims of crime, the community, and juvenile offenders as well should receive balanced attention from the juvenile justice system and each should gain tangible benefits from their interactions with the system.

At the time, the BARJ mission represented a dramatic new direction for Pennsylvania's juvenile justice system, which for generations had been predicated on the traditional *parens patriae* philosophy and the best interests of the offending youth. Most juvenile justice practitioners entered the field to work with these youth, having no inclination of working with crime victims and community members. True systems change begins with not only a firm foundation but a strong vision for moving forward. As a result, a huge cultural shift was necessary.

With that in mind, the PCCD's Juvenile Justice and Delinquency Prevention Committee (formerly known as the Juvenile Advisory Committee) crafted the juvenile justice system's mission statement along with a comprehensive set of guiding principles and beliefs to guide the overall operation of Pennsylvania's juvenile justice system. The mission statement is articulated as:

Pennsylvania Juvenile Justice:

- Community Protection
- Victim Restoration
- Youth Redemption.

Community Protection refers to the right of all Pennsylvania citizens to be and feel safe from crime. *Victim Restoration* emphasizes that, in Pennsylvania, a juvenile who commits a crime harms the victim of the crime and the community, and thereby incurs an obligation to repair that harm to the greatest extent possible. *Youth Redemption* embodies the belief that juvenile offenders in Pennsylvania have strengths, are capable of change, can earn redemption, and can become responsible and productive members of their communities. Further, all services designed and implemented to achieve this mission and all hearings and decisions under the Juvenile Act—indeed all aspects of the juvenile justice system—must be provided in a fair and unbiased manner (Juvenile Court Judges' Commission 2015).

Crime victims and survivors were front and center during the Special Session on Crime when the Pennsylvania Office of Victim Advocate (OVA) was created by Act 8 of 1995. The Victim Advocate has the authority and the duty to represent the rights and interests of all Commonwealth crime victims in general, including victims of juvenile offenders. Although originally the Victim Advocate was responsible for representing the rights and interests of crime victims before the Department of Corrections, the newly appointed Victim Advocate participated in efforts to enhance rights and services to victims of juvenile offenders and helped advance Act 86 of 2000 which created a "Bill of Rights" for victims of juvenile offenses. As a result, the Crime Victims Act now requires that victims of crimes committed by juvenile offenders can actively participate in the juvenile justice process. The legislative requirements and this clear, yet simple, mission statement laid a solid foundation for system enhancement efforts and continues to influence *all* policy and program development; planning and budgeting; resource allocation; and training requirements.

Building on a Strong Foundation
How We Got There

In comparison with other states, Pennsylvania's is a highly decentralized juvenile justice system, characterized by an unusual amount of local control and a remarkably diverse mix of private delinquency service providers that supplement the public services network. The state provides leadership, but the local juvenile courts administer the local juvenile court and probation departments. The Pennsylvania constitution gives the Courts of Common Pleas in each of the state's 67 counties unlimited original jurisdiction in juvenile delinquency matters (Juvenile Court Judges' Commission 2018).

Key state agencies and organizations responsible for juvenile justice matters boast strong partnerships and have been devoted to assisting the courts in achieving the "balanced attention" mandates in the Pennsylvania Juvenile Act. The success of Pennsylvania's effort to advance BARJ would not have been possible without the active involvement, expertise, and contributions from entities such as: the Juvenile Court Judges' Commission (JCJC); the Pennsylvania Council of Chief Juvenile Probation Officers (PCCJPO); the Juvenile Justice and Delinquency Prevention Committee (JJDPC) and the Victim Services Advisory Committee (VSAC) of the Pennsylvania Commission on Crime and Delinquency (PCCD); the Office of the Victim Advocate (OVA); the National Center for Juvenile Justice (NCJJ); and county-level juvenile courts, district attorneys, probation departments, and victim service agencies.

The JCJC is a statutorily created body that is mandated to advise juvenile court judges on all matters relating to the care of delinquent children. The JCJC also collects and disseminates Pennsylvania juvenile court statistics and establishes administrative and procedural standards for juvenile courts (Juvenile Court Judges' Commission 2018). Its member judges are leaders in advancing the juvenile justice mission and goals at the state and county levels through the development of standards of practice and judicial procedure as well as the administration of a grant-in-aid program to improve county juvenile procedure.

The PCCD initiates, validates, and financially supports justice-related programs put forth by practitioners and experts in the justice system. It focuses on research, policy, planning, training, evidence-based programming, technology, outreach, and support services. The Commission sets priorities for justice-related projects supported by the PCCD's funding streams through its various state advisory committees, such as the JJDPC and the VSAC.

The JJDPC is a federally mandated State Advisory Group with responsibility for juvenile justice planning, coordination, and policy recommendations as well as establishing priorities for juvenile justice projects supported by the various federal and state funding streams.

The VSAC is instrumental in enhancing rights and services to victims of crime. This group has responsibility for the dissemination of federal and state funds for victim service providers throughout the state. They are responsible for training, education, and system planning within the victim services community, and for the development of victim-sensitive strategies, policy, and programming.

The PCCJPO is a highly regarded membership organization of chief probation officers, deputy chiefs, supervisors, and probation staff that works closely with the JCJC on probation training, education, system planning, and legislative issues. The Council also works closely with all other juvenile justice system stakeholders and has been crucially essential to the successful implementation of this and other important initiatives.[1] The OVA advocates for the rights and needs of crime victims and survivors.[2] The NCJJ is the research arm of the National Council of Juvenile and Family Court Judges. Researchers at the Center provided pivotal guidance and technical assistance to the balanced and restorative juvenile justice reform efforts both nationally and to Pennsylvania.[3]

Gaining an understanding and a commitment to a new way of "doing business" is never an easy task, especially in a Commonwealth with 67 separate and different juvenile court operations. A mutual understanding of the philosophy, new values, principles, and goals underlying the new purpose clause of the Pennsylvania Juvenile Act (42 PaCS Section 6301) was imperative to the systemic, organizational, and cultural change that was required. Strong and informed leadership was needed at the top, but even more critical were the many practitioners conducting the actual work daily. It was from this perspective that change efforts in Pennsylvania began.

From the onset, Pennsylvania spent considerable time, effort, and resources to educate and train juvenile justice practitioners and the

---

1   https://pachiefprobationofficers.org
2   www.ova.pa.gov/AboutOVA/Pages/default.aspx
3   www.ncjfcj.org/national-center-for-juvenile-justice

judiciary in the principles of BARJ. Annual statewide conferences focused on BARJ were convened and numerous educational monographs, papers, and articles were published to support juvenile court judges and juvenile justice practitioners to understand and implement the BARJ mission in their local jurisdictions.

To explain the underlying philosophy of BARJ and the new purpose clause of the Juvenile Act, the JCJC organized multiple statewide policy forums and educational training opportunities for juvenile justice stakeholders and practitioners. The first statewide forum, held in 1996, was led by Dr. Gordon Bazemore and Dennis Maloney of the BARJ Project. Following this statewide event, county stakeholder teams consisting of Judges, Chief Juvenile Probation Officers, District Attorneys, Public Defenders, and victim advocates participated in a series of regional training sessions. These local teams were provided technical assistance, resources, and tools to assist them in their local implementation efforts.

A strategic planning process was convened by the Pennsylvania Council of Chief Juvenile Probation Officers to implement BARJ principles throughout the Commonwealth's 67 counties. The plan included the creation and addition of several new working committees to address implementation efforts: a BARJ Justice Committee which would focus on the broader implementation efforts, a Victims Services Committee whose focus was on inclusive attention to policy and program developments with the victims' services, and a Court and Community Collaboration Committee whose focus was enhancing experiences in communities to support the new juvenile justice goals. These committees remain viable contributors to the work of the Council and promote the ongoing juvenile justice system reforms.

The addition of crime victims as clients of the juvenile justice system was initially quite challenging. A statewide training entitled "Enhancing your Juvenile Court's Response to Victims" was offered for teams of juvenile justice stakeholders and practitioners from the counties to address these challenges by introducing the needs of victims of juvenile offenders, and the associated policies, practices, and services which would serve to include crime victims in the juvenile justice process.

Publications

A wide range of publications defining and describing BARJ were written and distributed statewide such as monographs, technical assistance articles and handbooks, and statewide and local newsletters. Critical resources for the judiciary were developed including the *Pennsylvania Delinquency Benchbook* (Juvenile Court Judges' Commission 2018), which outlines how judges may apply BARJ principles on and off the bench. This was published in 2003 and subsequently updated in 2018.

The Juvenile Court Procedural Rules Project originated in 1998 as an initiative to analyze national standards, case law, and local practices to respond to changes in the purpose of the Juvenile Act. The *Rules of Delinquency Procedure* incorporate provisions for BARJ to be addressed at every stage of the delinquency proceedings and provide unity of practice throughout Pennsylvania's juvenile justice system. The Rules also incorporated and expanded the rights and role for victims of juvenile offenders; subsequently victims of juvenile offenders began to be heard through the juvenile justice process. The presence of juvenile crime victims in the courtrooms and the recitation/sharing of their victim impact statements are all now part of the process.

Of special note are the Pennsylvania BARJ White Papers published and widely distributed throughout Pennsylvania and nationally. These significant publications served to provide definition and add clarity for BARJ in Pennsylvania's juvenile justice system. They laid out for Pennsylvania practitioners the legal, philosophical, and practical foundations of the BARJ goals by explaining each goal, why it is important, and how the specific goal can be achieved. The White Papers captured many of the foundations of the "what works" research for reducing recidivism and set the groundwork for future juvenile justice enhancements.

These White Papers were the start of an extended statewide discussion focused on continued collaboration, refinement, understanding, and action. Table 5.1 provides a summary of each White Paper/goal which addresses the definition of each goal and the new roles and responsibilities, and it provides reference to many programs and practices which are regarded as best practice.

Table 5.1 Summary of Pennsylvania BARJ White Papers

White Paper Title/BARJ Goal Definition	Juvenile Justice System Role	Practices and Programs
Advancing Community Protection (2008) Community Protection is the process of contributing to safe communities—with particular emphasis on known juvenile offenders—through prevention, supervision, and control	Identify static and dynamic risk factors (criminogenic needs) that put youth at risk for continued delinquent behavior Manage risk by using the least restrictive setting required to protect the community Minimize risk by selecting interventions that address the most critical criminogenic needs	Standardized risk assessments Cognitive behavioral approaches Skill training programs "Blueprints" programs Treatment protocols for mental illness, substance abuse, and sexual aggression Services and supports that help parents set clear expectations for and monitor the behavior of their children and learn other parenting skills
Advancing Competency Development (2005) Competency Development is the process by which juvenile offenders acquire the knowledge and skills that make it possible for them to become productive, connected, and law-abiding members of their communities and select five core competency domains—areas in which one could reasonably expect young people in trouble with the law to build and demonstrate competencies depending on their age and stage of development (pro-social skills, moral reasoning skills, academic skills, workforce development skills, and independent living skills)	Facilitate efforts that advance youths' competencies so that offenders are less likely to take part in anti-social, delinquent behaviors and better able to become responsible and productive members of their communities	Standardized needs (and strengths) assessment Supervision plan based upon assessment results Cognitive behavioral approaches Structured and specific skill-training programs Incentives and sanctions Opportunities to practice and demonstrate these new skills Document intermediate outcomes at case closing

Cont.

White Paper Title/BARJ Goal Definition	Juvenile Justice System Role	Practices and Programs
Advancing Accountability: Moving Toward Victim Restoration (2006) Accountability requires purposeful attention to offender participation in a process whereby juvenile offenders understand and acknowledge: <ul><li>the wrongfulness of their actions</li><li>the impact of the crime on the crime victim and the community</li><li>their responsibility for causing harm and take action towards repairing that harm</li></ul>	Determine what obligations juvenile offenders incur and provide the support and services necessary for offenders to fulfill those obligations and honor and protect crime victims' rights	Victim impact statements Victim community awareness curriculum/classes Community Justice Panels/Victim Impact Panels Apology statements Restitution Meaningful community service Crime Victims' Compensation Fund Restorative Processes (such as group conferencing and mediation), with sensitive inclusion of the crime victim and voluntary participation by all parties

Source: Pennsylvania Juvenile Court Judges' Commission White Papers, www.jcjc.pa.gov/Publications/Pages/default.aspx

The clearly articulated goals in the Juvenile Act and further defined through the White Papers have allowed the Pennsylvania juvenile justice system to develop and enhance performance measures and report goal-focused outcomes. The NCJJ assisted juvenile justice practitioners in the development of these intermediate outcomes and a protocol for probation departments to collect, analyze, and present intermediate outcome data. This data has become the basis for local and statewide "report cards" for the system. Statewide Juvenile Justice Outcome Measures are the aggregate quarterly reports of juvenile justice outcomes for the juvenile offenders in Pennsylvania. The reports reflect outcomes of juvenile offenders whose cases were closed during the report period and who have received a period of supervision from a county juvenile probation department. Outcomes associated with community protection, accountability, and competency development are reported annually. Data is collected on juveniles at the closing of their case and reported to the JCJC.

Based on the 2021 Pennsylvania Annual Outcomes Report (Juvenile Court Judges' Commission 2021), county juvenile probation departments supervised and closed 6961 cases. Of these cases, it is notable that:

- 88.1 percent (6315) of juveniles successfully completed supervision without a new offense resulting in a Consent Decree, Adjudication of Delinquency, ARD, Nolo Contendere, or finding of guilt in a criminal proceeding

- the total amount of restitution collected was $1,571,224

- 88.3 percent of juveniles made *full* restitution to their victims

- 95 percent of juveniles assigned community service completed their obligation resulting in a dollar value of $1,264,095

- 96.7 percent of juveniles successfully completed a victim/awareness curriculum/class when assigned

- 92.3 percent of juveniles whose cases were closed were employed or actively engaged in an educational or vocational activity at case closing

- 41.7 percent of the juveniles successfully completed a case plan that included goals; risk-reduction activities such as skill-building activities and cognitive behavioral group interventions; and treatment services to address the top two to three criminogenic needs identified by the Youth Level of Service (Juvenile Court Judges' Commission 2021).

Policy and Program Alignment

Policy and program alignment occurred as juvenile justice professionals incorporated the principles and goals of BARJ. The JCJC developed standards of practice around specialized juvenile probation positions and encouraged local jurisdictions to do the same. Counties developed their individual mission statements, developed strategic plans, set up implementation structures, and established performance measures to assess the outcomes based on the goals. The BARJ goals were integrated into court processes, dispositions, and court orders.

By 2001, the PCCD had awarded over $6.2 million to 32 counties specifically for the purpose of developing, implementing, and expanding BARJ programs, services, and initiatives. Funding for the BARJ Training and TA Project through the JCJC's Center for Juvenile Justice Training and Research (CJJT&R) was instrumental in establishing a focal point for training and technical assistance specific to the new BARJ mission and initiatives. In 1998, a BARJ Specialist position was created within the JCJC with funding made available for counties to create BARJ Coordinators positions in local juvenile courts.

Simultaneously, leadership of the victims' services community was mobilizing around the new juvenile justice reforms. Act 86, known as the Bill of Rights for Victims of Juvenile Crime, became effective on December 29, 2000. Act 86 amended the Crime Victims Act to expand the rights afforded to crime victims of adult offenders to be applicable to victims of juvenile offenders involved in the Pennsylvania juvenile justice system (Crime Victims' Bill of Rights 11.201). Pennsylvania's BARJ reforms established a demonstrable partnership between the juvenile court and victim advocacy groups that had been virtually non-existent. Due to the amendments to the Crime Victims Act in 2000, all victims of juvenile offenders receive information, rights, and services which include notification of major proceedings and input into critical decision-making points in the juvenile justice process, the right to submit victim impact statements, and an opportunity to have an apology from the offending youth. Remarkably, the passage of this legislation also came with a line item in the Pennsylvania state budget to fund Victim of Juvenile Offender (VOJO) advocates for all counties. Additionally, statewide VOJO advocates were appointed to provide training and technical assistance to local jurisdictions.

Youth are encouraged to acknowledge the harm they caused due to their behavior and be provided with opportunities to repair that harm to the extent possible and are also directed to participate in activities that focus on enhancing their skills and competencies. An impact of crime program specifically established for Pennsylvania entitled *The Victim Community Awareness: An Orientation for Juveniles* was developed by Ms. Valerie Bender, Restorative Justice Consultant, to provide youth with an awareness of the impact of their crime on victims and communities. This Pennsylvania program has become a standard practice for operationalizing the accountability goal in the majority of counties and throughout the service provider community.

Restorative practices, such as community justice panels, victim impact panels, victim-offender dialogue, and restorative group conferencing, all attracted attention and gained a foothold as means for holding offending youth accountable for repairing the harm they caused to individual victims and communities. Restitution and community service are two of the Juvenile Courts' most basic tools for ensuring delinquent youth are held accountable for repairing the harm that stems from their actions. The Juvenile Act authorizes judges to "order payment by the child of reasonable amounts of restitution as part of the plan of rehabilitation" (42 PaCS Section 6301). The Juvenile Act also includes provisions for counties to establish "restitution funds" from which crime victims can be reimbursed for financial losses once the youth "works off" their community services obligation ordered by the court.

Community service programs operate in all 67 counties in

Pennsylvania. Local programs used imagination and ingenuity to develop meaningful community service projects that would address all three primary BARJ goals. Juvenile offenders perform work that is of interest to local community members and crime victims. Service projects including graffiti removal, community clean-ups, and assistance to local community fairs and festivals provide communities with assistance from these youth people and provide the public with the knowledge that offending youth are held accountable and can earn redemption. Many youths may continue to volunteer at their community service site well beyond the obligatory assignment.

A few highlights of innovative projects include: working with master gardeners, many jurisdictions created community Gardening Projects where youth learned to grow and harvest fresh produce which is then delivered to local food pantries and families in need; skill building through Habitat for Humanity helped many youths learn construction skills by renovating and building homes for needy families; a recycling project in Lehigh County taught youth the importance of recycling and earned them cash for their restitution payments; stream restoration projects helped youth understand their natural environment and provided a needed service that helped prevent flooding by constructing erosion devices along rural streams. These meaningful community service projects obviously provide for the development of skills, the repair of harm, and structured time under supervision.

An emphasis on structured supervision strategies and probation and police partnerships provided increased safety measures to protect communities from the risk posed by delinquent youth. A focus on the goal of competency development reinforced the system's attention on academic and workforce development skills for youthful offenders. Anger management and conflict resolution programs became commonplace, and a few jurisdictions began to experiment with more formalized tools such as Aggression Replacement Therapy (ART), Thinking for a Change, and the use of resources from the National Curriculum and Training Institute (NCTI). However, the full impact of competency development remained somewhat elusive until application of evidence-based research became clear, setting the stage for the Juvenile Justice System Enhancement Strategy.

In 2005, ten years after Act 33 went into effect, Pennsylvania became the first of four states to participate in the John D. and Catherine T. MacArthur Foundation's Models for Change juvenile justice reform initiative to sustain and build upon the progress made toward the BARJ mission. Through this initiative, Pennsylvania addressed and improved the coordination of mental health and juvenile justice systems, the system of aftercare services and supports, and disproportionate minority contact concerns. Models for Change accelerated the pace of Pennsylvania's efforts at reform at both the state and local levels, and supported a series of evidence-based practices, including the introduction of screening and risk assessment instruments and targeted evidence-based interventions. Thus, Pennsylvania again embarked on a strategic approach to enhance the BARJ goals with a focus on the "what works" research.

In 2010, the JCJC and the PCCJPO created the Juvenile Justice System Enhancement Strategy (JJSES) out of recognition that the growth of knowledge derived from research evidence required juvenile justice stakeholders to adapt their practices to be more effective at achieving the BARJ goals. The first step in developing JJSES was to establish a statement of purpose and a plan describing the steps needed to integrate this growing research knowledge into existing practices. The statement of purpose is articulated as follows:

> We dedicate ourselves to working in partnership to enhance the capacity of Pennsylvania's juvenile justice system to achieve its mission of BARJ by:
>
> - Employing evidence-based practices with fidelity, at every stage of the juvenile justice process;
>
> - Collecting and analyzing the data necessary to measure the results of these efforts; and with this knowledge,
>
> - Striving to continuously improve the quality of our decisions, services, and programs. Statement. (Pennsylvania Commission on Crime and Delinquency 2012, 2015)

The publication commonly known as the "JJSES Monograph" (*Advancing BARJ through Pennsylvania's JJSES*) contains a detailed explanation of the JJSES, including the activities and practices that comprise the stages of the framework (Juvenile Court Judges' Commission 1997; Pennsylvania Commission on Crime and Delinquency 2012, 2015). A plethora of publications and resources were developed during this time in order to document and detail this research.

This initiative ignited a number of changes, including another revision of the purpose clause of Pennsylvania's Juvenile Act, mandating the employment of evidence-based practices whenever possible. The use of evidence-based practices is the cornerstone of the JJSES, compelling juvenile justice systems to achieve BARJ goals by aligning practice with research evidence.

The JJSES refocused and energized probation officers and juvenile justice stakeholders by leaning on empirical, data-driven tactics to guide structured decision-making; applying validated and reliable risk/needs actuarial assessments; making available evidence-based interventions; utilizing research evidence to shape case planning; and using data to inform performance measures, evaluation, and continuous quality improvement. JJSES also identifies resources for effective probation supervision. Many of Pennsylvania's 67 county probation departments have adopted practices and interventions including:

- Motivational interviewing: This is a counseling method that uses collaborative, client-centered, and goal-oriented communication to affect behavior change in individuals. A Pennsylvania-specific MI protocol was established to assist counties in implementing motivational interviewing skills.

- Structured decision-making: This is effected through the use of actuarial assessments for key decision-making points such as the Youth Level of Service (YLS) at intake, the Pennsylvania Detention Risk Assessment Instrument (PaDRAI) for secure detention, and the MAYSI, a mental health screening tool.

- Four Core Competencies: This is based on research that suggests that, to be effective, juvenile justice professionals must possess four fundamental competencies: establishing a professional alliance with youth, case planning, skills practice, and the effective use of rewards and sanctions.

- Evidence-based programming and interventions such as the

Carey Guides: This is a series of 33 web-based handbooks that help probation staff apply EBP to their clients. And Brief Intervention Tools (BITS). The guides are organized and presented in two sets—one that specifically addresses offenders' criminogenic needs and the other that addresses case management issues. The purpose of the BITS is to help juvenile justice professionals to effectively address key skill deficits in short, structured interventions (The Carey Group, Inc.).

- Cognitive-behavioral model: The cognitive-behavioral model suggests that criminal behavior is learned, that some risks and needs are more important than others, and that by addressing these risks and needs in the appropriate fashion, offender behavior may be changed.

- The Standardized Program Evaluation Protocol (SPEP): Based on the work of Dr. Mark Lipsey, Pennsylvania adopted the SPEP: a validated, data-driven rating system for determining how well a program matches what research tells us is effective for that particular type of program in reducing the recidivism of juvenile offenders (Lipsey et al. 2010).

The essence of the JJSES can be summarized as follows: it uses research-based evidence and data to guide policy and practice in all aspects of juvenile justice and, as such, enhances the capacity of Pennsylvania's juvenile justice system to achieve its BARJ goals. Evidence-based practices should guide stakeholders' actions at each decision point, whether those actions are to protect the community from further harm, develop competencies in youth to enable them to become productive members of their communities, and/or restore the harm done to victims and the community.

One of the primary tools used to measure the success of programs and policy within the juvenile justice system is to track recidivism, or the return to crime. Since 2012, Pennsylvania has tracked the outcomes of juvenile offenders for a period of two years after case closure to determine the percentage that remained law-abiding citizens. Special attention has been given to the recidivism rates of youth prior to versus after the implementation of the JJSES. Success is defined as no subsequent adjudications of delinquency or convictions in criminal court for a felony or misdemeanor offense within two years of case closure. Data from the 2018 case closing reports reflect a success rate for Pennsylvania delinquent youth of 85 percent and, overall, a 26 percent decrease in the statewide recidivism rate over the past five years (Pennsylvania Juvenile Court Judges' Commission 2022).

It is critical to understand and remember that reduction in recidivism is not the lone goal of juvenile justice. Accountability as measured by the degree to which offenders have worked to repair the harm caused by their actions is critical to a community that sees all its members as vital contributors to healthy families and safe neighborhoods. Ultimately, a key juvenile justice system goal is for delinquent youth to take full responsibility for their actions and gain the motivation and competencies to change their conduct behavior in the future. Probation officers, treatment providers, family members, and other pro-social people involved with juveniles must take advantage of the best available research and knowledge as they work toward these goals.

References

Juvenile Act, Pennsylvania State Statute, Chapter 63, Juvenile Matters, 42 PA C.S.A S6301, 1995.

Juvenile Court Judges' Commission (1997) "Balanced and Restorative Justice in Pennsylvania: A New Mission and Changing Roles Within the Juvenile Justice System." Harrisburg, PA: Juvenile Court Judges' Commission.

Juvenile Court Judges' Commission (2015) "Pennsylvania Court Dispositions." Harrisburg, PA: Juvenile Court Judges' Commission 26, no. 3. www.jcjc.pa.gov/Publications/Newsletters/2015/March.pdf

Juvenile Court Judges' Commission (2018) *Pennsylvania Juvenile Delinquency Bench Book*. Harrisburg, PA: Juvenile Court Judges' Commission. www.jcjc.pa.gov/Publications/Documents/Juvenile%20Delinquency%20Benchbook/Pennsylvania%20Juvenile%20Delinquency%20Benchbook_10-2018.pdf

Juvenile Court Judges' Commission (2021) "Pennsylvania Annual Outcomes Report." Harrisburg, PA: Juvenile Court Judges' Commission. www.jcjc.pa.gov/Research-Statistics/Documents/2021%20Statewide%20Outcome%20Measures%20Report.pdf

Lipsey, M.W., Howell, J.C., Kelly, M.R., Chapman, G., and Carver, D. (2010) "Improving the Effectiveness of Juvenile Justice Programs: A New Perspective on Evidence-based Programs." Washington, DC: Center for Juvenile Justice Reform. https://njjn.org/uploads/digital-library/CJJR_Lipsey_Improving-Effectiveness-of-Juvenile-Justice_2010.pdf

Maloney, D., Romig, D., and Armstrong, T. (1988) "Juvenile probation: The balanced approach." *Juvenile and Family Court Journal 39*, 3, 73-87. doi.org/10.1111/j.1755-6988.1988.tb00623.x

Office of Juvenile Justice and Delinquency Prevention (1994) "Balanced and Restorative Justice. Program Summary." Washington, DC: Office of Juvenile Justice and Delinquency Prevention. www.ncjrs.gov/pdffiles/bal.pdf

Pennsylvania Commission on Crime and Delinquency (2012) "Pennsylvania's Juvenile Justice System Enhancement Strategy: Achieving our Balanced and Restorative Justice Mission Through Evidence-based Policy and Practice." Harrisburg, PA: Pennsylvania Commission on Crime and Delinquency. www.pccd.pa.gov/Juvenile-Justice/Documents/JJSES%20Monograph%20Final%20version%20press%20ready%2005%2025%2012.pdf

Pennsylvania Commission on Crime and Delinquency (2015) "Advancing Balanced and Restorative Justice Through Pennsylvania's Juvenile Justice System Enhancement Strategy." Harrisburg, PA: Pennsylvania Commission on Crime and Delinquency.

Pennsylvania Juvenile Court Judges' Commission (2022) "Recidivism [Fact Sheet]." Pennsylvania Juvenile Justice System. www.jcjc.pa.gov/Research-Statistics/Documents/Slider%20Docs-Pics/2022%20Recidivism%20Fact%20Sheet.pdf

Snyder, H. and Sickmund, M. (1999) *Juvenile Offenders and Victims: 1999 National Report*. Washington, DC: Office of Juvenile Justice and Delinquency Prevention. www.ncjj.org/pdf/1999%20natl%20report.pdf

Torbet, P., Gable, R., Hurst, H., Montgomery, I., Szymanski, L., and Thomas, D. (1996) *State Responses to Serious and Violent Juvenile Crime*. Washington, DC: Office of Juvenile Justice and Delinquency Prevention. www.ncjj.org/pdf/statresp.pdf

— Chapter 6 —

School-Justice Partnerships

Building a Safe and Healthy Community
through Restorative Justice

JUDGE STEVEN TESKE (RET.)

In the Beginning, Circa 1995

It was the early 1990s; I was assistant director of field operations for the Georgia State Board of Pardons and Paroles and tasked by my director to travel the country and find the best practices in parole supervision and design a new supervision program that would reduce recidivism. I traveled from the east to west coasts shadowing parole and probation officers assigned to specialized units, observed multiple treatment programming, and listened to agency directors describe recent innovations in offender supervision and treatment. One of my tour of duties included a site visit to a new-style offender boot camp in central New York that boasted the addition of behavioral treatment modalities, a change from the military-only drills of marching in cadence, calisthenics, and yelling in your face, which still occurred but with treatment programs added to the regimen. I followed the boot camp graduates to their homes in New York City and tracked them to their offender programs, all designed to address their specific criminogenic needs.

Notwithstanding all the innovative practices thrown my way, the most impressive I found in my journeys that year was introduced to me by the pioneer of an emerging and effective approach at the time called restorative justice, Dr. Gordon Bazemore, though he made it clear that restorative justice was merely re-emerging. Bazemore was quick to inform his students that restorative justice existed in ancient civilizations only to be decimated when societies evolved to monarchs and removed the community as the deliverer of justice, which focused on the offender, victim, and community, and placed it in the hands of the monarch. A crime was an offense against the King and Crown, or *Lése-majesté*, and the victim was no longer an active participant in the search for justice. Even as monarchs began to fade or lose much of their authority, the deliverer of justice resided in the secular government, and the victim and community remained, for the most part, voiceless.

What I learned from Bazemore altered my universe of "What Works" in recidivist reduction, and not merely because it works, but it did what other best practices could not: force systemic changes to entire juvenile justice systems provided the leadership was serious about taking a holistic approach to restorative justice. Traditional evidence-based practices (EBPs) focus solely on the offender: cognitive behavioral intervention, moral resonation therapy, and mentoring just to name a few. There are some EBPs that include family members or others residing in the home with the offender such as multi-systemic therapy (MST) and family functional therapy (FFT), but only restorative justice focused on the victim, and it is the offender's role to repair the harm they did. For the offender to reintegrate into the community (be accepted), they must undergo a process Bazemore referred to as "earned redemption," a sanctioning approach that allows offenders to "make amends" to those they harmed (Bazemore 1999).

This shift from the focus of punishing or treating the offender to a holistic approach that includes those harmed, the victims, and the community informed me that collaboration would become a necessity to include the community. Regardless of what innovative approach I observed or heard during my journey that year, I remained indelibly impressed with restorative justice. And I was not the only one impressed with it. During that visit, I had the good fortune to visit Dr. Scott Peck, psychiatrist and author of *The Road Less Traveled* (1978), who took an interest in my journey and inquired into what I had found so far. I told him about what I had learned from Bazemore and that I was already working on ways to construct a supervision program framed by restorative justice. Dr. Peck listened intently and commented how the concepts of delayed gratification, accepting responsibility, and "balancing" mentioned in his book are closely aligned to the restorative justice principles I described, and in fact he made a written note of it during our conversation.

Upon returning to Atlanta, I wrote and presented my proposal entitled "Supervised Track and Phase Supervision" (STAPS). It collapsed the salient areas of criminogenic needs into tracks with each track broken down into graduated phases that include evidence-based modalities to address the criminogenic need specific to that track. Central to this approach was collaboration and partnerships between various public and private entities in each parole district. This was necessary for two reasons: (1) to garner the collective support needed to acquire the programming; and (2) to develop a restorative justice system to engage the community and the victims.

However, as is too often the case, good things fall casualty to timing and happenstance. There was a changing of the guard after I returned to Atlanta, and the new guard was less progressive. The proposal was shelved, except for my idea of consolidating parole offices to promote local collaboration. That part was economical and would save tax dollars even though more funds would be saved by reducing future victims of crime.

Well before this change of guard, I had graduated law school and passed the Bar. My bosses had convinced me to stay to build an innovative parole supervision program, and I did. My interest to remain was galvanized, or so I thought, during my sabbatical in search for a new and improved offender supervision program and my introduction to Bazemore being the peak of my enlightenment. My hopes for the future in community corrections were deflated by the oppressive fist of our new regime that crushed my proposal.

I was devastated. I saw no future in community corrections. I resigned to go practice law.

Political leaders are like the weather: one day it is sunny, and the next is stormy, and back and forth they come and go. After I left, the storm eventually turned to sunny days, and another new guard took the helm of the Board. My proposal was taken off the shelf, dusted off, and new life breathed into it by a group of progressive bureaucrats. They worked their magic, also integrating technology, resulting in national and international recognition (Bralley and Prevost 2001). They acknowledged my foundational work toward this innovative approach and invited me to one of those recognitions to share in the honor, and I went (APPA awards in 2001).

After several years of trial practice, I seized the opportunity to pursue a career as a jurist in the juvenile justice system and would become what the Governor of Georgia would later describe "a revolutionary jurist," a description I earned thanks to the teachings and inspirations of the likes of Bazemore (Deal 2013).

I was given a second chance in life to finish what I started, but this time working with kids. It was another opportunity to reengage with Bazemore for guidance and mentoring on ways I could assert my new role as a judge in utilizing restorative justice to reform a misguided juvenile justice system ravaged with ineffective anecdotal programs, punitive practices, racial and ethnic disparities, and little to no voice from victims and the community. This time around, Bazemore had a lot more to say, especially about juvenile court judges and their leadership role "as gatekeepers to restorative justice" (Bazemore 1998, p.2).

During my sojourn in the practice of law, Gordon took a deep dive into how judges perceived their role with victims as well as offenders by conducting focus groups in four states (Bazemore 1998). His results were published a year before I took the Bench, and it was during the "punitive era" of juvenile justice, an era not friendly to progressive practices, including restorative justice. Gordon made one thing quite clear to me: for restorative justice to be woven into the fabric of my juvenile justice system, "court practices" had to drastically change and "risk-taking" was necessary to make the drastic changes. That, he said, demanded leadership from the Bench and off the Bench. I recall Bazemore saying that "judicial leadership is uncommon" and going on to explain it has more to do with the immutable nature of the job than the person wearing the robe. The job, he said, "doesn't lend itself to risk-taking behaviors."

Bringing this full circle, one could guess that Gordon's counsel had much to do with inspiring my "revolutionary" ideas as a judge.

The remainder of this chapter is dedicated to Bazemore's influence on my work to build a School-Justice Partnership (SJP):

a collaborative approach to reduce student arrests on campus and replace those arrests with victim-centered reparative programs.

Suffice it to say, this is much more Gordon's story than it is mine.

What Did I Get Myself Into?

By the time I took the Bench in July 1999, I had made partner in the law firm. I was doing well, but I was exhausted. Trying cases and traveling the state on cases related to my work with the attorney general's office were wearing me down. And some clients I could do without. But it did not take long sitting the Bench to question what I got myself into. I was the junior judge out of three, which meant I did the initial hearings that decided probable cause. I was the gatekeeper deciding which kids stayed locked up or got to go home. The court had no metric system to guide judges on detention decision-making, much less for the intake workers who decide which kids arrested went to jail. Judging by the volume of detained kids in my court every day, their discretion favored lock-up. Just before my retirement, my court administrator and I reminisced about those days when I took the Bench and how far we had come in reducing detention rates. He chuckled and told me that his metric system before I introduced an objective admission tool was: "If they woke me up in the middle of the night, it was enough to lock 'em up."

In no time, I noticed that too many kids arrested were for misdemeanor offenses, and it seemed that many of them were for minor school offenses. Students wadding up a piece of paper and throwing it across the room, cursing in class, threatening to kick another student's "ass," or a school fight with no injuries other than one's pride. It did not take long for this to gnaw at me. I began to question why I left the thrill of trying cases, some involving millions of dollars, to sitting on a Bench all day listening to mostly school disruption cases.

The gnawing turned to a gall as one question led to another question. Why are the school police arresting kids for typical adolescent conduct? Why are the administrators allowing their students to be criminalized with handcuffs and taken to detention?

When it finally hit me, my gall turned to anger. I came to believe that we (court) were pawns of the school system and police using us to discipline their problem children. But the deeper I explored the circumstances underlying my feelings of anger, I realized what was happening to these kids was a betrayal, an injustice. It was the school administrator's betrayal of their duty to act *in loco parentis*, Latin for "in the place of a parent." Would a reasonable parent whose child acts up at home call the police and demand their child be arrested and locked up? Of course not. Why would school administrators act unreasonably while standing in the shoes of parents?

Arresting kids for acting immature, a neurological adolescent fact, is an injustice. If being arrested is a traumatic experience for most adults, imagine the impact to a child's psyche. Why would adults, with a college education, who have dedicated their profession to educating and helping children, commit acts of injustice against them? I concluded that their ignorance had made them indifferent to the needs of these students.

I realized in that moment of reflection that there is something worse than anger—witnessing betrayal, harm, or injustice. I was now beyond anger. I had to act.

Before acting, I had to understand the problem. I needed the data to prove that my anecdotal experiences that raised my ire were real. I knew that if I acted prematurely without hard evidence, the school system and police would go on the defense, and we would find ourselves in the blame game going in circles and getting nowhere.

I asked our IT folks to query the data and they came back with shocking numbers. Since 1995, when police were placed on school campuses, and until 2003, when I convened county stakeholders to discuss remedies, school-based arrests increased by 2643 percent. This represented about a 330 percent increase every year. Worse, misdemeanors—the low-level offenses that represent typical adolescent behavior—comprised 90 percent of all the offenses (see Figure 6.1).

My concern was that police were spending more time arresting students who posed no risk of harm to others. These are the kids who make adults angry, a characteristic typical of teenagers and supported in medical science. These circumstances begged the question: When did it become a crime to make adults mad?

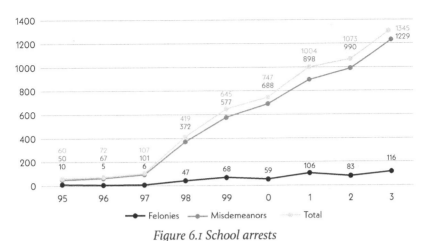

Figure 6.1 School arrests
SOURCE: C. WATSON (PERSONAL COMMUNICATION, JANUARY 2004)

And as if it could not get any worse, I contacted the school superintendent for graduation rates during this period. The graduation rates had fallen to an all-time low of 58 percent since police were placed on the campuses (see Figure 6.2). I was confident that the arrest rates were driving down the graduation rates. Later studies would confirm my suspicion showing that a student arrested on campus is twice as likely to drop out of school and if they appear in court the rate quadruples (Sweeten 2006).

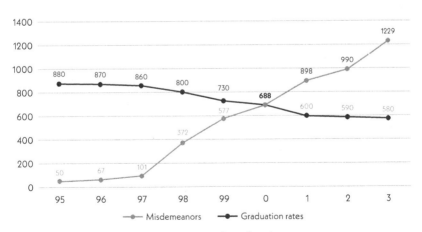

Figure 6.2 Arrests and graduation rates
SOURCE: C. WATSON (PERSONAL COMMUNICATION, JANUARY 2004)

My next query was to see if there was a relationship between graduation rates and crime rates. Knowing that studies have confirmed with empirical evidence that an increase in educational attainment significantly reduces subsequent violent and property crime, it made sense that how go graduation rates, so go crime rates (Lockner 2020). The hypothesis is that the more kids who graduate, the fewer crimes committed. This was confirmed by the data that showed as student arrests increased, the graduation rates decreased, and as the graduation rates decreased, the juvenile crime rate in the community increased (see Figure 6.3).

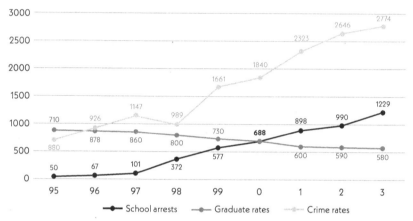

Figure 6.3 Arrests, graduation rates, and crime rates
SOURCE: C. WATSON (PERSONAL COMMUNICATION, JANUARY 2004)

Having confirmed my suspicions, and my anger now justified, I presented the problem to my two senior judges, and both agreed something should be done. The chief judge requested a meeting with the chief of police. I took the lead at the meeting to present the data and our theory that criminalizing non-delinquent youth will increase crime rates, a theory grounded in studies at the time showing that arrests and detention of low-risk youth increases delinquent behaviors (Teske 2013). Unfortunately, the chief was not impressed and matter-of-factly told us that his officers will continue to make arrests if they have probable cause.

I did not let this go.

School Offense Diversion: The Path to Restorative Justice

Enter Gordon Bazemore for the second time in my life.

I knew the next step involved a re-structuring of the court that included enhancing our diversion program. The chief judge gave me carte blanche authority to take the bull by the horns and re-direct these students from formal court hearings. This was 2001, and the study showing that kids arrested on campus are twice as likely to drop out of school and four times more likely if they appear in court would not be published for another five years.

I had that same feeling that Jerome Miller had in the early 1970s that inspired him to empty the training schools (prisons) in what would be dubbed the "Massachusetts Experiment." Miller led a 100-car caravan to the Lyman School for Boys and transported all the kids to dorms on the campus of the University of Massachusetts (Miller 1991). From there, he sent them home to their parents or relatives and diverted the money spent to house them to develop programs in their communities. I was part of a celebration in late 2011 honoring Miller and his experiment. Miller shared the story of "deconstructing" the secured youth facilities in Massachusetts. Miller confessed that he did not have the benefit of the evidence-based research that we enjoy today, but he knew that doing anything pro-social with these youth was better than what they had endured in the institutions (Schiraldi 2015). Subsequent studies would prove Miller's intuitions right. Those kids fared better than in prison.

Upon hearing his confession, I immediately recalled my feelings a decade earlier. I did not have the benefit of the studies that came later that school arrests and appearances in court are harmful, but my gut was telling me that treating teenagers like criminals was bad for the kids and bad for the community. I could not stop the police from arresting the kids, but I could divert them from court appearances to minimize the harm.

But first, said Gordon, I had to build a restorative justice framework and a "balanced" intervention model to redefine the mission of the juvenile justice system whereby the victim is at the center. By doing so, reparative programs would be elevated and programs dedicated solely to the offender would drive the rehabilitative process. But Gordon made clear that it would require me to step off the Bench, engage the community and other agency stakeholders, and, most importantly, work internally to shift the culture of the court from an offender-targeted treatment-only system to a system informed by reparative programming.

This required building an infrastructure of internal decision-making processes equipped with objective decision-making tools that would assess who should and should not be detained. Among those not detained, we required another objective decision-making tool to guide intake on those who should be diverted from prosecution and into reparative programs. It was the latter that reintroduced me to Gordon Bazemore.

It became obvious that a path towards building a restorative justice system would require structural changes, internal decision-making tools, and building a collaborative whereby the community can civically participate in the transformation to repair the harm to victims while simultaneously creating an opportunity for offenders to make amends to their victims to the satisfaction of the victim and the community, or as Bazemore says, an opportunity for the offender to earn their "redemption."

My first step toward executing Gordon's advice was the creation of a program coordinator position dedicated to researching and developing reparative programs. We created a school-offense diversion program to divert students arrested away from court and into reparative programs. Initially, students involved in altercations were sent to victim offender mediation facilitated by a certified mediator and one well versed in restorative justice practices, including peace circles. This continued for three years and netted a 15 percent reoffense rate among the students. This overwhelmingly positive outcome proved beneficial later as we moved forward to stop arrests on campus as well as expanding reparative programs to the community.

During these three years, I worked on stopping the bleeding of detained youth. I knew I could not build a restorative justice framework to expand reparative programs throughout the court, school system, and the community while simultaneously over-criminalizing kids with harsh detention policies that increase the risk of criminality. Studies have shown that a stay in pre-trial detention increases a youth's likelihood of felony recidivism by 33 percent and misdemeanor recidivism by 11 percent (Walker and Herting 2020). That would be counterproductive.

I needed a detention infrastructure that gave my intake staff objective risk and assessment tools. I sought the technical assistance of the Juvenile Detention Alternatives Initiative (JDAI) and the Annie E. Casey Foundation, a leader in building local collaboratives, designing objective screening tools, and developing alternatives to detention. Although JDAI's focus at that time was limited to pre-detention, who is detained and not, and had minimal if any focus on diversion from formal hearings, the detention assessment tools were the first ground-up measure toward quantifying who should not go to the prosecutor. If we can identify who should not be detained, the next question is who among those not detained has no business going to court.

This latter question led us to develop a Diversion Assessment Instrument to identify those who, although they have committed a delinquent act, are not delinquent. This concept is foreign to many because they are most familiar with the adult system. If you do the crime, you must do the time. But kids are neurologically prone to risk-taking behaviors and less equipped at resolving conflicts. Hence, why teenagers drag race, play chicken, and get into school fights. Consider the crime-age curve in Figure 6.4 illustrating the point in life at which humans commit the most crimes—about age 16—and which falls sharply after (Laub and Sampson 2003).

During this process of tool building, I sent letters to every stakeholder agency, public and private, describing a Juvenile Justice and Child Welfare Collaborative, its purpose to build a detention alternative and restorative justice system, and to meet periodically to review data and discuss the state of the system and any necessary tweaks. I emphasized in my letters and brochures that crime victims are invited and integral to building a new juvenile justice system. This included letters to the churches and civic organizations requesting volunteers to attend a meeting to participate in the collaborative.

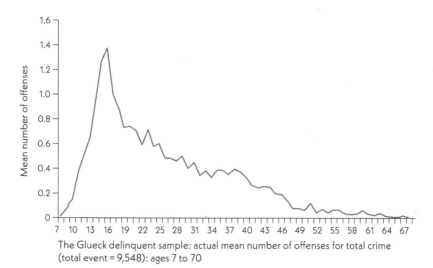

Figure 6.4 Delinquent sample mean number of offenses for crimes
SOURCE: LAUB AND SAMPSON (2003)

Our first meeting of the collaborative focused on introductions, orientations, and a discussion of our mission: to create a restorative justice framework, ridding the system of practices that harm kids, including indiscriminate arrests, arbitrary detention of youth, indiscriminate shackling of kids in court, and more.

It was the second meeting of the collaborative that hastened our path to restorative justice and moved the needle on school-based arrests. A JDAI delegation was sent from Multnomah County Juvenile Court in Portland, Oregon, one of their five model courts, to help us develop a strategic plan for detention reform. This technical assistance was not designed to address restorative justice, but the deeper we delved into our data and what stages of detention should be addressed and in what ways, the consensus was to attack the school arrests problem first. These arrests represented one-third of all arrests and detentions, and in terms of solving it, they were the low-hanging fruit, the easiest to solve. The dynamics had changed because the chief of police who had shut us down earlier had retired, and a progressive chief replaced him.

With the community behind me, an ad hoc committee was created by the collaborative to develop an inter-agency agreement to reduce school-based arrests within a restorative justice framework.

Building a Framework for Restorative Justice: The School-Justice Partnership

Following Gordon's advice, I used my role as a juvenile court judge to convene the stakeholders involved in those decisions of which students are arrested and sent to court: police and school administrators, those involved in building reparative programs, students, victims, and citizen volunteers. During the time it took to align the stars and come together, my programs division continued to coordinate the School Offense Diversion program, including mediation and peace circles. Others who participated included members of the community, NAACP, social services, behavioral health, a couple students, and citizen volunteers to represent the community at large (and who were victims of juvenile crime). I brought in a neutral facilitator, and I acted as the convener.

As the meetings progressed, the discussion on how to reduce school referrals generated more questions. What are school administrators to do with these disruptive students no longer referred to the court? When should police intervene in school disruption matters? How do we identify the underlying problems causing the disruption? What do we do to address those problems given the limited capacity and resources of the schools? How do we ensure the safety of schools? The collaborative process generated new and difficult questions that extended the time to develop a system to meet the goal.

I convened the meetings at least twice a month, with the facilitator assigning tasks to each member between meetings. The process to develop a system for reducing referrals to the juvenile court took nine months and a memorandum of understanding (MOU) was signed by all. Following cross-training of police, school administrators, and other relevant personnel; mental health; social service providers; and the court's Programs and Mediation units, the newly developed system was implemented at the beginning of the 2004–05 academic year.

We agreed that two MOUs were required to accomplish a reduction in suspensions and arrests while simultaneously securing alternative restorative justice measures. The first MOU, titled the "School Reduction Referral Protocol," called for the reduction in the arrests of students for certain misdemeanor offenses using a three-tier process. The student and parent received a warning on the first offense, a reparative program on the second offense, and a referral to the court on the third offense unless a reparative program is better suited.

The second MOU targeted those students identified as chronically disrupted students typically diagnosed with Adverse Childhood Experiences (ACEs) and who required clinical intervention. While reparative programs were not disregarded for this population, the evidence informed us that the complex trauma experienced by these students required clinical intervention. This cooperative inter-disciplinary body dedicated to addressing the chronically disruptive students is called the Clayton County Collaborative Child Study Team (Quad C-ST). This body would later serve as a Reparative board in addition to screening traumatized students.

Within four years (2008), school arrests and referrals to the court were reduced by 67.4 percent. As previously shown in Figure 6.1, we see that the school police spent most of their time arresting students for low-level offenses. Although the protocol suspended the arrest of students for the commission of certain misdemeanors, the data informed us that the protocol produced a residual effect in the felony referral rate with a decrease of 30.8 percent. According to school police, the warning system and reparative programs were used for some felony offenses involving typical adolescent behavior. The decision by school police over time to extend their discretion to use the warning and reparative programs for felony offenses outside the scope of the protocol indicated a shift in cognition; that is, an understanding that discipline should be applied on a case-by-case basis. This resulted in greater reductions in referrals.

After the protocol was implemented, the number of students detained on school offenses was reduced by 86 percent. The number of youths of color referred to the court on school offenses was reduced by 43 percent. Another by-product of the protocol was a reduction in serious weapons on campus by 73 percent. These involved weapon offenses for which police had no discretion in the law, meaning that the protocol nor police discretion was a factor contributing to the reduction in weapons at school.

Our collaborative explored this phenomenon and found,

according to police, that the change in police culture toward students over time, shifting from an incident-driven to a problem-oriented approach, also impacted how the students related to the police. Students shared in surveys that their School Resource Officer (SRO) was helpful and worked to solve conflicts, and the majority stated that they would go to their SRO before approaching the teacher or principal for advice or help. The SROs pointed to the student's cognitive shift as the underlying reason for the decline in weapons on campus. The students had become the most valuable source of intelligence for the police, allowing police to prevent weapons coming onto campus.

Based on this information, the collaborative agreed to enter a new MOU that conformed to the data and surveys. The new MOU re-branded the protocol the "School-Justice Partnership" (SJP) and expressly authorized police on campus to use their discretion in a felony offense to forego an arrest and refer students to reparative programs.

It was 2011 and the time was ripe to elevate restorative justice to a whole new level and make it the central framework, and, in so doing, bring reparative programming to all facets of the court. In addition to replacing school arrests with reparative programs and diverting juvenile complaints in general to reparative programs, these programs were made available to probation. At the center of this framework was a new division called the Restorative Justice Division (RJD). I staffed it with nine full-time employees supervised by a seasoned manager. The mediation unit was attached to the RJD. The mediation unit included three certified mediators also trained in peace circles and Family Group Conferencing.

Guided by Bazemore, our juvenile justice system was framed by restorative justice with access to reparative programs through every conceivable entry to the court, but more impactful was making it available in the community through the schools and the Quad C-ST so to avoid the filing of a juvenile complaint.

The implementation of reparative programs in school-related matters yielded anywhere between a 7 and 15 percent recidivist rate. For example, in the school year 2011–12 (see Figure 6.5), there were 420 students referred to reparative programs in lieu of arrests. Yet, of those 420 only 13 percent re-offended. This data begs the question:

Why were we arresting students in the first place if reparative programs work better to improve the behaviors of students while restoring victims?

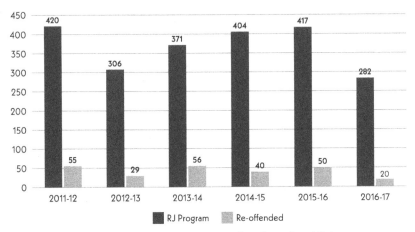

Figure 6.5 Reparative program referrals and recidivists
SOURCE: C. WATSON (PERSONAL COMMUNICATION, JANUARY 2018)

A three-year recidivist study conducted of youths referred to the court by police on patrol showed that only 30 percent re-offended. Between 2011 and 2013, youth re-offended at a rate of 17, 8, and 5 percent respectively, a decrease of 13 percent in the three years (see Figure 6.6).

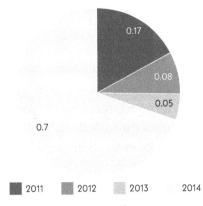

Figure 6.6 Re-offense rate
SOURCE: C. WATSON (PERSONAL COMMUNICATION, JANUARY 2014)

Restoring Victims and the Community

At the time of my retirement in 2021, school arrests fell by 76 percent (see Figure 6.7)[1]. All too often, people are awestruck when presented with this dramatic statistic. But the whole story is not the decline in school arrests. The goal was to reduce crime among our youth, which eventually would reduce crime among adults because all youth become adults. It is a matter of being patient. Reducing school arrests was merely the first step. The key to our goal to reduce juvenile crime was what we did in lieu of arrests, and this is where Bazemore played the most significant role in achieving our goal. It was not convincing us to implement reparative programming, though his instruction was helpful toward that end, but in how to do so holistically to increase its effectiveness and impact on the community.

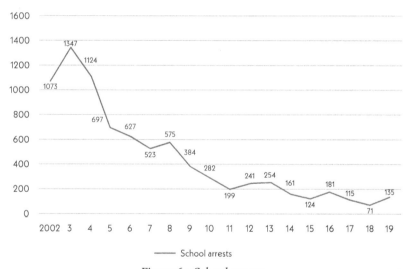

Figure 6.7 School arrests

SOURCE: C. WATSON (PERSONAL COMMUNICATION, JANUARY 2020)

A holistic system is one in which all its parts are interconnected. Sadly, juvenile justice systems are too often defined linearly by constricting them to juvenile courts and community and institutional corrections. This definition forces policymakers to develop policies

---

1   The 2020-21 school year is not included because the shut down of schools during COVID-19 skewed the numbers and would show a greater decline in school arrests. 2019 is the 19-20 school year, the last full academic term before COVID hit.

that hopefully will reduce recidivism or prevent juvenile crime within the powers, regulations, and resources of these institutions. But what if more resources are required to accomplish a serious reduction in recidivism? And what if those needed resources are outside the linear boundaries of the juvenile justice system? For example, how does a juvenile justice system improve school connectedness, a significant factor to reduce recidivism, if that ability rests squarely inside another linearly defined system called education? The answer is, it cannot unless the two decide to become partners.

Bazemore's teachings revealed that a holistic approach to restorative justice demanded that for reparative programming to be impactful and bring positive results to the entire community, we must reframe the definition of a juvenile justice system to include all other systems that share or have contact with the same youth, or may have future contact (i.e., delinquency prevention).

It was not enough to bring restorative justice to a linearly defined juvenile justice system in order to effect global changes in crime rates. Global impact demands global application. Limiting reparative programming to a linearly constrained system will bring constricted results.

By building a partnership between the juvenile justice system, schools, and police, reparative programming was implemented to all youth in the county, not just to those who were referred to the court system. By adhering to Bazemore's mantra—that it is not enough to do restorative justice—risks must be taken to make it the central framework of the juvenile justice system. But Bazemore led me to the revelation that a juvenile justice system meant something much bigger than the court system, and that for restorative justice to be effective, it required judicial leadership willing to take risks to forge partnerships that will expand the reach of reparative programs.

There is no doubt that stopping the arrests of many students played a role in promoting an increase in graduation rates, but the devil is in the details. A bigger role was played by what we did in lieu of those arrests that was also holistic in that it employed reparative programs to promote the restoration of the victim and give the student offender the opportunity to earn their redemption. Since 2002 when our graduation rates hit an all-time low of 58 percent, and unnecessary arresting of students stopped and reparative programs were instituted inside the courts, probation, and the entire school system, the rates increase to nearly 80 percent by 2021 (see Figure 6.8).

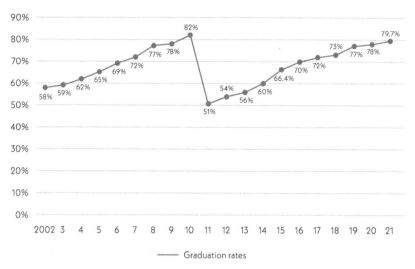

Figure 6.8 Graduation rates
SOURCE: C. SLAY (CANYON SOLUTIONS, INC. JANUARY 2021)

Restorative justice played a significant role in promoting school climate, which is the most significant factor when it comes to increasing graduation rates. In a massive synthesis study of research on school climate, it was concluded that "sustained positive school climate is associated with positive child and youth development, effective risk-prevention and health-promotion efforts, student learning and academic achievement, *increased student graduation rates*, and teacher retention" (Dary and Pickeral 2013, my emphasis). Restorative justice was so impactful that the school system created an assistant superintendent position dedicated to overseeing restorative justice.

Just as the replacement of student arrests with reparative programs resulted in an increase in graduation rates, the more students graduating resulted in fewer youth committing crimes. As shown in Figure 6.9, within four years of implementing SJP to reduce school arrests and create a reparative system, and the number of students graduating increased, the number of youths committing crimes throughout the county declined by 76 percent.

It also meant that 76 percent fewer citizens are victimized.

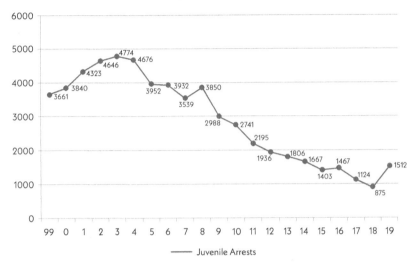

Figure 6.9 Juvenile crime
SOURCE: C. WATSON (PERSONAL COMMUNICATION, JANUARY 2020)

Final Thoughts

Up until my retirement, I served on the Georgia Juvenile State Advisory Group, the state agency that decides the distribution of federal juvenile justice funding that states receive from the Office of Juvenile Justice and Delinquency Prevention (OJJDP), US Department of Justice. States are audited by OJJDP about every three years. During one of these audits, the auditors wanted to visit a school campus that employed police. They were concerned about police being used as disciplinarians and the criminalization of typical student behavior. Our juvenile justice specialist asked me for suggestions on what school they could visit. It so happened that we would be visiting a youth prison in Macon, Georgia later in the week. It also so happened that a delegation from the Macon school system came to my court to spend a couple days learning about the SJP and restorative justice. Later, I took my technical assistance team to Macon and spent two days helping them to develop an SJP using reparative programs. I called the school superintendent for help, and a school was chosen for our visit.

Upon arriving at the high school later that week, we were escorted to a large conference room. The assistant superintendent and principal entered and informed us that last week a student was murdered in a drive-by shooting. They explained that an assembly was held yesterday in memorial to the murdered student who was described as a very affable and well-liked young man. Just as the assembly was closing and students were exiting the gymnasium, a loud commotion erupted. Three male students were taunting a female student who was wearing a t-shirt with the name and facial profile of the murdered student. All four students considered themselves a friend of the murdered student, but the word on the street was that the shooter was the cousin of the female student. The male students did not appreciate her wearing the shirt in honor of their friend given that her cousin murdered him. They were pulling at her shirt yelling at her to "take it off" and accusing her of "disrespecting" him (the murdered student). The commotion grew as other students began to jump into the affray yelling at the female student and pulling at her shirt. Campus police had to call in back up, and the campus was placed on lock-down. After breaking up what was described as a riot, the four students were escorted to the main office and separated. They were sent home, told to report back the next morning, and go directly to the office. The principal, certified in peace circles (also called healing circles and talking circles), informed us that he would be facilitating a peace circle. Based on the facts he just described, the female student is the victim.

Before bringing the students into the room, the principal provided the auditors with a description of a peace circle. He explained it was a reparative program deeply rooted in the traditional practices of indigenous people. He stated that circles include at a minimum the victim and offender(s), but can also include victim supporters, offender supporters, justice staff, police, and interested community members. For reasons of the Family Educational Rights and Privacy Act (FERPA), this circle he explained would involve the victim and three offenders. The principal pointed to the middle of the room where five chairs were situated in a circle. He stated that he would sit the students around the circle with the victim seated in the chair next to him. He informed us that typically the facilitator holds a talking stick and passes it to persons in the circle when it is their turn to speak. No one can interrupt the person who is holding the stick. He told us he uses a bean bag instead and held one up in his hand. With a chuckle he said, "Just in case it gets out of control," and explained that a bean bag "doesn't hurt like a stick when thrown."

The four students entered the room and took their seats. The principal described the circle process, held up the bean bag and described its purpose and the rules, and asked the students if they had any questions about the process. They answered "no" and the principal threw the bean bag to student A (one of the male students; the other male students are referred to as B and C). The exchanges went like this:

Principal: Tell us why you were upset with Jamilla (victim).

Student A: She was wearing a t-shirt with our friend's picture and name on it. She was disrespecting our murdered friend and disrespecting us, his friends.

Principal: Help me understand how her wearing a shirt with his profile and name is disrespectful to Damarius (murdered student) and to you.

Student A: Because it was her cousin that pulled the trigger. (The student throws the bean bag back to the principal)

Principal: (Throws bag to Student B) Do you feel the same way?

Student B: Yeah. She had no business coming to school wearing that shirt after what her cousin did. (Principal tells him to throw the bean bag to Student C and he does)

Principal: (Looking at Student C) How do you feel? Do you agree with them?

Student C: Same. Why would she think it's okay to wear that shirt knowing her cousin killed our friend? What did she expect? That we would be okay with it? (Rhetorically asking and throws the bean bag to the principal)

Principal: (Looking at the victim seated next to him and hands her the bean bag) Jamilla, is there anything you want these young men to know about why you wore the shirt to the assembly, especially given the word on the street that it was your cousin who did the shooting?

Jamilla: Damarius was my friend too. (Her eyes begin to water, and tears slowly trickle down both cheeks. Principal reaches over to table and gets a Kleenex and hands it to her)

(As she reaches into her pocket, she pulls out her cell phone and taps on the screen with her finger and begins to talk) I texted my cousin when I heard what he did and told him I hated him and that he killed my best friend. (Tears flowing freely and Jamilla is breathing heavy, and she is gasping trying to hold back the tears)

(She is now reading from her cell phone) This is what I texted him. "I hate you. You killed my best friend. Don't you ever contact me again. You are dead to me forever." (She hands her phone to the principal. He reads the texts to himself)

Principal: (Looking at Jamilla) Can I show this to them?

Jamilla: Yeah. (Wiping the tears)

(Principal stands and tells the students to stand and he holds the phone in front of all three to read. After reading the texts, the three students take their seat)

Principal: (Throws the bean bag to Student A) Any thoughts about what you just heard?

Student A: I didn't know. Had I known all that I wouldn't have come after you and say all those things. I am sorry Jamilla. (Principal tells him to pass the bean bag to Student B)

Principal: (Looking at Student B) What are your thoughts?

Student B: The same as his. I am sorry too. (Principal tells him to pass the bean bag to Student C)

Principal: (Looking at Student C) What are you thinking?

Student C: I feel bad now. I wouldn't have done all that if I knew all that you told your cousin. I am sorry. Really sorry. (Principal asks for the bean bag and Student C tosses it to him)

Principal: (Passes bean bag to Jamilla) Anything else you want to say, Jamilla?

Jamilla: (Jamilla has stopped crying. Her eyes are red and watery) Y'all didn't know. I understand why you were upset, and I don't blame you for being mad at me. I would have been angry too if the shoes were on the other feet.

Principal: (Tosses bean bag to Student A) Is there any lesson you can take away from this?

Student A: Yeah. Control my anger and go to Jamilla and ask in private why she would wear the shirt when it was her cousin who killed our friend instead of jumping to conclusions and causing her more pain.

Principal: (Directing the bean bag be tossed to Student B) What about you? What, if anything, have you learned today?

Student B: Same thing. I feel really bad about what I did.

Principal: (Directing the bean bag be tossed to Student C) And you, what have you learned?

Student C: Don't jump to conclusions. There can be other reasons and I won't know unless I ask first. I am sorry Jamilla for not coming to you for an explanation.

Jamilla: I forgive you. I forgive all of you.

Principal: (Throws the bean bag to Student A) What are you going to do once you leave this room?

Student A: I am going to let everyone know the truth. That we were wrong and jumped to conclusions. That Jamilla loved Damarius and turned her back on her cousin.

(Students B and C chime in and say "Me too")

Student A: (Still holding the bean bag) Jamilla, is it okay to give you a hug?

(Students B and C ask if they can too)

Jamilla: I would like that.

(The three offending students approach Jamilla, and they all embrace in a group hug)

The auditors along with the juvenile justice specialist were in tears. Once the students left the room, the principal stated that his school today is safer because of this peace circle. He elaborated by describing the tensions among the student body over this murder involving gang rivalries, and the animosity toward Jamilla. Jamilla, he said, "was not safe at this school so long as these students didn't know the truth about what really took place. Now the truth will get out and it will come from the students who attacked her. They owe it to Jamilla, and to our school community."

And for that, "Those young men have earned their redemption." I know Gordon would be proud.

References

Bazemore, G. (1998) "Crime victims and restorative justice in juvenile courts: Judges as obstacle or leader." *Western Criminology Review 1*, 1, 1–38. www.westerncriminology.org/documents/WCR/v01n1/Bazemore/Bazemore.html

Bazemore, G. (1999) "Restorative justice, earned redemption and a communitarian response to crime." *The Communitarian Network: Position Papers and Case Studies*, 1–76.

Bralley, J. and Prevost, J. (2001) "Reinventing community supervision: Georgia Parole's result driven supervision." *Corrections Today 63*, 2, 120–139.

Dary, T. and Pickeral, T. (2013) *School Climate Practices for Implementation and Sustainability: A School Climate Practice Brief*, Number 1. New York: National School Climate Center. https://safesupportivelearning.ed.gov/sites/default/files/School%20Climate%20Practices%20for%20Implementation%20and%20Sustainability.pdf

Deal, N. (2013) Letter of Recommendation in Support of Judge Teske Nomination for Henry Toll Fellowship Program, March 27.

Laub, J.H. and Sampson, R.J. (2003) *Shared Beginnings, Divergent Lives: Delinquent Boys to Age 70*. Boston, MA: President and Fellows of Harvard College.

Lochner, L. (2010) "Education Policy and Crime," *National Bureau of Economic Research*, Cambridge, MA. https://www.nber.org/system/files/working_papers/w15894/w15894.pdf

Miller, J. (1991) *Last One Over the Wall: The Massachusetts Experiment in Closing Reform Schools*. Columbus, OH: Ohio State University Press.

Schiraldi, V. (2015) "45 Years Later, Massachusetts Experiment Still has Lessons to Teach." *Juvenile Justice Information Exchange*, August 15. https://jjie.org/2015/08/13/45-years-later-massachusetts-experiment-still-has-lessons-to-teach

Scott Peck, M. (1978) *The Road Less Traveled.* London: Arrow Books.
Sweeten, G. (2006) "Who will graduate? Disruption of high school education by arrest and court involvement." *Justice Quarterly 23,* 4, 462–480. doi.org/10.1080/07418820600985313
Teske, S. (2013) "OP-ED: Breaking the Cycle of Hyper-recidivism." Juvenile Justice Information Exchange, July 17. https://jjie.org/2013/07/17/breaking-the-cycle-of-hyper-recidivism
Walker, S.C. and Herting, J.R. (2020) "The impact of pretrial juvenile detention on 12-month recidivism: A matched comparison study." *Crime & Delinquency 66,* 13–14, 1865–1887. doi.org/10.1177/0011128720926115

— Chapter 7 —

Mitigating Harm and Restoring Trust

A Restorative Justice Approach to Campus Policing

SYDNEY PIDGEON AND DAVID KARP, PHD

> *Effective, principled implementation of restorative policing depends on a holistic, systemic vision that seeks to incorporate restorative justice principles in all aspects of policing.*
>
> BAZEMORE AND GRIFFITHS 2003, P.345

In this chapter, the authors provide a case study of restorative policing on a university campus. Policing across the United States is particularly fraught with high levels of community distrust and crises of adequate staffing. Since 2020, a recent dramatic decline in police staffing has limited many departments to rely upon calls for service as their primary response to crime (Young, Sayers and Sanchez 2022). A new vision is needed for policing, and one place to start is on college and university campuses.

Gordon Bazemore was a pioneer in the work of restorative policing, an approach to policing that incorporates restorative principles along with a focus on community policing. His contributions were invaluable for activating restorative policing within police departments and calling upon the community to serve as active partners in creating sustainable and effective solutions to crime. Hines and Bazemore (2003, p.411) argued that "effective policing without the active support of the community is all but impossible," that the burden of crime control can be the full responsibility of police officers and a significant role for the community is needed. Restorative policing includes components: crime prevention, community involvement, and problem solving (Hines and Bazemore 2003). When incorporated, they can not only reduce crime but also improve police-community relations.

College and university police departments can benefit from restorative policing as a foundation for engagement with their populations of service. The unique structure and role of campus police departments naturally align with restorative policing. It is common for campus police officers to engage in collaborative community safety work and support campus events and activities, rather than simply respond to calls for service.

Karp and Schachter (2019, p.259) argue that "colleges and universities have become great laboratories for restorative justice." Traditionally, this experimentation has been for adjudication of student misconduct, but campus police departments can use a restorative justice approach to develop better relationships with their campus communities and rebuild trust. The implementation of restorative practices within campus police departments serves as a way to not only engage restoratively after harm offered, but also in the service of prevention. Campus police departments already work alongside staff and students as co-producers of campus wellbeing, and this particular policing disposition toward community-oriented policing makes them particularly well-suited as pioneers of restorative policing. By applying restorative principles to their work, campus police can achieve a new level of collaboration, harm mitigation, and trust building, as well as serving as a restorative policing model for municipal police departments.

Student Perceptions of Campus Police

Nearly every campus across the nation employs a police or public safety department (Reaves 2015), but there has been almost no research on this unique subset of policing. Recently, demands for police reform and/or abolition are growing (Childress, Farolen and Stein 2020; Davidson 2020; Rogers and Gravelle 2020) and college students have maintained a prominent voice in this movement (Hernández and Ravani 2019; Kingkade 2011; Rodríguez 2012; Summers and Gougelet 2020; Thacker 2006), with groups forming such as "Cops Off Campus," "a crowdsourced, nationwide study of the interrelations of universities and policing, coordinated by an all-volunteer collective of abolitionist researchers" (Abolitionist University 2020, para. 1). Students have been unsettled by how much campus policing has grown to mirror municipal policing (Inoue 2019). This transition blurs lines of distinction between municipal and campus police and is reinforced by campus police often being staffed by former municipal officers, and how these officers engage their on-campus communities similarly to how they responded in their former communities (Allen 2015; Allen and Jacques 2020). This is coupled with an increase in firearm presence for campus safety officers. Currently, 75 percent of non-municipal campus safety officers are armed, which increases the perceived intensity of response (Margolis and Shtull 2012; Reaves 2015). Some colleges have even abolished an independent university policing system completely and turned to local police as sole responders to campus incidents (Savasta 2013). Regardless of where a campus is present on the spectrum of legalized police authority, the perception of municipal police often colors how campus police are viewed despite being separate entities (Summers and Gougelet 2020). This fear and distrust negatively influence satisfaction, willingness to report, cooperation, and perceived effectiveness of campus police (Aiello and Lawton 2018; James 2015).

Distrust is present during interactions between students and campus officers and can escalate and lead to physical harm if unaddressed. Restorative justice has been implemented in the aftermath of harm, as is described in a case study discussed in Karp and Schachter (2019). The authors shared the story of Jenna, an African American student who had a panic attack induced by cannabis consumption, and a campus security officer who restrained Jenna in an attempt to keep both her and the campus community safe in her moments of distress until the ambulance arrived. In his restraint and her resistance, Jenna injured both herself and the officer. In the restorative process that followed the incident, Jenna and her friends shared their intense distrust for the police, Jenna sharing that her perception was that police were "out to get them," while on the contrary, the security officer's intention was to keep the student safe. Further, he shared that the reason he chose to work on a campus was to support students, not to get them in trouble. Misunderstanding between campus police and students is showcased in this example, and it exists widely. During their restorative process, Jenna and the campus safety officer were able to have a transformational conversation that led to an embrace. The officer shared gratitude for the opportunity to follow up with a student in this way, and both parties were able to learn of their differing perceptions and were able to identify some actions for how to move forward to improve the image of campus safety among the campus community. Without the existence of restorative practices within this experience, more harm and distrust may have existed than before on campus. But, with the opportunity to participate in powerful dialogue, the participants were able to mitigate harm and restore trust that had a positive impact on the harmed parties and can have a domino effect on the campus population.

Mitigating Harm and Restoring Trust

Nowhere is trust more broken than between police and minority communities, and mistrust is highest between police and youth (Johnson and Weisberg 2021). As higher education continues to include a more diverse population, campus police must recognize this historical mistrust.

Current policing practices place youth who come from marginalized communities or identities at increased risk for incarceration or injury. Once they have a criminal record, they experience consequences that further exclude them from full participation in society, impacting their employment opportunities, housing, and access to public services. These disparities make it difficult for those most affected to believe the justice system is fair, especially when they may have negative, traumatic, and dangerous personal experiences with law enforcement. Their experiences, especially for youth of color, connect to and perpetuate historical traumas and align with folklore about oppressive police officers, perpetuating a cycle of mutual distrust, anxiety, and animosity (Johnson and Weisberg 2021, p.36).

A promising approach to police/community distrust is the implementation of "Police Youth Dialogues [which] encourage difficult conversations around transparency and accountability and different issues that come up between police, community members, and young people" (Johnson and Weisberg 2021, p.90). Such dialogues have been implemented in various communities across the United States, including Florida, Colorado, and Massachusetts. In Florida, for example, the River Phoenix Center for Peace facilitated over 100 Police Youth Dialogues over an eight-year period with over 1,200 officers and 2,000 youth (Johnson and Weisberg 2021, p.6). Evaluations have shown that Police Youth Dialogues have improved each group's attitudes about each other, youth have increased their willingness to talk with police, and that there is a renewed sense of safety with police presence, and a greater willingness to report crimes. Police have increased their awareness of racial dynamics and have a greater desire to proactively and positively engage with youth (Johnson and Weisberg 2021; Williams and Crifasi 2020).

Partnerships between campus police and the campus community can identify community concerns and implement new approaches to restore trust and re-engage community participation. Previous research has indicated the implementation of restorative and community policing methods (Griffith et al. 2004; Hancock 2015), collaboration with the campus community (Gelpi 2019; Johnson and Bromley 1999), and increased partnership with crisis professionals (Canto et al. 2017; Deane et al. 1999; Reuland, Draper and Norton 2010; Segal 2014; Wright 2002) have supported mitigating harm during campus police response. In addition to assessing current policies and procedures, with specific attention to the above strategies, Lewicki and Tomlinson (2014) provided methods of managing calculus-based distrust: collaboration between groups, development of alternative courses of action, and increased awareness of others' perceptions, partnered with an adoption of restorative practices (Pointer 2019). When combined, trust develops between the campus community and university police.

Based on previous research and applying Bazemore's principles of restorative policing, we describe here a case study at the University of San Diego. Specifically, a restorative approach was used to rebuild trust between the Department of Public Safety and the Department of Residential Life over a one-year period. Bazemore's three components of restorative policing—crime prevention, community engagement, and problem solving—were intentionally utilized to mitigate harm, restore trust, and provide an example of how campus police can engage restoratively with their community. In the case study, both populations were able to (a) understand the current and historic harms and needs of university public safety and residential life departments and (b) identify ways to improve the relationship and trust between residential life and campus public safety. The trust and collaboration that was built between these two student-facing departmental units impacted the larger student and departmental populations and showcased the success that is possible when implementing restorative policing on college campuses.

CASE STUDY: UNIVERSITY OF SAN DIEGO

The University of San Diego (USD) is a mid-size, private Catholic institution located in San Diego, California. USD's ten residential facilities house about 2,500 students (University of San Diego Department of Public Safety 2019). These residential facilities are managed by the 13 on-call professional staff members and 80 student resident assistants in the Department of Residential Life (hereinafter referred to as "Residential Life") in partnership with the Department of Public Safety (DPS). The DPS provides "a full range of crime prevention and crime control services to contribute to the safety and security of the campus community" (University of San Diego 2022, para. 1) and is a non-sworn agency, which means its officers do not have full arrest powers granted by local authority (Reaves 2015). However, DPS officers are fully armed. The DPS responded to 1,391 incidents in the residence halls in 2019, and nearly all of these responses elicit a co-response with the residential life community (University of San Diego Department of Residential Administration 2021; J. Miyashiro, personal communication, March 29, 2021).

Despite these consistent interactions in crisis and incident situations, the sources of planned, intentional interaction between the residential life community and the DPS officers outside of incident response are nearly nonexistent. Further, there was a known deterioration in the relationship between the residential and public safety communities over the last five to ten years and undisclosed concerns present for both communities heightened by the national climate on policing that further impacted the relationship. Given the frequent collaboration of the residential life community and the DPS, a functioning and collaborative partnership between Residential Life and the DPS is essential to best serve students in the event of an incident.

In the wake of social unrest and demands of police reform (Childress et al. 2020; Davidson 2020; Rogers and Gravelle 2020), the University of San Diego had a unique opportunity to join the national conversation about policing in our country occurring throughout 2020 by presenting restorative justice as a way to understand harms and needs of their community and as an intervention tool to mitigate harm and restore trust between the communities. In particular, the communities used restorative circles as a medium to understand and identify harms, obligations, and engagement for each group. The unique nature of the circle method allows for flexibility to hold space for each of these pillars, while still maintaining the integrity of the structure. With attention to each of the essential elements of a circle (Pranis 2015, pp.6-9), participants engaged in three circle processes. Each circle built upon the other and laid the groundwork for the groups to come together and create sustainable change within their departments.

Phase One: Understanding Needs and Igniting Active Engagement

Ultimately, what some view as the third core principle of restorative justice (Van Ness and Strong 1997; Bazemore and Walgrave 1999) comes closest to full compatibility with the vision of community policing in its most ambitious form. This principle suggests a need for a transformation in the relationship between the government/criminal justice system and the community which places the community in a much more active role in promoting both public safety and justice.

GORDON BAZEMORE AND CURT GRIFFITHS 2003, p.337

The goal of the first phase of the project was to truly understand the dynamics between Residential Life and the Department of Public Safety in order to properly engage both communities separately and together. In addition to pre-engagement research and discussion, the purpose of the first phase was to provide space for both communities to reflect on the concerns surrounding the relationship between the DPS and Residential Life, identify possible avenues for healing between both communities, and deepen their commitment to repairing the relationship. An independent circle was held for each group: one with five Residential Life professional staff, one with eight resident assistants, and one with seven DPS. Of the Residential Life and DPS participants, all were individuals with the longest tenure and highest positions within their respective departments. During these circles, the conversations were centered around the values participants believe should be at the center of the partnership between Residential Life and the DPS, and during the dialogues, participants shared stories of challenges or concerns they or their communities had regarding the partnership or the corresponding department, later naming various solutions or action steps that they believed could mitigate the harm of the most significant concerns.

In the beginning of each circle, most participants had some concern or hesitation about participating due to the uncertainty that existed surrounding restorative processes and engaging in the complex relationships between the departments. But by using a circle process that enabled participants to get to know each other, at first in a lively and fun way, and then inviting consideration of the challenges they faced and ideas for addressing them, the circles helped forge hope in transforming the relationship between the departments.

At the end of this process the energy had shifted, and there was an openness and an appreciation for the process. The following words were used by the three groups to describe what they are taking away from the process: *hope (x3), openness (x2), vigilance, change, awareness, insight, perspective, excitement, productive, moving forward, fruitful conversations, continued participation (x2), desire to be a part of these conversations, continue giving and receiving feedback, optimism, the commitment to strengthening of individual relationships.* These reflections embody both the commitment to improved relationships, and the power of restorative processes as a method for understanding complex harms and needs.

In addition to the emotional investment in the partnership and openness to restorative justice, some significant lessons were gained from this phase. A variety of themes emerged in all three circles that both departments identified as shortfalls in their partnership.

Communication: Both groups expressed an immediate need for improved communication, as many incidents that created distrust, division, or frustration were rooted in miscommunication or lack of communication between the departments. Increased frequency of communication and additional avenues for communication during and after incident responses were identified as the two essential needs to improve interdepartmental communication.

Mutuality: "They don't understand...," "They don't get...," and "They don't see..." were common phrases stated by both departments in their discussion of challenges in the partnership. Mutuality is a strong need between the two departments to allow for respect and understanding that can foster teamwork and trust. There were various concerns that each group raised that have not been addressed with the other department. As an example, student leaders said that there was often a large officer response to many calls and confusion (and sometimes frustration) for why so many officers were present. The DPS similarly recognized this student concern and described how current policy required supervisor involvement and multi-officer response for many types of calls. This example, as with others, was a missed opportunity for mutuality that had created a lack of understanding and frustration on both sides.

Compassion: Ensuring student safety requires a balance between clear and consistent procedures and flexibility to be responsive to the psychological needs of students in the moment. To allow students to feel safe and supported most fully, there is a need for increased compassion and sensitivity. Given the positionality and mission of the DPS, the opportunity to lean into the distinction between public safety and local police allows for a reframing of DPS officers as full members of the USD community, rather than an intrusive enforcer of policy. When focusing on compassion, the perception, experience, and partnership with the DPS can mitigate harm and improve trust.

Engagement Outside of Incident Response: The majority of interactions Residential Life has with the DPS is during or surrounding a crisis/incident. Interacting in only these circumstances creates an association of crisis and concern as the foundation for the partnership. One Residential Life staff highlighted this concern by stating "I don't meet officers until something happens." Limiting this interaction to incident responses prevents meaningful relationship building required for a functioning partnership outside the confines of crisis.

Trust: By taking the needs described above seriously, trust can be built between these campus partners. Trust, or confidence in one another, is required to support the partnership and best serve students.

The insights learned in this first phase provided the framework for moving forward, while also meeting the goals of identifying areas of harm and needed healing, and sparking a commitment to culture change within the departments. The intentional curation of circle prompts led the groups to a deeper commitment to improving the relationship and critically thinking about the status of the partnership and what it needs to flourish. These prompts embedded in a restorative philosophy allowed for a depth of response that might not have been possible outside of a restorative process.

Phase Two: Exploring Accountability

In restorative policing, we are attempting to recreate this shared ownership of responsibility.

HINES AND BAZEMORE 2003, P.414

The initial circles were beneficial to each group, but to move towards repairing harm, accountability is required through inter-departmental dialogue. As Howard Zehr highlights, "accountability means they should be encouraged to understand that harm. Those who have caused harm should begin to understand the consequences of their behavior" (Zehr 2014, p.33). To help both groups understand the layers of harm that exist for one another, all participants were provided a report with a consolidated data analysis outlining notable themes of needs named by both departments in Phase One. Participants were given a week to review the report and then participated in pre-circle dialogues (Residential Life staff only and DPS staff only) with the purpose of understanding past harms and moving towards responsibility through sharing observations, reactions, and reflections from the themes presented in the report. In an attempt to be restorative in process and honor the desire for sustainable culture change, leadership from each department who participated in prior cycles were invited to continue participation moving forward.

The pre-circle dialogues proved to be difficult as confronting harm was challenging for both groups. The dialogue cycled through *defensiveness*, to *curiosity*, to *openness*. Upon learning of the harms that exist for the other, both groups made some defensive comments, offering reasons why they were not personally responsible, such as saying the issue was outside their control, required by policy, beyond their capacity given staffing and resources, or simply a one-off experience and not a relevant pattern. After that initial defensiveness, participants began earnestly exploring why these harms do exist for the other group and even contemplating what solutions could mitigate them. The foundation of restorative work that was done among the participants led to an openness to hearing other perspectives, understanding and taking accountability for harm, and the desire for implementing action to improve the relationship. This prepared the groups to come together and begin a culture shift for the partnership between Residential Life and the Department of Public Safety.

Phase Three: Coming Together in Partnership

In the world of the justice system the police are at the bottom of the system hierarchy, but that also makes the police the base upon which all the rest depend. While it is the police who provide the system with cases, it is the community that initiates everything for the police. When looked at in this way a partnership of police and community seems inevitable and it is clearly in the best interest of the police to cultivate this community partnership.

HINES AND BAZEMORE 2003, P.426

The idea of these two groups coming together to discuss harm and engage in planning action to restore their relationship was a hopeful outcome of this case study, but one that many believed was overly optimistic. However, the commitment and courage of both populations, their desire to work together to support student safety, and the foundation of restorative practices allowed for success.

One week after participants engaged in Phase Two, all participants gathered for a catered lunch prior to joining in the circle. Engaging in a casual meal and conversation together prior to the circle helped participants become comfortable before they began the more difficult circle process. The purpose of this final circle was to give both departments a space to affirm their commitments to the partnership, reconcile the ways they may have not been serving the partnership, find hope in what a partnership can look like, and actualize the next steps for transformation.

The beginning of the circle was connective, as participants fixed their eyes on the restorative centerpiece (Pranis 2015) that included a picture of the combined values from all three individual circles naming the values participants believed should be at the center of the relationship between Residential Life and the DPS:

Partnership Values Word Cloud

diligence community
understanding partnership
curiosity
communication professionalism
integrity
trust Jesus respect
care openness compassion

After centering on these values, participants shared what they do in their roles without sharing their titles. This leveled the hierarchy of positions and highlighted the shared responsibility for the work ahead. Most shared how their role is dedicated to supporting students and the larger campus community in crisis or in student development, which created a common bond across roles and departments. Individuals named *trust, understanding, integrity, respect, adaptability,* and *problem solving* as values essential to their work, while also holding the challenge of their individual and collective positions. As the circle proceeded, a set of notable turning points indicated the evolution of the group process.

A Proclaimed Need. In a circle process, sometimes someone shares a comment or a story that helps frame the purpose of the circle. In this circle, one of the Residential Life participants stated that trust is the value they lead with and "being able to give and receive trust is really important since nobody is solely responsible for that." This comment named "trust" as the central need for the group and simultaneously released the group from individual responsibility of building trust between the departments. A participant set this tone early in the circle significantly contributing to the openness and transformation that remained present during their time together. As the circle proceeded, expressions of hope for renewed partnership helped strengthen their resolve.

Confronting Harms and Needs. As participants confronted the harms and needs identified in the report, it was apparent that the preparatory dialogues served both groups, as many shared variations of what was mentioned in the individual circles, with enhanced reflection and thoughtfulness. Each department named and affirmed issues that they themselves were not quite fulfilling including transparency, communication, and engagement outside of crisis. The vulnerability offered by each department made for productive conversations around creating sustainable action and maintaining accountability in cross-departmental collaboration. Holding both a sense of obligation and feeling of hopefulness, there was cautious optimism for what a better partnership could look like.

Participation. Given the structure of restorative circles, each of the previous discussions had a natural transition to planning action. At this point, both groups had two formal opportunities for robust planning, and this was the first time they would bring their ideas together and assess feasibility as a group. As participants shared proposals, agreement emerged quickly and naturally. The teamwork that was hoped for at the beginning of the circle was realized. Multiple times, the formality of the circle broke as participants affirmed a speaker's ideas or called out, "I would like to help you with that." Recognizing that the recommendations required action from all of the officers and Residential Life team members, one participant proclaimed, "We are planting seeds for that eventual moment when stuff does hit the fan. We know who is around us and helping us and supporting us."

There were statements hinting that their plans would persist. They shared: "I am feeling excited, I am feeling really affirmed and the ways we have recommitted to each other and the work"; "I am excited for the continued partnership and working together"; and "Some great things are going to come out of this partnership."

In the final round, a Residential Life team member stated, "I am committed to developing the strategy and putting the structure behind the intention, and it's clear that the intention is there," and a member of the DPS turned to this person and shared, "I am committed to meet with you so we can start on that and continue it." Immediately after the circle adjourned, the two connected to share contact information and find time in their joint calendars to set up recurring strategy meetings to support ongoing partnership and collaboration. The following commitments were made and also speak generally to how other campuses might engage in relationship building between the departments.

Commitments
Nightly Desk Check-Ins
Nightly Desk Check-Ins were created so that DPS officers assigned to the night shift could briefly meet with a residential assistant (RA) working a residential desk to: (a) inform the RA about who is on duty and responding to calls; (b) provide an opportunity for the RA and DPS officer to discuss upcoming events of the night or possible concerns; and (c) allow for increased facetime between the two groups outside of incident response to build connection. Through this implementation, trust and collaboration could be built between officers and RAs, as the majority of facetime interactions between the two groups would likely be in this casual and collaborative space rather than at the scene of an incident.

Debrief Protocol
Both departments felt the need for RAs, who were the student leaders responding to incidents, to be further trained and expected to provide thorough debriefs of the incident to officers upon the officer's arrival to a scene. Training RAs in debrief methods and institutionalizing a debrief protocol as soon as the DPS arrives on scene means the incident response could be more efficient, collaborative, and victim centered. In addition, debriefs would include sharing what went well, if anything needs to be improved, and what next steps look like. This debrief was meant to offer space for shared reflection and discussion rather than relying solely on duty reports or supervisor escalation.

Training
Training, in many forms, was a recommendation that was consistently discussed. Although training is often implemented as a performative "fix" for an institution's problems, the participants

discussed moving beyond a "checkbox" of training and toward true collaborative engagement where each group could learn from one another. The group determined two training additions: expanding the Residential Life "Behind Closed Doors" incident role-play training to include public safety; and similarly, as an opportunity to increase collaboration outside of incidents, they planned to jointly offer future trainings on various topics of interest or concern on a bi-annual basis.

Social Engagement

The group agreed that hosting social events following joint training would allow for additional facetime, relationship building beyond the uniform and job title, and trust building between the departments. Ideas included taco truck socials, DPS attending the Student Leader Banquet, DPS providing an award to an RA who provided exemplary support to a student of concern, extending invitations to DPS for socials and dinners during training, and any additional informal opportunities that can allow for increased facetime and conversation outside of an incident.

Officer Liaison

Strategic partnership often requires the identification of individuals responsible for maintaining an initiative or goal. To properly institute change, a long-term recommendation was the creation of an officer liaison position to be the point of contact and collaboration to build continued initiatives between the departments. This person would support the Director of Residential Life in the development and implementation of the recommendations from this restorative process and additional initiatives determined by the larger groups, provide maintenance of the commitment to partnership, and offer adjustments and changes as necessary to meet the current needs of the groups.

Ongoing Strategy Meetings

Climate change and partnership improvement require significant maintenance, so ongoing strategy meetings would be implemented among a small group of Residential Life team members (including at least one Community Director, Residential Life Leadership team member, and RA) and DPS officers and leadership. This group would meet monthly or bimonthly to provide updates on what they are seeing in terms of residential student needs, assess the current implementation of partnership strategic plans, plan social gatherings, and offer new ideas and suggestions to better support the partnership and student safety.

Sustainable Change Through Restorative Policing

Dr. Gordon Bazemore inspired the development of restorative policing by theorizing the role of restorative justice in police–community relations. Two decades after his seminal research, his ideas were put into practice and transformed the relationship between the Department of Public Safety and the Department of Residential Life at the University of San Diego. Nearly two years after its restorative process, both departments remain committed to their renewed partnership. In particular, the social engagement and training adjustments have led to a dynamic shift between the departments. Although this case study reflects the restorative work of only one university, it suggests a promising model that might expand to other campuses and perhaps to policing more broadly.

At the heart of this work is the problem of trust. Policing in the US has a legacy of harm, particularly in how police have engaged with communities of color. Applying restorative practices when working with complex social, political, and historical harms enables communities to quickly and meaningfully identify harms, community needs, and paths forward that can lead to transformation. Higher education is the home of research and experimentation. Campus safety departments can play a significant role in the future of policing by embracing their campus's intellectual curiosity, interdepartmental and interdisciplinary collaboration, and mission to support students and create safe and welcoming communities for all.

References

Abolitionist University (2020) "Cops Off Campus Research Project." *Abolitionist Journal.* https://abolition.university/cops-off-campus-research-project

Aiello, M.F. and Lawton, B.A. (2018) "Campus police cooperation and legitimacy: Extending the procedural justice model." *Deviant Behavior 39*, 10, 1371–1385. doi.org/10.1080/01639625.2017.1410618

Allen, A. (2015) "Campus police-citizen encounters: Influences on sanctioning outcomes." *American Journal of Criminal Justice 40*, 4, 722–736. doi.org.sandiego.idm.oclc.org/10.1080/01639625.2018.1519133

Allen, A. and Jacques, S. (2020) "'He did that because I was Black': Black college students perceive municipal police, not campus police, as discriminating." *Deviant Behavior 41*, 1, 29–40. doi.org/10.1080/01639625.2018.1519133

Bazemore, G. and Griffiths, C. (2003) "Police reform, restorative justice, and restorative policing." *Police Practice and Research 4*, 4, 335–346. doi.org/10.1080/15614260310001631244

Canto, A.I., Becker, M.S., Cox, B.E., Hayden, S., and Osborn, D. (2017) "College students in crisis: Prevention, identification, and response options for campus housing professionals." *Journal of College & University Student Housing 43*, 2, 44–57. www.nxtbook.com/nxtbooks/acuho/journal_vol43no2/index.php#/p/44

Childress, C., Farolan, C., and Stein, A. (2020) *Who is protected and who is served? The gap between Massachusetts campus police authority and action.* National Lawyers Guild Review. www.nlg.org/wp-content/uploads/2020/01/Who-is-Protected-and-Who-is-Served_-final.pdf

Davidson, M. (2020) "Activists demand change in policing on Catholic campuses." *National Catholic Reporter 57*, 6, 1–10.

Deane, M.H., Borum, R., Veysey, B., and Morrissey, J. (1999) "Emerging partnerships between mental health and law enforcement." *Psychiatric Services 50*, 1, 398–402. doi.org/10.1176/ps.50.1.99

Gelpi, A. (2019) "Improve community relations, prevent critical incidents with equitable policing practices." *Campus Security Report 16*, 3, 1–6. doi.org/10.1002/casr.30530

Griffith, J.D., Hueston, H., Wilson, E., Moyers, C., and Hart, C.L. (2004) "Satisfaction with campus police services." *College Student Journal 38*, 1, 150–156.

Hancock, K. (2015) "Community policing within campus law enforcement agencies." *Police Practice & Research 17*, 5, 463–476. doi.org/10.1080/15614263.2015.1108194

Hernández, L. and Ravani, S. (2019) "Students Protest UC Berkeley Police Arrests They Say Were Racially Motivated." *San Francisco Chronicle*, March 20. sfchronicle.com/crime/article/Students-racially-profiled-brutalized-by-13701947.php

Hines, D. and Bazemore, G. (2003) "Restorative Policing, Conferencing and Community." *Police Practice and Research 4*, 4, 411–427. www.tandfonline.com/doi/abs/10.1080/1561426031001631307

Inoue, M. (2019) "Between surveillance and surveillance: Or, why campus police feel vulnerable precisely because they gain power." *Journal of Contemporary Ethnography 49*, 2, 229–256. doi.org/10.1177/0891241619880323

James, V. (2015) *Campus Rape Victims: How They See the Police.* El Paso, TX: LFB Scholarly Publishing.

Johnson, M.E. and Weisburd, J. (2021) *The Little Book of Police Youth Dialogue: A Restorative Path Toward Justice.* New York: Good Books.

Johnson, R.P. and Bromley, M. (1999) "Surveying a university population: Establishing the foundation for a community policing initiative." *Journal of Contemporary Criminal Justice 15*, 2, 133–143. doi.org/10.1177/1043986299015002002

Karp, D.R. and Schachter, M. (2019) "Restorative Justice in Colleges and Universities: What Works When Addressing Student Misconduct." In T. Gavrielides (ed.) *The Routledge Handbook of Restorative Justice*. New York: Routledge.

Kingkade, T. (2011) "University of California Campus Police Have a History of Excessive Force Against Protesters." *Huffington Post*, December 9, 2011. www.huffpost.com/entry/california-campus-police-clash-with-protesters-ows_n_1125537

Lewicki, R.J. and Tomlinson, E.C. (2014) "Trust, Trust Development, and Trust Repair." In P.T. Coleman, M. Deutsch, and E.C. Marcus (eds) *The Handbook of Conflict Resolution: Theory and Practice*, 3rd edn. San Francisco: Jossey-Bass/Wiley.

Margolis, G. and Shtull, P. (2012) "The police response to mental illness on campus." *Journal of College Student Psychotherapy 26*, 4, 307–321. doi.org/10.1080/87568225.2012.711179

Pointer, L. (2019) "Restorative practices in residence halls at Victoria University of Wellington, New Zealand." *Conflict Resolution Quarterly 36*, 3, 263–271. doi.org/10.1002/crq.21240

Pranis, K. (2015) *Circle Keepers Handbook*. St. Paul, MN: Living Justice Press.

Reaves, B. (2015) "Special Report: Campus Law Enforcement, 2011–12." The Bureau of Justice Statistics, U.S. Department of Justice. https://bjs.ojp.gov/content/pub/pdf/cle1112.pdf

Reuland, M., Draper, L., and Norton, B. (2010) "Improving Responses to People with Mental Illness: Tailoring Law Enforcement Initiatives to Individual Jurisdictions." Council of State Governments, Justice Center. https://csgjusticecenter.org/wp-content/uploads/2020/02/Tailoring_LE_Initiatives.pdf

Rodríguez, D. (2012) "Beyond 'police brutality'": Racist state violence and the University of California." *American Quarterly 64*, 2, 303–313.

Rogers, C. and Gravelle, J. (2020) "Implementing a police foundation degree: Insights from South Wales." *Policing: A Journal of Policy & Practice 14*, 2, 349–361. http://dx.doi.org/10.1093/police/paz028

Savasta, M. (2013) "Good communication, customer service focus make a major transition successful." *Campus Security Report 10*, 2, 1–3.

Segal, E. (2014) "The Crisis Intervention Team (CIT) model for law enforcement: Creative considerations for enhancing university campus police response to mental health crisis." *Creative & Knowledge Society 4*, 1. http://dx.doi.org/10.2478/cks-2014-0001

Summers, L. and Gougelet, K. (2020) "Whose university? When police pass the baton to campuses." *Society for the Anthropology of Work*. doi.org/10.21428/1d6be30e.8cc96f6f

Thacker, P. (2006) "Shock and Anger at UCLA." *Inside Higher Ed*, November 16, 2006. www.insidehighered.com/news/2006/11/17/shock-and-anger-ucla

University of San Diego (2022) "About Public Safety." www.sandiego.edu/safety/about

University of San Diego Department of Public Safety (2019) Annual campus incident report. Internal DPS report.

University of San Diego Department of Residential Administration (2021) "StarRez Occupancy Report." Internal USD report.

Van Ness, D. and Strong, K.H. (1997) *Restorative Justice*. Cincinnati, OH: Anderson Publishing.

Williams, R. and Crifasi, C. (2020) "Evaluating the impact of Baltimore Community Mediation Center's Youth-Police Dialogue Circle Program." *Injury Prevention 26*, 1, A1-56. https://injuryprevention.bmj.com/content/26/Suppl_1/A38.1

Wright, J.C. (2002) "Partnership with community resources-campus police: Revisiting policies to reflect the 21st century." *Reference Librarian 36*, 75/76, 287–292. doi.org/10.1300/J120v36n75_26

Young, R., Sayers, D., and Sanchez, R. (2022) "'We Need Them Desperately': US Police Departments Struggle with Critical Staffing Shortages." *CNN*, July 20, 2022. www.cnn.com/2022/07/19/us/police-staffing-shortages-recruitment/index.html

Zehr, H. (2015) *The Little Book of Restorative Justice*, 2nd edn. Intercourse, PA: Good Books.

― Chapter 8 ―

Readiness Assessments Matter

A Case Study of Two US Middle Schools' Organizational Capacity to Implement Restorative Justice in Education

MARTHA BROWN, PHD

I was among the last cohort of Dr. Gordon Bazemore's graduate students before he retired, long before he should have. I only knew him for a few years, but there were things that I learned from him that impacted me deeply.

The first was how to write and publish—something I love to do. Gordon and Mara Schiff asked me to be third author on a peer-reviewed article they were invited to submit. I was still a Master's student and was deeply honored (and terrified) to have the opportunity to learn how to publish and publish with Gordon Bazemore! While I fumbled my way around attempting to write a literature review, he was steadfast in his encouragement and positive feedback. That's how Gordon always was. I also realized that he personally knew almost every scholar that he cited. They were not just anonymous names in parentheses—they were real people to him, and he often told humorous stories about them. When I attended a restorative justice conference in Vermont in 2014 and met people I had cited in my dissertation, I thought, "Gordon was right—they are indeed real people!"

The second lesson I learned from him was how to value relationships—and I have a long way to go here to even get close to how Gordon was. When Gordon, Mara, and I worked together in 2010 trying to get schools interested in restorative justice, I witnessed that relationships were his number one priority. He truly loved people. He loved talking with them and then pondering things they said. He reflected deeply without judgment. It was like he knew he was building a field, and everything people said to him was both valuable and worthy of consideration. Even though Gordon was a genius and highly respected academic, he had the ability to make everyone feel comfortable because he treated them like they were his equals. That is truly a rare quality.

Finally, Gordon Bazemore taught me a valuable secret. Gordon was a prolific writer, and once I asked him how he could write so much and still have time for teaching and his family. He told me the secret to publishing prolifically: to use what you publish as content for the next publication. That is something I've clung to and used all these years—including in this chapter. Instead of starting each article or chapter from scratch, he took a piece of a previous article and expanded on it, rethought it, or applied the theory to a new context. In this way, Gordon contributed volumes of deep thinking about restorative justice when the field was still very young. My hope is that even though restorative justice in education is now a teenager, today's practitioners and academics will take time to know this amazing human being through his written works.

Special thanks to Marg Thorsborne who reviewed the chapter draft and provided clarification on a few points.

Introduction

Restorative justice in education (RJE) is a whole-school approach that involves building and nurturing relationships, creating just and equitable classrooms, and repairing harm and transforming conflict (Evans and Vaandering 2022). Readiness assessments, organizational change theories, and implementation science can provide schools with the frameworks, processes, and tools needed to implement RJE with fidelity so that schools are more likely to achieve their desired outcomes. However, few schools take advantage of these instruments and processes. Instead, they tend to rely on meetings or workshops where certain restorative practices are explained and demonstrated, with teachers and staff then being sent off to train their peers and/or implement RJE with little or no leadership, structure, coaching, or additional training. Attempting to implement RJE without first assessing readiness could lead to poor implementation, unmet goals, and, ultimately, initiative failure (Attrill, Thorsborne and Turner 2019). In the book *Getting More Out of Restorative Practice in Schools: Practical Approaches to Improve School Wellbeing and Strengthen Community Engagement* (Thorsborne, Riestenberg and McCluskey 2019), Australian RJ practitioners Sue Attrill, Margaret Thorsborne, and Beverly Turner published case studies of the readiness process they developed. Their process has also been employed in schools in the US and UK, illustrating that regardless of the instrument a school chooses, the basic tenets of readiness can be applied globally.

Readiness assessments allow schools (and other organizations) to determine their capacity and motivation for change and to decide whether they have the structure and strengths needed to successfully implement a complex initiative like RJE. This chapter begins with a brief review of the literature on implementation science, change theories, and readiness. The author will then introduce the R=MC^2 Readiness Assessment (hereinafter referred to as the R=MC^2), describe its components and sub-components, and discuss how it is administered and analyzed. The next section includes a discussion of data gleaned from two readiness assessments done in middle schools in the United States, and how these data informed the school implementation teams' next steps. The chapter will conclude by describing how readiness assessments can be used to help monitor implementation integrity, inform course adjustments, support school transformation, and change efforts over time.

The Problem

Most whole-school reforms have no record of sustainability (Fullan 2008). Splett and colleagues (2022) conducted a study of the implementation barriers encountered by schools testing the effects of a single complex intervention and concluded:

> It is well-documented that implementing and sustaining interventions in educational and community settings is fraught with

many challenges. For example, in a systematic review of sustaining school-based health interventions after external funding concludes, Herlitz et al. (2020) identified 24 studies where no interventions were sustained in their entirety with fidelity to the original model. Yet, reviews of implementation fidelity overwhelmingly suggest implementation fidelity influences outcomes. In an extensive review of the influence of implementation fidelity on program outcomes, Durlak and DuPre (2008) found that interventions with high fidelity can be up to 12 times more effective at achieving outcomes than those that are poorly implemented. Three prominent barriers to implementing and sustaining school-based interventions with quality are turnover, inadequate administrative support, and limited time. (Herlitz et al. 2020, p.5)

These three prominent barriers and others can be identified early in the implementation process by administering a valid readiness assessment, such as the R=MC^2 described in this chapter. Readiness assessments give schools the information they need to identify and address problems that might hinder implementation fidelity before expending too much time, money, and energy on an initiative.

Assessing readiness can be compared to gardening. A successful gardener spends time preparing the soil long before planting seeds. The gardener knows that healthy soil is the key to hearty and productive plants. Yet in schools, seeds in the form of initiatives, programs, policies, and innovations are frequently scattered on infertile soils, namely, schools that are not ready to implement those initiatives. These schools will likely fail to see the fruits of their labors. It is not uncommon for schools to then blame the quality of the initiative for the failure rather than examining their own implementation processes.

Restorative justice literature often recommends assessing school climate and culture, as well as staff attitudes, behaviors, and perceptions (Moore 2008; Wearmouth, McKinney and Glynn 2007; Youth Justice Board for England and Wales 2004). However, only a few practitioners advocate for also assessing school readiness (Attrill et al. 2019; Brown 2021). Although some consultants, school districts, and state departments of education have developed their own readiness assessments, it is unclear whether these instruments are validated and grounded in the research on organizational change or how the results are used to inform decision-making.

Berkowitz (2019) modified a tool created by the New Zealand Ministry of Education called the *Restorative Justice Practices Tiered Fidelity Inventory for School-Wide Implementation*. One of the strategies to be assessed via a rubric was called "Implementation Readiness," characterized by the following levels:

- **Level 1: Foundational.** Few site stakeholder groups are introduced to restorative justice practices (RJP) with limited opportunities for implementation input. Minimal baseline data are collected, and school climate goals are not established.

- **Level 2: Progressing.** Less than 80 percent of site stakeholder groups have been introduced to RJP with some opportunities for implementation input. Some baseline data are collected, and school climate goals are partially established.

- **Level 3: Well Established.** Eighty percent or more site stakeholder groups are introduced to RJP and are given opportunities for implementation input. Baseline data are collected and used to inform the school climate SMART (Specific, Measurable, Achievable, Relevant, and Time-bound) goals with identified measures of success.

In this case, the term "readiness" was used to determine whether the school had set SMART goals, determined measures of success, and collected baseline data. This is not the definition in the readiness literature on organizational change (Attrill et al. 2019; Scaccia et al. 2015). Rather than readiness for implementation, this strategy would perhaps be more accurately called "Evaluation Readiness."

Herein lies the problem: the fields of education and restorative justice have failed to utilize organizational learning and change theories, despite the proliferation of readily available literature, seminars, and practices. Education is a notoriously siloed field that would benefit from opening up to cross-disciplinary and multi-disciplinary influences outside of education. Indeed, the R=MC^2 described in this chapter is grounded in multi-disciplinary research literature on organizational change (Scaccia et al. 2015) and offers schools a valid instrument and process to assess how their people, systems, and structures function in ways that help or hinder the successful implementation of RJE.

Review of the Literature

Literature from the fields of education, organizational change, evaluation, and restorative justice in education inform this chapter.

Organizational Change Theories

RJE requires a systematic approach to implementation as well as structural and philosophical change (Evans and Vaandering 2022; Hopkins 2004; Morrison 2007a, 2007b; Morrison, Blood and Thorsborne 2005). Zins and Elias (2006) found that implementing schoolwide change is a complicated and multifaceted process that requires leadership, time, collaboration, shared values, training, and ongoing effort (all of which can be assessed using the $R=MC^2$).

Engaging all members of the school community—students, staff, parents, teachers, administrators, and community members—is essential for successful implementation (Attrill et al. 2019; Brown 2018; Zins and Elias 2006). School communities need structures that reflect mutual respect as well as clear information about what RJE is and what it is not; how it will be implemented and by whom; what commitment, time, and resources will be required from the school; initial and ongoing training; and integration into behavior policies (Brown 2018; Hopkins 2004; Sumner, Silverman and Frampton 2010; Youth Justice Board for England and Wales 2004).

Principals play a pivotal role in molding schools, setting priorities, initiating collaborations and innovations, and shaping the school culture by being effective role models themselves (Hoppey and McLeskey 2013; May, Huff and Goldring 2012; Sammons et al. 2011). The ability of school leaders to create, foster, and sustain a shared vision that reflects clear and common values, beliefs, and assumptions that result in a cohesive and collaborative school environment among all school personnel is essential to sustainable and effective change

(Boyes-Watson 2005; Hall and Hord 2011; Morrison 2007a). Morrison (2007a) emphasized that in line with restorative justice, the process of leadership must go beyond the procedural aspect of engagement to the emotional aspect of engagement, stating that not only do leaders need to "walk the talk," but they also need to create safe spaces where others can engage socially and emotionally (p.174).

While the principal may act as leader, motivator, and coach in the process of change, classroom teachers ultimately implement the initiative. Therefore, initial and ongoing professional development and coaching is central to giving teachers the tools they need to effectively implement change interventions with integrity and enhance positive outcomes for teachers and students. Schools undergoing change rely heavily upon teacher collaborations that function to support both lateral and vertical capacity building (Fullan 2006a).

Because RJE requires a paradigm shift and the consistent application of specific philosophies, pedagogies, and processes across school environments (Amstutz and Mullet 2005; Evans and Vaandering 2022; Hopkins 2011; Riestenberg 2012), it is vital that the person introducing RJE to the school community be experienced and credible so that all members of the school community have sufficient information to decide whether or not they will buy in to RJE (Brown 2021; Sumner et al. 2010). It is important for a school to have either a dedicated, well-trained staff person or consultants from outside organizations to support the initiative, train existing and incoming staff, evaluate progress, and maintain the momentum (Brown 2018, 2021; Morrison 2007a; Wearmouth et al. 2007).

Advocates of RJE understand that school-wide implementation takes a minimum of three to five years to scale up. Embedding restorative practices across all school environments is a continual process that is never finished, given that schools are dynamic institutions that are constantly changing (Brown 2015; Hopkins 2004; Karp and Breslin 2001; McCluskey et al. 2008; Morrison 2007a, 2007b; Riestenberg 2012). Additionally, what RJE looks like is highly contextual and may differ from school to school even within a single district, which is why using an implementation science framework such as the one described in the following section would be helpful.

Implementation Science

Implementation science is defined as "the scientific study of methods and strategies that facilitate the uptake of evidence-based practice and research into regular use by practitioners" (The UW Implementation Science Resource Hub, n.d., para 2). Implementation science promotes a systems approach to organizational change and breaks down the adoption and implementation of a new initiative into four stages: exploration, installation, initial implementation, and full implementation (see Table 8.1).

Table 8.1 Four stages of implementing school-wide restorative practices

Stage	Description
Exploration "Should we do it?"	Decision of making a commitment to adopt and enact the processes and procedures to support implementation of RJE with fidelity
	Create a shared vision that embraces diverse perspectives and allows for the nuances of school culture and context
	Develop a restorative justice community
Installation "Let's get ready to do it!"	Train staff and setting up infrastructure required to successfully implement RJE
	Involvement of students, staff, families, and community members
	Create a core team to plan, hold the vision, implement, and collect baseline data
Initial Implementation "Let's do it!"	Adoption of restorative practices and policies into all systems within the school
	Staff members are actively engaged in the practices
	Students and families are knowledgeable about practices and active participants
	Clear evidence of restorative practices is visible
	Data collection is ongoing
Full Implementation "Let's make it better!"	Data has been collected and reviewed with all stakeholders
	There is ongoing professional development for all staff
	Benefits are present, celebrated, and made known
	Reflection happens and adjustments are made as needed

Note: Modified from Brown (2018). Used with permission from Living Justice Press. Adapted from the Minnesota Department of Education's Trainer's Guide for Working with Schools to Implement Restorative Practices by Kara Beckman and Nancy Riestenberg, who adapted this chart from the Los Angeles County (CA) Office of Education.

An appropriate time to assess readiness for implementation and obtain baseline data is between the exploration and installation phases. Then once the initial implementation stage begins, it is vital that feedback loops and other evaluative processes be implemented so the school can recognize where the process is and is not going according to plan and address those issues. The ultimate goal is to change from systems that support punishment to systems that support repair, restoration, and transformational restorative justice (Reimer 2018). This involves systemic change beyond the school itself and invites community-based, district, state, and even federal agencies to collaborate and provide the resources needed to support transformation (Brown 2021). But are all schools ready for change?

What Is Readiness?

We define readiness as a measurement of an organization's willingness and ability to implement a particular program or initiative (Scaccia et al. 2015). According to Scaccia and colleagues (2015, p.485), "readiness is considered a necessary precursor to successful organizational change and is often embedded within larger program planning and implementation frameworks." The readiness of individuals and organizations can be assessed at multiple stages of the implementation process (Kingston et al. 2018). Organizational readiness for change is key to bridging the gap between evidence-based innovations such as RJE and implementation fidelity, or integrity, as some practitioners prefer.

Many schools fail to achieve their desired outcomes of an initiative, including RJE, because they are "unprepared for the significant work and systems change required to achieve outcomes" (Splett et al. 2022, p.2). The $R=MC^2$ offers schools quantitative data that can help them prepare for systems change. For instance, perceptions and attitudes are scored in the "RJE-Specific Capacity" component of the $R=MC^2$, and an additional assessment, such as those mentioned previously, could be used as a companion if desired. Results may guide implementation teams on how to shift attitudes and behaviors so that buy-in and motivation for RJE increases. The readiness assessment and/or other pre-determined instruments (e.g., school climate surveys) would then be re-administered every two to three years to determine which aspects of the school culture and organization have changed, and to what degree. Gathering baseline data only makes sense if the same data will be collected in ensuing years so that progress can be tracked. An initial readiness assessment provides a baseline of comparison to later assessments to determine whether schools have increased their capacities and motivation (Kingston et al. 2018). As previously stated, these ongoing data collections, analyses, and interpretation processes and their timelines should be described in an implementation plan. Schools that fail to plan are planning to fail.

Ready or Not?

The author is often asked the question, "What if we find out we are not ready?" To answer that question, we need to define "not ready." Attrill and colleagues (2018) categorized schools as being ready or not ready according to the results of their assessment, and schools assessed as not ready for RJE are provided with recommendations for alternative actions and improvements that could help them to get ready for successful RJE implementation. However, there is an alternative to this dichotomous definition of readiness:

> Organizational readiness is often described as a categorical, and sometimes dichotomous, construct with pre-defined cut-points or thresholds (Flaspohler et al. 2012; Hawkins and Catalano 2002; Oetting et al. 1995; SAMHSA 2010). When organizational readiness is categorized this way, there is a premise that organizations that are "ready" will be able to effectively implement an innovation. This is problematic for two reasons. First, we often do not have empirical guidelines to help us understand when an organization is ready versus when it is not ready. Second, if an organization is deemed "not ready" to implement, it can often be difficult to determine what conditions are needed in order for implementation to be successful. In our heuristic [$R=MC^2$], organizational readiness is more nuanced than simply a category or stage. Rather, differences in readiness are a matter of degree. Further, organizations can be high in some components of organizational readiness (e.g., motivation) while low in others (e.g., innovation-specific capacity). Variability can be seen in the three different components. (Scaccia et al. 2015, pp.6–7)

This variability allows schools to approach any organizational weaknesses from a position of strength, which builds motivation and capacity for RJE.

Are there schools that are not functioning well that want to implement RJE? Absolutely—and this means that getting ready for RJE may take major restructuring, new leadership, and more time than anticipated. That said, schools are complex and dynamic organizations that are microcosms of their surrounding communities. Assessing readiness can be used to prioritize which schools in a district should be first in line to receive the always-limited resources available for training and support. Schools that score low in one or more components—those that may not yet be ready for implementation—should be given the support they need to increase their capacity and motivation for RJE and be budgeted to come online at a later date. Additionally, as schools change over time, so does their readiness, which is why readiness should be assessed over time to determine what specific aspects of the organization have changed, for better or for worse. Readiness should not be a one-time assessment.

The R=MC² Readiness Assessment

The R=MC² is an assessment grounded in empowerment evaluation, implementation science, and organizational change literature (Scaccia et al. 2015; Watson et al. 2022). The R=MC² is a heuristic of organizational readiness consistent with practical implementation science that includes three components: general organizational capacities, innovation-specific capacities, and motivation. The R=MC² Readiness Assessment provides all school community members with an opportunity to assess the three main components needed for change: the school's general capacity for change, the school's capacity for RJE specifically, and the staff's motivation to embark on the long, often difficult road toward systemic change (Scaccia et al. 2015). The goal of the R=MC² is to suggest practical directions for improved implementation. Should the results of the assessment show that a school scores low in one or more of the three essential components, schools can work toward addressing those issues that are most likely to interrupt or hinder implementation before moving ahead into the initial implementation stage (see Table 8.1).

There are 72 scaled-response items in the R=MC² designed specifically to assess a school's readiness for RJE. The three main components and their subcomponents are described below.

General Capacity

General Capacity consists of the attributes of a functioning organization and are associated with the ability to implement any innovation successfully. Data from this section of the assessment points to organizational strengths or to weaknesses that negatively impact the school's ability to function well. There are eight subcomponents in General Capacity:

- Culture
- Climate
- Innovativeness
- Resource Utilization
- Leadership
- Structure
- Staff Capacity
- Process Capacity.

Schools that are beginning major change efforts, including the adoption of RJE, will benefit from high levels of General Capacity components that include support from leadership, adequate staff capacities, and a culture of innovativeness (Scaccia et al. 2015).

Innovation (RJE)-Specific Capacity

Innovation-specific capacities are the "human, technical, and fiscal conditions that are important for successfully implementing a *particular* innovation with quality" (Scaccia et al. 2015, p.4). These strategies change from innovation to innovation. The RJE-specific items on the R=MC² described in this chapter were informed by

Brown's (2015) research on RJE in schools and were incorporated with assistance from the Wandersman Center. There are five sub-components in RJE-Specific Capacity:

- RJE-Specific Knowledge and Skills
- Program Champion
- Supportive Climate
- Inter-organizational Relationships
- Intra-organizational Relationships.

Schools with high RJE-Specific Capacity know about RJE, believe it is a better alternative than other initiatives, and are willing to do the often complex and time-consuming work of changing the culture of their school (Scaccia et al. 2015).

Motivation

Motivation in the context of the $R=MC^2$ refers to the perceived incentives and disincentives that contribute to the desirability of RJE. Data gleaned from this component can be used to assess the collective expectations of the school community, perceptions about RJE, perceptions of anticipated outcomes of RJE implementation, pressures for change, and emotional responses about RJE. There are six subcomponents of Motivation:

- Relative Advantage
- Compatibility
- Complexity
- Ability to Pilot
- Observability
- Priority.

Schools with high motivation to adopt RJE typically prioritize RJE, recognize the advantage of the RJE over other initiatives, and see how it aligns with the school's mission (Scaccia et al. 2015).

Several considerations preclude administering a readiness assessment. First, it is important that schools use a *validated* instrument grounded in the literature on organizational change, such as the R=MC². Second, the school community should be engaged enough in RJE to ensure high response rates; people need to know enough about RJE to respond to the RJE-Specific Capacity items. Regardless of which readiness assessment a school chooses, there is a process for administering it and sharing the results (Attrill et al. 2019).

In the following section, the process that RJAE Consulting used with two middle schools that chose the R=MC² as their readiness assessment is described.

The Assessment Process

As described by Attrill et al. (2019), the assessment process starts with an on-boarding period to learn more about the school's context and history with RJE. Readiness consultants communicate with the school's leader and core implementation team to determine: a) what their experience with RJE has been thus far, b) what kind of training was done by whom and to what extent, c) why they want to assess readiness at this time, and d) if they will build energy around the assessment and take actions to ensure both representation across the school community and high response rates.

Once it has been determined that it is indeed the right time to move ahead with the assessment, school leaders provide consultants with the names and email addresses of administrators, teachers, support staff, educational assistants and paraprofessionals, other staff including those who work in the custodial and food service, and, if appropriate, parents and volunteers. When using the R=MC², those emails are then entered into SurveyMonkey®, which allows the consultant to track completed surveys and schedule automated reminders to those who have not yet completed the assessment. This is done to obtain the highest possible response rates.

Before emailing the link to the R=MC², at least two emails are sent to everyone invited to take the assessment. In the first email, the external consultant makes their introduction and ensures participants that their responses will be confidential and anonymous.

This email also provides the schedule of the assessment process, including the date it launches, how long it remains open, the date it closes, and when and how the results will be available. In the next email, the consultant includes a five-minute video explaining the R=MC^2 assessment and provides a few examples of its items so participants know what to expect. The goals of the pre-assessment communications are to educate participants about the assessment, build excitement, improve response rates, and establish a connection with participants. When it is time to launch the survey, an email containing the link to the online assessment is sent. Every two to three days, response rates are monitored, and reminders are sent to those who started but did not finish the assessment or those who did not open or start the assessment. These reminders continue until the survey is closed.

Typically, a school should strive for a 75 percent response rate or higher so that the school's implementation team can be reasonably confident that the responses are representative and accurate. If the reminders do not generate enough completed surveys, it may be necessary to ask the principal to gently nudge faculty and staff about the assessment and its purpose and encourage them to complete it. It is important to build community and encourage all members of the school community to express their voice rather than issue a mandate. In other words, the assessment process should be done restoratively.

After the survey is closed, results are analyzed using Excel, and consultants create a report and present the results to the principal and implementation team. If the school is already working with a restorative justice trainer, that person or team should be included in meetings about the assessment so they can assist with planning strategies for improvement. It is best practice that consultants, trainers, and staff spend time together, often in circle, processing the findings and discussing how a school might use the results to increase their capacity and motivation to implement RJE. The following case studies provide real-life examples of how schools can use information from the R=MC^2 to address issues that help and hinder implementation.

The R=MC² in Two Schools

The results of the R=MC² described here are taken from unpublished reports. All information, including the schools' names, has been changed or deidentified.

Data Analysis

In the assessment, respondents were asked to express how strongly they agreed or disagreed with individual survey items, or statements, in the various components and subcomponents. Respondents selected from a 7-degree Likert scale, where 1 represented *strongly disagree* and 7 represented *strongly agree*. Responses were aggregated to determine the average score of each component and each subcomponent. Then, the scores of the whole group as well as those of each subgroup were visualized in charts. Scores of 3 or lower were interpreted as low; scores between 3.1 and 5.4 were considered moderate; and scores of 5.5 or higher were considered high.

While reporting results of component and subcomponent scores by group provides insightful information to schools, honing in on individual assessment items can be even more revealing. Thus, individual items were analyzed using the Test of Symmetry and Disagreement (TSD) (see Morris and Lieberman 2018). The TSD is an Excel spreadsheet that includes embedded formulas that calculate variance, effect size, standard deviation, p-values, and other inferential statistics. This is a powerful test even with small sample sizes. The TSD also includes visual features: "cell text in the 'Description' column is underlined and colored red if the lean is significantly to the right, green if significantly to the left, and a red-green shading is applied if disagreement is significant" (Morris and Lieberman 2018, p.6).

In any Likert-type survey item where respondents are asked to state how strongly they agree or disagree with a statement, respondents' choices may lean in the positive (*strongly agree*) or negative (*strongly disagree*) directions. The TSD test revealed some items that had no lean in any direction, which warranted further attention because it illustrated that responses were distributed across the scale from *strongly disagree* to *strongly agree* without suggesting any consensus among the respondents. The TSD called out items with response lean toward agreement or disagreement, but also those items with a significant number of responses that leaned in the opposite direction—known as statistical disagreement. These items are of particular interest, as the significant number of respondents who disagreed with the majority could play a vital role in hindering or helping implementation. Failing to test items for statistical disagreement silences the voices of respondents whose choices lean in the opposite direction of the majority. Thus, it is more than helpful to know the strength of agreement or disagreement to individual items as well as to determine whether there was statistical disagreement in any items. Both the R=MC² and the TSD were used to analyze responses and the results were communicated in a final report that was presented to the schools' principals and implementation teams. Select data from two reports are discussed here.

CASE STUDY 1: HARRIS JUNIOR HIGH SCHOOL

Harris Junior High School had been attempting to implement RJE for several years, but the principal was not satisfied with its progress. The principal contacted me after hearing my presentation on the R=MC², hoping that the results of the assessment could guide their next steps and breathe new life into their RJE implementation work.

Sample

A total of 89 people from Harris Junior High School took the R=MC² Readiness Assessment, representing 78 percent of the 114 members of the school community who had been invited to take it. Respondents were divided into five groups: administrators ($n = 4$); behavioral health ($n = 12$); teachers ($n = 49$); educational/teaching assistants ($n = 14$); and other ($n = 10$) which included nurse, AmeriCorps Fellow, cashier, clerical, kitchen supervisor, media specialist, nutrition services, technology support specialist, and one parent.

Main Component Scores: Harris Junior High School

Analysis of the three main components revealed that Harris appeared to have a moderate General Capacity for change (5.19), a moderate RJE-Specific Capacity (5.05), and moderate Motivation (4.84).

GENERAL CAPACITY

Early in data analysis, a trend appeared between the combined group scores and each individual group: scores in the administrator and other groups were observably higher than scores of those in the teacher, behavioral health, and educational/teaching assistants' groups (see Table 8.2). It seems that those who worked most closely with students throughout their day rated items lower than those who had less student contact.

Table 8.2 Harris's scores on General Capacity subcomponents by group

Subcomponents of General Capacity	Average of all groups ($n = 89$)	Administrator ($n = 4$)	Other ($n = 14$)	Behavioral health ($n = 12$)	Teacher ($n = 49$)	Teaching/ educational assistant ($n = 10$)
Culture	5.52	5.75	5.93	5.13	5.41	5.38
Climate	4.97	5.20	5.39	4.63	4.64	5.01
Structure	4.95	5.39	5.23	4.78	4.75	4.62
Innovativeness	5.30	5.38	5.75	4.69	5.05	5.61
Resource Utilization	4.63	4.81	4.93	4.40	4.11	4.89
Leadership	5.91	6.20	6.22	5.65	5.88	5.59
Staff Capacity	5.03	5.33	4.90	4.81	4.78	5.30

In this instance, a school community could ask itself: Why do administrators and some support staff believe capacity for change is higher than those who work directly with students? A circle dialogue around this single question could reveal important attitudes, beliefs, and/or actions that influence how different people in different positions feel about the school, and how these attitudes impact implementation. The point here is that the scores are more than numbers, and school implementation teams should take time to interrogate the data, looking for trends and patterns that could indicate potential strengths or weaknesses.

Next, the Test of Symmetry and Disagreement (TSD) (Morris

and Lieberman 2018) allowed a deeper look at specific items, particularly those with no definitive lean in one direction or another, or where there was significant disagreement.

Figure 8.1 illustrates this concept using histograms from certain items on Harris's test. A statement whose polarity leans toward agreement, which in this case was "Our school has a common purpose," depicts an asymmetric right lean.

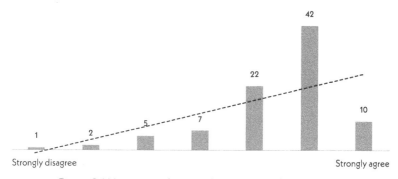

Figure 8.1 Histogram of an item leaning towards agreement: responses to "Our school has a common purpose"

The visually obvious polarity to the right toward the *strongly agree* end of the scale can be interpreted as indicating that Harris's school community agrees that the school has a common purpose, which is a strength that can support RJE implementation.

Items with no polarity—where responses were spread evenly among response choices *strongly disagree* to *strongly agree*—may look like Figure 8.2.

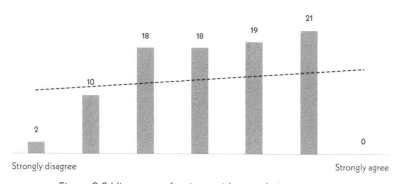

Figure 8.2 Histogram of an item with no polarity: responses to "Teachers trust students in this school"

An item like this one, which in Harris's case was "Teachers trust students in this school," warrants attention because it shows a range of agreement and disagreement. The R=MC² alone would have only shown the scores on this item, not its lack of polarity, which could be illustrative of a possible trust issue in the school. What is behind the lack of polarity? And how might a lack of trust in some groups impede implementation? Using the R=MC² results alongside the results of the TSD gives schools more detail that could inform actions they may want to take to improve trust (like keeping circles with students and teachers).

Items with significant disagreement are also of interest. The TSD revealed significant disagreement on the item "I feel physically safe in this school," in the subcomponent Climate. Figure 8.3 shows responses to this item ranging from *disagree* to *strongly agree*.

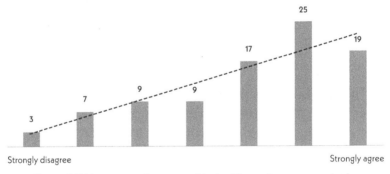

Figure 8.3 Histogram of an item with significant disagreement in the Climate subcomponent: responses to "I feel physically safe in this school"

While the majority of responses leaned toward the right, or *strongly agree*, end of the scale, there were enough responses in the middle and at the left end of the scale to trigger significant disagreement. This begs the question, why do a number of Harris's school community members feel unsafe? Again, it is recommended that Harris's staff and faculty sit in circle together to explore this question and determine what can be done to increase people's feelings of safety.

Although the TSD does not separate scores by group, we can look at the group scores of the R=MC² assessment and make some reasonable assumptions or ask some salient questions. In the Climate subcomponent (see Table 8.2), administrators scored 6.25 while teachers scored 4.14, a difference of 2.11 points. Why the difference between these groups? Additionally, the item with significant disagreement on the TSD, "I feel physically safe in this school," is in the Climate subcomponent. Is there a connection between the 2.11-point difference between administrator and teacher scores and some members of the school community feeling unsafe? It would behoove Harris to spend time in community talking about these results and uncovering potential issues like these and others that impact implementation.

Another item of interest on Harris's TSD was "Staffing levels are sufficient right now to accomplish our day-to-day tasks" in the subcomponent Staff Capacity. As shown in Figure 8.4, responses leaned toward the *strongly disagree* end of the scale, which in and of itself indicates something that hinders implementation, but there was also significant disagreement.

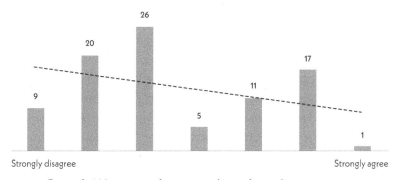

Figure 8.4 Histogram of an item with significant disagreement in the Staff Capacity subcomponent: responses to "Staffing levels are sufficient right now to accomplish our day-to-day tasks"

It would be worth exploring the reasons for so much disagreement on this item. On the R=MC², the score across all groups for subcomponent Staff Capacity was 5.03, which is moderate, and differences in scores of each group were small (< .55). Where, then, is the disagreement, and how does this school community define "sufficient?"

Additional Findings

In this section, data and items are drawn in both the RJE-Specific Capacity and Motivation components to illustrate how the R=MC² assessment and the TSD work together to uncover issues critical to implementation (see Table 8.3). First, notice the 1.18-point difference between administrator and teacher scores regarding RJE knowledge and skills. This suggests that teachers do not feel as knowledgeable and skilled as administrators do, which begs the question, why? What additional training do teachers feel they need? This difference in perceptions also calls into question the type and frequency of training and professional development for teachers and teaching/educational assistants. Conversations with the principal revealed that this school had initially contracted with a well-known restorative justice training organization that uses the "train and pray" model, one of the misimplementation models identified by Gregory and Evans (2020). Was the training less effective for teachers? This is hard to say, as most training is not evaluated for its effectiveness (see Brown 2021). Still, because teachers are the ones who implement the innovations (Fullan 2008), it is important that they are well-equipped to do so.

Next, notice the low average score (3.33) for the Complexity subcomponent, with teachers again being the lowest scoring group (3.01) and administrators being the highest (3.58), a trend that persisted across all components.

Table 8.3 Examples of how scores differed among the groups

Component	Subcomponent	Administrator ($n = 4$)	Behavioral health ($n = 12$)	Teacher ($n = 49$)	Teaching/educational assistant ($n = 10$)	Other ($n = 14$)	Average of all groups ($n = 89$)
RJE-Specific Capacity	RJE Knowledge and Skills	5.69	5.35	4.51	4.90	5.38	5.17
Motivation	Complexity	3.58	3.31	3.01	3.27	3.50	3.33

Results of the TSD revealed significant disagreement on three very important items: two, "We have the knowledge needed to implement restorative justice in our school" and "We have the concrete skills needed to implement restorative justice in our school," are in the RJE-Specific Capacity component. On both items, responses ranged from *strongly disagree* to *agree*. The third item that revealed significant disagreement, "It's difficult to implement restorative justice because it is complicated," is in the Motivation component (see Figure 8.5).

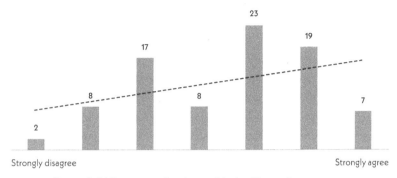

Figure 8.5 Histogram of an item with significant disagreement in the Motivation component: "It's difficult to implement restorative justice because it is complicated"

Similarly, responses to the item "Restorative justice is easy to implement" clearly leaned to the left, or *strongly disagree*, end of the scale (see Figure 8.6).

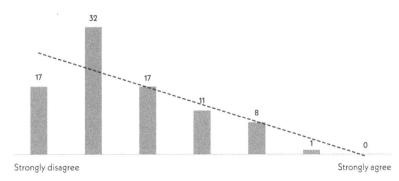

Figure 8.6 Histogram showing strong disagreement with an item in the Motivation component: "Restorative justice is easy to implement"

The $R=MC^2$ and TSD revealed that the Harris school community considered RJE to be a priority, yet it was hesitant to fully embrace RJE because many in the school community did not think they had the skills and knowledge to effectively implement it, and they felt that RJE was too complex and complicated.

Is there a connection between the four items discussed above? The quality, length, and type of training matter, as do messaging, communication, and support. As stated in *Creating Restorative Schools* (Brown 2018), training must be ongoing and adjusted to meet the needs of the school community, including new staff and those who want more advanced training. If school communities do not have effective ongoing training, and do not use implementation science to plan for and guide implementation, it is no wonder they feel that RJE is complex and difficult. The danger of perpetuating this pattern is that schools could reach a point where they throw up their hands and quit. The "train and pray" model, while very profitable to those who provide this kind of training, may ultimately be detrimental to the implementation process (Gregory and Evans 2020).

Harris Junior High School's Overall Readiness

Results of the readiness assessment and the TSD suggest that using an implementation science framework could strengthen Harris's capacities and motivation for RJE. The entire school community could benefit from learning more about RJE in the exploration stage (see Table 8.1), bringing all school community members on board, and implementing RJE strategically, ensuring that there are resources in place for systematically monitoring implementation integrity. Careful implementation planning could break down RJE implementation into digestible pieces so that it did not seem overwhelming and difficult.

It is not surprising that Harris hit a bump in the road to implementation and requested a readiness assessment. Most schools start with training and pay little attention to implementation integrity or monitoring. Results of the R=MC² Readiness Assessment and Test of Symmetry and Disagreement revealed that Harris Junior High School was in a moderate state of readiness and that they would benefit from:

- using an implementation science framework to guide the work

- developing a sound three- to five-year implementation plan that includes baseline and comparative data collection
- ensuring that all staff, including teaching/educational assistants, are trained appropriately, initially, and continually
- keeping regular circles to explore different groups' perspectives and concerns, including those raised by the assessment.

CASE STUDY 2: DOUGLAS MIDDLE SCHOOL

In this case, a district administrator heard my readiness assessment presentation and reached out for help with moving RJE implementation forward at Douglas Middle School. They informed me that the principal had applied for positions at other schools and wanted to leave Douglas, and that there were relational problems between that principal and the staff. Staff did not know the principal intended to leave, and the researcher could not disclose this information. Despite this uncomfortable situation, the principal, assistant principal, and the district administrator agreed that a readiness assessment was warranted. The same process was used at Douglas Middle School and Harris Junior High School.

Sample

A total of 54 staff took the R=MC², representing 81 percent of the 67 people who were invited to take it. Respondents were divided into five groups: administrators (n = 3); counselors (n = 3); teachers (n = 34); educational/teaching assistants (n = 4); and other (n = 10), which included the nurse, cafeteria, custodial, library, and secretarial staff.

The purpose of examining some results from this school is not to compare Douglas to Harris, but rather to broaden our understanding of how a readiness assessment can support RJE implementation under a variety of circumstances.

Main component scores at Douglas Middle School were in the moderate range: Motivation was the highest (4.27), followed by RJE-Specific Capacity (4.07) and General Capacity (4.06).

Table 8.4 Douglas's scores on General Capacity subcomponents by group

Subcomponent	Administrator (n = 3)	Counselor (n = 3)	Teacher (n = 34)	Teaching/ educational assistant (n = 4)	Other (n = 10)	Average of all groups (n = 54)
Culture	3.61	3.44	3.67	3.61	4.48	3.76
Climate	4.43	3.67	3.50	4.22	3.94	3.95
Structure	4.45	3.94	3.54	3.35	3.83	3.82
Innovativeness	4.22	4.28	3.55	4.04	3.99	4.02
Resource Utilization	4.25	3.25	2.73	3.19	4.06	3.50
Leadership	6.15	5.09	3.87	3.84	4.01	4.59
Staff Capacity	5.44	5.33	4.27	4.75	4.05	4.77

Table 8.4 reveals that four of the seven subcomponents had low-moderate average scores: Culture (3.76), Climate (3.95), Structure (3.82), and Resource Utilization (3.5). Within the Leadership subcomponent, administrators' (6.15) and counselors' (5.09) scores were much higher than teachers' (3.87) and teaching/educational assistants' (3.84) scores. They were two to three points apart, reflecting a large disparity in agreement ratings within the statements about leadership. These large differences illustrate problems between these groups that need to be explored and addressed, especially considering the important roles both leaders and teachers play in implementation. Given what was known about the principal, it was possible that teachers were very unhappy with leadership, and that leadership was over-rating itself, perhaps to look good to the district. It was no coincidence, then, that the TSD revealed a lean toward disagreement on these items regarding the principal: "I trust the principal at their word" and "The principal works to create a sense of community in this school."

All groups scored Resource Utilization the lowest (3.5), and the teachers' score (2.73) was 1.52 points fewer than that of the administrators (4.25). Some aspects of this subcomponent were addressed in a meeting when we discovered that the approximately 20 people on the RJE implementation team were also on a number of other committees and felt stretched very thin. The staff were asked to draw a chart of all the committees and decide which had similar purposes so that they could be combined or eliminated, which they did. It did not take long to construct an alternative to the existing committee structure—one that respected and honored teachers' time and allowed them to be more efficient and effective.

Analysis of the General Capacity component and its subcomponents and items revealed a serious disconnect between the perceptions of administrators and counselors and those of the teachers and teaching/educational assistants. Scores also revealed a need to improve communication, structure, processes, and morale. The greatest disagreement among the groups occurred in items about the principal's ability to create trust and community and unite the school around a common purpose, the importance of which is discussed in Brown's (2015, 2018) studies.

Other Findings of Interest

Low scores and disagreement with statements were found among the remaining components as well. In the RJE-Specific Skills and Knowledge subcomponent of the RJE-Specific Capacity, administrators scored the lowest (3.92) of all the groups, revealing they were the least knowledgeable and skilled group in the school. For organizational change to happen, leaders must be knowledgeable and skilled, have the ability to lead the change, and buy into the innovation being implemented (Brown 2015, 2018; May et al. 2012; Nor and Roslan 2009).

Second, Complexity scored the lowest (3.8) of all subcomponents in the Motivation component. On the TSD, there was a lean toward *strongly disagree* in 23 items, including the following:

- Restorative justice is better than other practices we have considered using in our school.
- Restorative justice is easy to implement.
- It's difficult to implement restorative justice because it is complicated.

Overall, staff perceived RJE to be complicated and difficult to implement.

Douglas Middle School's Overall Readiness

At Douglas Middle School, the R=MC² was not enough to tell the whole story of its state of readiness. The TSD identified multiple areas of concern that had real potential to derail the successful implementation of RJE. While many in the Douglas school community and some district administrators were aware of problems with the principal, the readiness assessment revealed other issues that would need to be addressed in addition to identifying a strong principal who would support and lead the change effort.

Was Douglas ready for RJE? Even though respondents did not know or were not sure that the principal was trying to secure other positions in the district, the disconnect between administrators and teachers was clear in all the scores, as was the alignment of counselors' and administrators' scores. The data implied the existence of a strong alliance between administrators and counselors and a disconnect between them and other faculty and support staff. Data alone suggested an "us vs. them" situation—a problem that must be rectified in order for this school to unite in their efforts to implement RJE with integrity. The TSD revealed strong disagreement with 23 items on the R=MC² across all three main components. This was not a healthy position for a school to be in when considering implementation of RJE. The relational ecology of the school was unhealthy, and the leadership support that is so critical for implementing any initiative with fidelity was weak (Brown 2015, 2018; Morrison and Vaandering 2012).

The principal of Douglas Middle School ultimately left the school, but the story does not end there. The readiness assessment report gave district administrators, faculty, staff, and the incoming principal critical information on where to begin the work of getting the school community ready for RJE. It was made clear in the report that unifying the Douglas community and establishing trust between all groups in the school should be a top priority. We also discussed the need for harm reparation and healing processes so that the community could move forward under a new leadership that more fully embraced the restorative vision. We believed that once past harms were addressed and healed and new, trusting relationships were built, Douglas could (and would) address other issues raised in the readiness report and continue implementing RJE.

Lessons Learned

Harris and Douglas were different schools in many ways and were implementing RJE under different circumstances. However, both school communities perceived RJE to be too difficult to implement. This is an important finding and calls for both schools and RJE trainers to scrutinize their message and methods and course correct accordingly. Gregory and Evans (2020) described seven misimplementation models found in US schools, including the "train and pray" model so frequently employed. In 2021, Brown published a critique of the way many schools and trainers tend to approach RJE training and professional development and suggested that research and evaluation be done to develop an evidence-based training curriculum grounded in implementation science that can be adapted to any school. The results of these assessments and tests discussed in this chapter lead to these questions:

- What messages did RJE trainers send to schools about implementation that left them feeling that RJE is too complex and difficult to implement?

- Did trainers use, recommend, and model implementation science frameworks?

- What prevents the development of an evidence-based RJE training curriculum that is grounded in implementation science and is adaptable to any school? Who would construct such a curriculum?

- Why do schools and districts resist investing in long-term organizational change solutions that produce results, such as readiness assessments and implementation science, and instead choose "train and pray" models that produce results and/or problems like those described in this chapter?

The RJE community, including trainers and training organizations, should embrace these and other questions and work together to create a more unified and consistent approach to creating restorative schools.

The Role of Process Evaluation in Implementation

An important part of implementing RJE is developing an implementation plan that includes and emphasizes process evaluation. Whole-school reformers agree that evaluating the implementation process is critical (Brown 2018; Fullan 2006a, 2006b, 2008; Morrison 2007a). Morrison (2007a) explained that data gathered during implementation should be used to make course adjustments going forward, paying careful attention to what is going well, what needs attention or course correction, and what should be discarded altogether. Answering those questions is the very purpose of a process evaluation. Process evaluation should be used for the first three to five years of a school's restorative journey to track the school's progress toward its goals and determine the degree to which RJE has been implemented with integrity (Beckman 2020). Schools should consider what data will be collected, what existing data would be included, what new instruments or methods are needed, when to collect data, how to analyze data, who will analyze data, and how the school will make sense of and utilize evaluation findings. The circle practice can be used to discuss how implementation efforts are progressing and to co-create solutions to challenges and problems (Brown and Di Lallo 2020). No matter the methods chosen, feedback loops are vital. Measuring change in a school requires the school to understand its starting point by collecting baseline data and then collecting and analyzing data at pre-determined milestones to determine whether, how, and where systemic change is happening (see Brown 2021). Readiness assessments offer an empirical method for assessing change and can provide some important baseline data. If re-administered periodically throughout implementation, readiness assessments can contribute a myriad of ways to understand and document change. There is a direct correlation between implementation fidelity and achieving desired outcomes and goals. Schools and districts must accept that systemic change and full implementation of RJE takes time and a commitment of resources.

Conclusion

Research by Brown (2015) in Oakland schools found that RJE implementation is messy and non-linear. While systems change is never easy or quick, implementation science, process evaluation, readiness assessments, and effective ongoing training and support can ease the complexity and stress of RJE implementation. Many lessons were learned from the Douglas and Harris readiness assessments. However, there still remains a high need for more schools to use readiness assessments to support implementation of RJE. These assessments shine light into the dark recesses of systems change, and create opportunities for school communities to discuss, question, and make sense of many intricate and interconnected aspects of their school. Readiness matters.

References

Amstutz, L. and Mullet, J.H. (2005) *The Little Book of Restorative Discipline for Schools: Teaching Responsibility; Creating Caring Climates.* New York: Good Books.

Attrill, S., Thorsborne, M., and Turner, B. (2019) "Assessing Readiness for Restorative Practice Implementation." In M. Thorsborne, N. Riestenberg, and G. McCluskey (eds) *Getting More Out of Restorative Practice in Schools: Practical Approaches to Improve School Wellbeing and Strengthen Community Engagement.* Philadelphia, PA: Jessica Kingsley Publishers.

Beckman, K. (2020) Implementation Integrity Measures for School-wide Restorative Practices in Saint Paul Public Schools [Unpublished compilation of measures]. Minneapolis, MN: University of Minnesota. https://prc.umn.edu/sites/prc.umn.edu/files/2021-12/SPPS%20Implementation%20Measures_12_2021.pdf

Berkowitz, K. (2019) "The Art of Integrating School Climate Initiatives." In M. Thorsborne, N. Riestenberg, and G. McCluskey (eds) *Getting More out of Restorative Practices in Schools: Practical Approaches to Improve School Wellbeing and Strengthen Community Engagement.* Philadelphia, PA: Jessica Kingsley Publishers.

Boyes-Watson, C. (2005) "Community is not a place but a relationship: Lessons for organizational development." *Public Organization Review* 5, 4, 359–374. doi.org/10.1007/s11115-005-5096-5

Brown, M.A. (2015) "Talking in Circles: A Mixed Methods Study of School-wide Restorative Practices in Two Urban Middle Schools." PhD dissertation, Florida Atlantic University. https://fau.digital.flvc.org/islandora/object/fau%3A32067/datastream/OBJ/view/Talking_in_Circles__A_Mixed_Methods_Study_of_School-wide_Restorative_Practices_in_Two_Urban_Middle_Schools.pdf

Brown, M.A. (2018) *Creating Restorative Schools: Setting Schools up to Succeed.* St. Paul, MN: Living Justice Press.

Brown, M.A. (2021) "We cannot return to 'normal': A post-COVID call for a systems approach to implementing restorative justice in education (RJE)." *Laws 10*, 68, 1–18. doi.org/10.3390/laws10030068

Brown, M.A. and Di Lallo, S. (2020) "Talking Circles: A culturally responsive evaluation practice." *American Journal of Evaluation 41*, 3, 367–383. doi.org/10.1177/1098214019899164

Evans, K. and Vaandering, D.D. (2022) *Little Book of Restorative Justice in Education: Fostering Responsibility, Healing, and Hope in Schools* (first published 2016). New York: Good Books.

Fullan, M. (2006a) "The future of educational change: System thinkers in action." *Journal of Educational Change 7*, 3, 113–122. doi.org/10.1007/s10833-006-9003-9

Fullan, M. (2006b) "Change theory: A force for school improvement" [Seminar series paper no. 157]. Center for Strategic Education. www.michaelfullan.com/media/13396072630.pdf

Fullan, M. (2008) "Curriculum Implementation and Sustainability." In F.M. Connelly (ed.) *The Sage Handbook of Curriculum and Instruction*. Thousand Oaks, CA: Sage Publications.

Gregory, A. and Evans, K. (2020) The Starts and Stumbles of Restorative Justice in Education: Where Do We Go From Here? [Policy brief]. National Education Policy Center. https://nepc.colorado.edu/publication/restorative-justice

Hall, G.E. and Hord, S.M. (2011) *Implementing Change: Patterns, Principles, and Potholes*, 3rd edn. Upper Saddle River, NJ: Pearson Education.

Herlitz, L., MacIntyre, H., Osborn, T., and Bonell, C. (2020) "The sustainability of public health interventions in schools: A systematic review." *Implementation Science 15*, 4 (January), 1–28. doi.org/10.1186/s13012-019-0961-8

Hopkins, B. (2004) *Just Schools: A Whole School Approach to Restorative Justice*. London: Jessica Kingsley Publishers.

Hopkins, B. (2011) *The Restorative Classroom: Using Restorative Approaches to Foster Effective Learning*. New York: Optimus Education.

Hoppey, D. and McLeskey, J. (2013) "A case study of principal leadership in an effective inclusive school." *Journal of Special Education 46*, 4, 245–256. doi.org/10.1177/0022466910390507

Karp, D.R. and Breslin, B. (2001) "Restorative justice in school communities." *Youth & Society 33*, 2, 249–272. doi.org/10.1177/0044118X01033002006

Kingston, B., Mattson, S.A., Dymnicki, A., Spier, E. et al. (2018) "Building schools' readiness to implement a comprehensive approach to school safety." *Clinical and Family Psychology Review 21*, 433–449. doi.org/10.1007/s10567-018-0264-7

May, H., Huff, J., and Goldring, E. (2012) "A longitudinal study of principals' activities and student performance." *School Effectiveness and School Improvement 23*, 4, 417–439. doi.org/10.1080/09243453.2012.678866

McCluskey, G., Lloyd, G., Kane, J., Riddell, S., Stead, J., and Weedon, E. (2008) "Can restorative practices in schools make a difference?" *Educational Review 60*, 4, 405–417. doi.org/10.1080/00131910802393456

Moore, M. (2008) Restorative Approaches in Primary Schools: An Evaluation of the Project Co-ordinated by the Barnet Youth Offending Service. https://restorativejustice.org.uk/sites/default/files/resources/files/Restorative%20Approaches%20in%20Primary%20Schools%20An%20Evaluation%20of%20the%20Project%20Co-ordinated%20by%20the%20Barnet%20Youth%20Offending%20Service.pdf

Morris, J.D. and Lieberman, M.G. (2018) "Treatment of Single Likert-type Items in Surveys." Paper presentation. American Educational Research Association Conference, New York. April 2018.

Morrison, B. (2007a) *Restoring Safe School Communities: A Whole School Response to Bullying, Violence and Alienation.* New South Wales: The Federation Press.

Morrison, B. (2007b) "Schools and Restorative Justice." In G. Johnstone and D.W. Van Ness (eds) *Handbook of Restorative Justice.* Cullompton: Willan Publishing.

Morrison, B., Blood, P., and Thorsborne, M. (2005) "Practicing restorative justice in school communities: The challenge of culture change." *Public Organization Review* 5, 4, 335–357. http://dx.doi.org/10.1007/s11115-005-5095-6

Morrison, B. and Vaandering, D. (2012) "Restorative justice: Pedagogy, praxis, and discipline." *Journal of School Violence* 11, 2, 138–155. http://dx.doi.org/10.1080/15388220.2011.653322

Nor, S.M. and Roslan, S. (2009) "Turning around at-risk schools: What effective principals do." *The International Journal on School Disaffection* 6, 2, 1–29. https://files.eric.ed.gov/fulltext/EJ853212.pdf

Reimer, K. (2018) *Adult Intentions, Student Perceptions: How Restorative Justice is Used in Schools to Control and Engage.* Charlotte, NC: Information Age Publishing.

Riestenberg, N. (2012) *Circle in the Square: Building Community and Repairing Harm in School.* St. Paul, MN: Living Justice Press.

Sammons, P., Gu, Q., Day, C., and Ko, J. (2011) "Exploring the impact of school leadership on pupil outcomes: Results from a study of academically improved and effective schools in England." *International Journal of Educational Management* 25, 1, 83–101. doi.org/10.1108/09513541111100134

Scaccia, J.P., Cook, B.S., Lamont, A., Wandersman, A. et al. (2015) "A practical implementation science heuristic for organizational readiness: R = MC2." *Journal of Community Psychology* 43, 4, 484–501. doi.org/10.1002/jcop.21698

Splett, J.W., Perales, K., Miller, E., Hartley, S.N. et al. (2022) "Using readiness to understand implementation challenges in school mental health research." *Journal of Community Psychology* 50, 7, 3101–3121. doi.org/10.1002/jcop.22818

Sumner, M.D., Silverman, C.J., and Frampton, M.L. (2010) "School-based Restorative Justice as an Alternative to Zero-tolerance Policies: Lessons from West Oakland" [Report]. Thelton E. Henderson Center for Social Justice. www.law.berkeley.edu/files/thcsj/10-2010_School-based_Restorative_Justice_As_an_Alternative_to_Zero-Tolerance_Policies.pdf

Thorsborne, M., Riestenberg, N., and McCluskey, G. (2019) *Getting More Out of Restorative Practice in Schools: Practical Approaches to Improve School Wellbeing and Strengthen Community Engagement.* London: Jessica Kingsley Publishers.

The UW Implementation Science Resource Hub (n.d.) "What is Implementation Science?" University of Washington. https://impsciuw.org/implementation-science/learn/implementation-science-overview

Watson, A.K., Hernandez, B.F., Kolodny-Goetz, J., Walker, T.J. et al. (2022) "Using implementation mapping to build organizational readiness." *Frontiers of Public Health* 10, 904652. doi.org/10.3389/fpubh.2022.904652

Wearmouth, J., McKinney, R., and Glynn, T. (2007) "Restorative justice: Two examples from the New Zealand schools." *British Journal of Special Education* 34, 2, 196–203. http://dx.doi.org/10.1111/j.1467-8578.2007.00479.x

Youth Justice Board for England and Wales (2004) "National Evaluation of the Restorative Justice in Schools Programme" [Report]. http://dera.ioe.ac.uk/5926/1/nat%20ev%20of%20rj%20in%20schoolsfullfv.pdf

Zins, J.E. and Elias, M.J. (2006) "Social and emotional learning: Promoting the development of all students." *Journal of Educational and Psychological Consultation* 17, 2&3, 233–255. http://dx.doi.org/10.1080/10474410701413152

— Chapter 9 —

Measuring What Really Matters in Juvenile Justice

An American Case Study

DOUGLAS THOMAS

Introduction

The measure of a man comes down to moments, spread out like dots of pain on the canvas on life. Everything you were, everything you'll someday be, resides in the small, seemingly ordinary choices of everyday life... Each decision seems as insignificant as a left turn on an unfamiliar road when you have no destination in mind. But the decisions accumulate until you realize one day that they've made you the man that you are.

KRISTIN HANNAH

Dr. Gordon Bazemore made the most of his moments and had a knack for making the right kinds of decisions. He was eulogized in his obituary as a man who "excelled in academics, athletics, music, and to most kids in his neighborhood, coolness." Likewise, the totality of a person's career is measured in accomplishments great and small. Gordon Bazemore had many extraordinary professional accomplishments. He was a teacher, a college professor and administrator, a prolific writer, and a pioneer in restorative justice. As Director of the national Balanced and Restorative Justice (BARJ) Project, funded by the Office of Juvenile Justice and Delinquency Prevention (OJJDP), US Department of Justice, Dr. Bazemore worked together with other scholars, researchers, practitioners, and policymakers at the local, state, national, and international level to bring the promise and practice of restorative justice to institutions and communities around the world. The sum of his life choices seems to indicate that he had a talent for choosing well.

Bazemore (2006) made the choice to write a monograph with the daring and provocative title of *Measuring What Really Matters in Juvenile Justice*. The title challenges several fundamental assumptions about juvenile justice. First, it suggests that it is possible to measure juvenile justice, and second, that it is possible to identify and measure what matters. Further, the title doubles down on the second challenge by emphasizing that it will focus on what *really* matters.

While allowing that measurement is not a new concept to juvenile justice, Bazemore argued that data collected by juvenile justice agencies often has unrelated outcomes, while seldom allowing for the citizenry to assess and critique the performance in a meaningful way. As a result, traditional efforts to measure juvenile justice have resulted in information that has not helped juvenile justice systems and organizations determine the impact and cost-effectiveness of their interventions; failed to provide input to juvenile justice professionals regarding public awareness and support for these efforts; and rarely provided citizens and other government stakeholders with a sense of what it is that juvenile justice systems and agencies are really accomplishing or trying to accomplish (Bazemore 2006).

Dr. Bazemore's monograph was written in support of a mission-driven system of performance outcomes and measures for juvenile justice systems based on the BARJ model (OJJDP 1998) developed in response to frustration with traditional measurement efforts in juvenile justice that have little to do with outcomes at all (Harp et al. 2006). The focus on process measurement (e.g., number of clients served, number of contacts with clients) rather than outcomes was attributed in large part to the historical absence of a clearly articulated mission for juvenile justice. However, the widespread adoption of the BARJ model for juvenile justice in the late 1990s and early 2000s (see also publications by Bazemore, Pavelka, Pavelka and Thomas, and OJJDP) provided a strong conceptual basis for developing measurement standards grounded firmly in community needs and expectations.

Measuring What Really Matters in Juvenile Justice provided a detailed rationale and defense for each set of measures and outcomes proposed under the three balanced approach mission goals—accountability, public safety, and competency development—described in the *Guide to Developing and Implementing Performance Measures for the Juvenile Justice System* (Harp et al. 2006).

This chapter presents a case study of an effort led by Dr. Gordon Bazemore and colleagues to develop a mission-driven system of performance outcomes and measures for juvenile justice systems based on the BARJ model in response to frustration with traditional measurement efforts in juvenile justice that appeared to have little to do with outcomes. *Measuring What Really Matters in Juvenile Justice* provided a detailed summary and rationale and defense for each set of measures and outcomes proposed under the three balanced approach mission goals—accountability, public safety, and competency development. This chapter attempts to describe the enduring legacy of *Measuring What Really Matters in Juvenile Justice* which exceeded its original purpose and provided a defensible basis for a unique approach to measuring performance in juvenile justice. By laying out the practical and theoretical framework for performance measures for BARJ, Dr. Bazemore also built a framework for expanding conventional perspectives on measuring justice outcomes beyond recidivism.

Measuring Performance

Albert Einstein famously defined *insanity* as doing the same thing repeatedly and expecting a different result. Caren Harp and Dennis Maloney took this concept to the next level and, with the juvenile justice system in mind, defined *beyond insanity* as doing the same thing repeatedly and not expecting *any* results. For many juvenile justice practitioners—neophytes and grizzled veterans alike—the juvenile justice system may indeed appear to be "beyond insane." This is not due to a lack of curiosity or lack of data. Juvenile justice organizations regularly collect uncountable pieces of information and produce data-filled reports on all sorts of things. The problem is that very little of the data gathered to document, describe, quantify, or otherwise memorialize juvenile practices are dedicated to measuring performance.

> Usually, what is measured has to do with inputs (e.g., funding, number of referrals to court), processes (e.g., time to process cases, case processing rates), or outputs (e.g., number of juveniles placed, number of contacts with probationers). While these data are important and useful, they do not *necessarily* provide measures of performance. (Thomas 2006, p.1)

Measuring "What Really Matters" Matters

There is no easy way to determine precisely what *really* matters and what should be measured. The juvenile justice system is, in fact, prolific in its ability to collect, process, report, and publish data-filled reports and websites. And while these data matter, they usually have had little to do with documenting expected outcomes or measuring performance.

> There is clearly little rationale or "theory" behind such counts that would link these activities to change in offenders or any other outcome. And there is also no apparent link to any philosophy of justice. At best, juvenile justice agencies and systems have measured inputs and processes or activities linked to practice such as making contacts, making court appearances, and completing paperwork. Most have failed to measure or even articulate intermediate outcomes associated with such practices, and the connection between such practices and long-term outcomes relevant to the public (e.g., community safety) is almost never articulated. (Bazemore 2006, p.1)

Bazemore (2006) attributed the traditional scarcity of performance measures in the juvenile justice system to an "historical absence of a true mission." Indeed, the juvenile justice system may sometimes seem like a system in search of a common purpose. The historical conflict within and limitations of juvenile justice philosophies were succinctly described in *Measuring What Really Matters in Juvenile*

Justice, starting with the original "best interest of the child" approach followed by a parade of competing points of view, including those that emphasized crime control and public safety; treatment and rehabilitation; hands-off and diversion from system contact; and even abolishment of the system as out of date and failed (Feld 1991).

The philosophical and theoretical turbulence in which the juvenile justice system operated in the late 1990s and early part of the twentieth century had a broad impact on every aspect of the system, including state-level legislation and policy (Pavelka 2016).

Despite the rehabilitative purpose that the juvenile justice system was originally created to achieve, there no longer exists a common design in America's juvenile justice system. Different philosophies on how the juvenile justice system should handle serious juvenile offenders appear throughout the United States. The statutory language of each state's juvenile justice code basically represents a piecemeal approximation of a legislature's intent. The competing interests of enforcing the rehabilitative ideal upon which the juvenile justice system was created, and of administering punishment to protect society from delinquent children, present a nationwide dilemma (Giardino 1996, p.224).

Given the historic roller coaster rationale for juvenile justice, it is not difficult to imagine why defining what really matters has been so elusive.

Balanced and Restorative Justice: A Unifying Mission for Juvenile Justice

The BARJ model came about as a response to generational conflicts over the purpose of the juvenile justice system and an attempt to clarify and reconcile the competing approaches that failed to satisfy basic needs of individual crime victims, the community, and juvenile offenders. This model, described by Bazemore (1997), provided an alternative philosophy—restorative justice—and a new mission, "the balanced approach," which requires juvenile justice professionals to devote attention to: holding offenders accountable while making amends to the victims and community; developing offender competencies; and providing a safe public with the victims, community, and offenders as active participants (Maloney, Romig and Armstrong 1988). In this context, instead of an act against the state, crime is understood as an act that creates harm for the victim and the community. As described, BARJ is an ancient idea common to tribal and religious traditions of many cultures. Practitioners have used techniques consistent with this approach for years; however, they have lacked a coherent philosophical framework that supports restorative practice and provides direction to guide all aspects of juvenile justice practice. Many believed, and many still believe, that the BARJ model provides a "better approach" to juvenile justice.

> Balanced consideration of the stated goals of balanced and restorative justice—community protection, offender accountability, and competency development—"brings clarity and reason to juvenile justice issues" (Harp 2002, p.1). This comprehensive philosophy speaks to every aspect of delinquency, punishment, treatment, and prevention. These three principles, fully implemented, create a juvenile justice system that truly operates in the best interests of the child and the community.

BARJ provided a vision for juvenile justice built on both traditional and innovative practices as well as ancient core values that have guided justice-related practices in communities for centuries. Because BARJ provided a framework for systemic reform and offered hope for preserving and revitalizing the juvenile justice system, the model was quickly embraced by many juvenile justice organizations, practitioners, and researchers.

The OJJDP introduced the National BARJ Project in 1992. This project provided intensive training, technical assistance, and guideline materials in three selected sites, which had committed to implementing major systemic change to conform to the BARJ model. This project, led by Dr. Gordon Bazemore and Dr. Mark Umbreit, caught on fast. By the end of 1995, at least 24 states had adopted or were exhibiting juvenile codes or administrative procedures that include the balanced approach or restorative justice concepts (Freivalds 1996; Pavelka 2016).

The BARJ Project launched a national movement in juvenile justice reform. Since its start described above, BARJ continues to grow but perhaps at a slower rate; it has been a long journey that is more evolution than revolution (Pavelka and Thomas 2019). In addition to being adopted as the legislatively mandated juvenile justice purpose clause in over half the states, several states engaged in systematic statewide initiatives to implement policies and programs that reflect the BARJ mission (Pavelka 2016). Further, many local jurisdictions across the nation strategically embrace BARJ in their mission statements and conduct their operations with an eye toward specifically meeting BARJ goals. BARJ opened the door to developing and implementing a far-reaching variety of non-traditional programs and interventions designed to enhance youth accountability while supporting competency development and maintaining community safety (Pavelka and Thomas 2019).

Effective Mission Statements Point the Way, Performance Measures Confirm Arrival

Even the most enthusiastic supporters of a popular way of doing business are bound to ask at some point in time, "Well, does it work?" Proponents of alternative points of view are likely to be quicker to ask that question. As Susan Blackburn describes in her chapter on Pennsylvania's BARJ journey, the value of developing and reporting performance outcomes that support BARJ goals—community protection, accountability, and victim involvement—was recognized early in the process. Pennsylvania was not alone. The national BARJ Partnership, other jurisdictions, and notably OJJDP also recognized the urgent need to develop performance-based outcomes to guide and support implementation of BARJ initiatives.

To that end, in 2003, the US Congress directed OJJDP to fund the American Prosecutor's Research Institute (APRI), the BARJ Project, and the National Center for Juvenile Justice to carry out a national project to demonstrate that it is both possible and valuable to measure the performance of juvenile justice systems. The performance measures developed through the National Demonstration Project were based on the BARJ model and were designed to establish effective measures of the ability of jurisdictions to provide community safety, offender accountability, and competency development. These goals were selected because of the extensive research, development, and implementation of BARJ and the efforts to establish BARJ as a strategic mission for juvenile justice which provides "a more inclusive and well-defined approach to juvenile justice than the traditional child-centered, offender-oriented approach that has guided juvenile courts since their inception in the late 1800's" (Harp et al. 2006).

Four jurisdictions were selected to participate in the one-year national demonstration project—Allegheny County (Pittsburgh), PA; Cook County (Chicago), IL; Deschutes County (Bend), OR; and the State of South Carolina. Each jurisdiction was requested to implement a protocol to collect case-level data on a set of ten benchmark measures linked to BARJ goals and to produce a system-wide "report card" on the actual measures related to community safety, offender accountability, and competency development. Each jurisdiction received training and technical assistance for implementing the performance measures implementation protocol that described methods for defining mission and goals (e.g., inclusive of key stakeholders), developing effective performance measures (e.g., demonstrate results), data collection (e.g., mission-driven, accurate, complete), and application of performance measures (e.g., meaningful, useful, and demonstrate effectiveness) (Thomas 2006).

Defining Mission and Goals

Mission does matter. Studies on the impact of mission statements confirm that a well-written and well-implemented mission statement has a lasting impact on the organization's performance and values (Berbegal-Mirabent, Alegre and Guerrero 2020). A clearly defined, system-wide philosophy aligning the efforts of all system stakeholders is critical to successful measurement of system performance. In *Measuring What Really Matters in Juvenile Justice*, Bazemore described a clear distinction between traditional statements of mission in juvenile justice and the BARJ mission.

> A good mission statement should be more than a broad statement of values that is used for political purposes. While such statements as "serve the best interests of the child" or "protect the public from youth crime" do little to create internal or external understanding of the priorities of a system or agency, a useful mission statement

identifies the "clients" of the system; specifies performance objectives; and prioritizes practice while guarding against adoption of fad programs; identifies roles of staff, offender, victim and community in the juvenile justice process. A mission also implies action and can only be effective if it helps managers plan, execute, and monitor change. (Bazemore 2006, p.12)

Bazemore argued that the BARJ mission meets the criteria of a "good" mission statement. Its origins can be found in a reconsideration of the needs and expectations of community members who are likely to expect that any "justice" system will support fundamental community needs to sanction youth crime, to rehabilitate and reintegrate offenders, and to enhance public safety by assisting the community in preventing and controlling crime. In addition to these fundamental expectations, he noted that "increasingly, justice systems have also been expected to address a fourth need, to attempt to restore victim loss" (Bazemore 2006, p.12).

The origins of BARJ are found in the balanced approach, an earlier manifestation of a balanced mission for juvenile justice. The authors of the balanced approach suggested three overall purposes for juvenile justice intervention:

- *Community Protection.* Public safety needs are best met when community groups increase their ability to prevent crime, resolve conflict, and reduce community fear and when known offenders are adequately monitored and develop internal controls.

- *Competency Development.* Rehabilitation needs are best met when young offenders make measurable and demonstrated improvements in educational, vocational, social, civic, and other competencies that improve their ability to function as capable, productive adults.

- *Accountability.* Because an offense incurs a primary obligation to crime victims, accountability cannot be equated with simply taking one's punishment, or with being responsible to the court or to juvenile justice professionals (e.g., obeying curfew, complying with drug screening). Rather, sanctioning needs are best met when offenders take responsibility for the crime and the harm caused to victims, take action to make amends by restoring the loss, and when communities, offenders, and crime victims play active roles in sanctioning and feel satisfied with the process.

The *Restorative* part followed quickly. BARJ is not simply a matter of finding equilibrium between community protection, competency development, and accountability. Indeed, an essential component of the model is the restorative justice framework. Restorative practices are essentially different ways of "doing justice" by seeking to repair the harm of crime wherever it occurs (Bazemore and Walgrave 1999). The restorative justice framework also includes such reparative obligations or sanctions as restitution, community service, apologies, and victim service, as well as a variety of policies and orientations that support these practices and are grounded in a commitment to change system roles and relationships to empower communities to better address the needs of victim, offender, and community as primary "stakeholders" in the justice process (Bazemore 2006, p.14).

Bazemore points out that the normative theory of restorative justice is based on three "big ideas" that most clearly distinguish restorative justice from other orientations, and define the core outcomes, processes, practices, and structural relationships that characterize restorative approaches (Bazemore 2006):

- *The Principle of Repair:* Justice requires that we work to heal victims, offenders, and communities that have been injured by crime.

- *The Principle of Stakeholder Participation:* Victims, offenders, and communities should have the opportunity for active involvement in the justice process as early and as fully as possible.

- *The Principle of Transformation in Community and Government Roles and Relationships:* We must rethink the relative roles and responsibilities of government and community. In promoting justice, government is responsible for preserving a just order, and community for establishing a just peace (Van Ness and Strong 1997).

Developing Performance Measures

While the BARJ model provides an excellent framework for developing performance-based measures, the actual measures must be designed, developed, tested, and implemented. The participants in the National Demonstration Project actively engaged in a facilitated, consensus-based process to identify mission-driven performance outcomes that could be measured at the time of case closure. From this process, ten measures were selected by consensus vote of demonstration site representatives and included:

- Community Safety: Juvenile courts have an obligation to protect victims and communities from further victimization by court-involved juveniles, as measured by juvenile crime trends (e.g., rate of delinquency adjudications), law-abiding behavior (e.g., completion of court supervision with no additional charges filed), and adult criminal convictions (e.g., long-term recidivism).

- Accountability: Juvenile courts have an obligation to help juvenile offenders to take responsibility for their behaviors and take action to repair harm caused by crime, as measured by payment of restitution obligations, completion of community service, and victim satisfaction.

- Competency Development: The juvenile court has an obligation to help court-involved youth to enhance or develop pro-social skills, as measured by resistance to drug and alcohol use, school participation, employment, and volunteer/citizen involvement (see Table 9.1).

Table 9.1 Measuring balanced and restorative justice: goals, activities, and outcomes

Goal	Activities	Outcomes
Community Protection All citizens have a right to feel safe from crime	Implementation of a graduated system of interventions, supervision, and, where necessary, secure placement of juvenile offenders	No new offenses or serious violations of conditions of probation committed while under supervision of the juvenile court
Offender Accountability When a juvenile commits a crime, he or she incurs an obligation to individuals and the communities in which it was committed	Activities designed to help offender repair harm to individuals and community to the extent possible	Community service ordered/completed Restitution ordered/paid Participation/successful completion of victim awareness classes
Competency Development Juveniles should acquire knowledge and skills that make it possible for them to be productive, connected, and law abiding	Activities designed to provide juveniles with knowledge, tangible skills, and increased capacity to live in their communities without supervision	Successful completion of educational, vocational, skill building, moral reasoning, and independent living programs/activities

Source: Thomas (2006)

Collecting the Data

Most of the data required to measure performance-based outcomes are likely to be included in juvenile justice data systems. However, juvenile justice information systems are not designed with measuring performance in mind, and they may not contain some of the data required for measuring performance against expected outcomes (e.g., participation and completion of competency development activities). As a result, a separate process for collecting data had to be developed that included:

- a clearly defined unit analysis—case-level data representing the sum of juvenile court activity from the time the case is opened (e.g., probation disposition) to the time the case is closed (e.g., formal court order ending juvenile court involvement)

- a stand-alone data collection instrument—a form completed at case closing that includes the specific expected outcomes of the case (e.g., remaining crime free, completing community service, paying restitution, completing treatment or competency building activities)

- reliable data collection/entry agents—juvenile probation officers or active case managers served as the data collectors and were responsible for accurately and thoroughly completing the case closing forms immediately upon termination of the case

- regular and consistent outcome reports—system-wide "report cards" that provide information regarding specific benchmark outcomes for jurisdictions and other summary outcome reports for individual juvenile probation officers, juvenile probation supervisors, and juvenile court judges.

The Juvenile Justice Report Card

Most people who have attended school are familiar with the concept of a report card. Report cards inform the parents of children about their child's academic progress at several points during the school year. For many parents it is the most important document that they receive from the school; for some parents it may be the only document they receive from the school. Traditional report cards are brief, uncomplicated documents that focus on critical educational goals and provide students and parents alike with familiar and meaningful benchmark performance measures.

Likewise, the juvenile justice report cards developed through the Juvenile Justice Performance Measures Project created a powerful tool for communicating the juvenile justice goals of each of the participating jurisdictions and basic information regarding the capacity of juvenile courts and juvenile court professionals throughout the state to achieve those goals (Thomas 2006). However, these performance data were reported in multiple other ways as well, including in budget requests, monthly progress reports for individual staff and operational units, annual department-wide performance reports, and as support for individual case closing recommendations.

While familiar to educators, these juvenile justice *report cards* represented a new way for juvenile justice practitioners to consider and report critical performance outcomes. Anticipating hesitancy among juvenile justice practitioners to embrace these intermediate outcomes, Dr. Bazemore explained in *Measuring What Really Matters in Juvenile Justice* that collecting data on these outcomes "will signal to communities and staff that achieving objectives relevant to these goals is of the utmost importance and should promote shared ownership of mission performance outcomes" (Bazemore 2006, p.41).

The benefits of mission-driven performance measures were quickly recognized by the original demonstration sites. The Allegheny County Juvenile Court Services Director recognized that case-level outcomes "take away the guess work of managing the Department, allow us to analyze case specific outcomes, and make it possible for us to apply data-driven corrections to our operations" (Thomas 2006, p.17).

The wide-ranging, inclusive, and collaborative nature of the performance measures initiative was not lost on the Director of a drug and alcohol prevention and intervention project in Marquette County, MI who described broad-based participation in the development of juvenile court performance measures: "Participation extended beyond juvenile court personnel and included schoolteachers and superintendents, law enforcement, prosecuting and defense attorneys, substance abuse and mental health therapists and supervisors, youth serving agencies, county data specialists, the mayor and county administrator" (Thomas 2006, p.17).

In Deschutes County Oregon, the Circuit Court Judge hailed the County's Juvenile Justice Report Card's capacity to educate and inform the public about the true mission and goals of juvenile justice in his jurisdiction:

> While the report card has been helpful in providing information to the public, it, more importantly, has provided the public information of what the juvenile justice system deems important to measure. This "education" about what is important to measure changes the focus of the community discussion. Rather than discussing issues related to how long or whether a juvenile is detained (the proverbial

"pound of flesh"), the public discussion turns toward how has the community been made whole from the conduct of the individual and what is the system doing to prevent the conduct/harm in the future. (Thomas 2006, p.12)

The South Carolina Department of Juvenile Justice (DJJ) was the only statewide agency to implement juvenile justice performance measures. The DJJ Director was unequivocal in his description of what the DJJ Report card means to South Carolina's Department of Juvenile Justice:

> For the South Carolina Department of Juvenile Justice (DJJ), the Report Card represents an unprecedented effort to offer citizens a forthright and honest appraisal of the performance both at DJJ and the larger juvenile justice system of South Carolina in serving the state's juvenile population, crime victims, and communities. (Thomas 2006, p.12)

The Allegheny County Juvenile Probation's Balanced and Restorative Justice Report Card is available by way of example here.[1]

Establishing a Defensible Basis for Measuring Performance of Juvenile Justice Systems

The National Demonstration Project described above was based largely on the experience, enthusiasm, and commitment of a relatively small group of juvenile justice practitioners, researchers, and policymakers for the BARJ model and for measuring performance. And while experience, enthusiasm, and commitment (not to mention substantial financial support from OJJDP) can go a long way towards a good start, long-term sustainability requires a solid theoretical and philosophical foundation.

Bazemore was asked to provide that foundation for this project and for the larger principle that juvenile justice performance can be measured, and those measures are powerful contributors to providing balanced justice for youth, families, victims, and communities. In his introduction to *Measuring What Really Matters in Juvenile Justice*, Bazemore explained the purpose of the monograph was "to make

---

[1] www.alleghenycourts.us/wp-content/uploads/2022/10/Report-Card-2022.pdf

the case for a consistent, meaningful, and practically useful system of performance outcomes" (Bazemore 2006, p.2).

He understood the task, describing some of the possible obstacles to widespread support or adoption, including policymakers and researchers who may not view the proposed measures as terribly important among a potentially wide range of possible choices, juvenile justice professionals who might find little of interest in the ten outcome measures offered by the project, and restorative justice advocates who may find the measures offered to be too restrictive, shallow, or superficial. In a preemptive response to these possible (and not unreasonable) objections, Bazemore (2006, p.3) indicated that "the current effort in no way precludes, and may even encourage, other ongoing attempts—through evaluation research or surveys, or qualitative methodologies—to examine more refined indicators of impact and implementation of restorative justice and other juvenile justice reform objectives."

Performance Measures Defined

Defining the idea or process one is defending is a reasonable first step. Dr. Bazemore went to a credible source, the Center for Accountability and Performance, which defines performance measurement as a method of gauging progress of a public program or activity in achieving the results or outcomes that clients, customers, or stakeholders expect. Basically, performance measures tell people what public programs are doing and how well they are doing them. It is important to define *success* as well as establishing reference points against which success can be measured. Performance measurement, then, is the act of assessing an organization's ability to do things, including measures of productivity (how much they do), effectiveness (how efficiently they do it), quality (how well they do it), and timeliness (how long it takes them to do it). The performance measures proposed by the National Demonstration Project were the result of the collective efforts of many people in several jurisdictions to answer those questions and to develop a consistent, locally relevant process for measuring productivity, effectiveness, and quality of juvenile court service agencies.

A Growing Acceptance of Performance Measurement

The participants in the National Demonstration Project were not alone in their quest for effective performance measures. There were (and are) other "advocates of performance outcomes in a wide variety of government and private agencies [which] strive to select a finite series of performance indicators that resonate with public concerns, have practical significance for guiding intervention and achieving mission objectives, and can be shown to be linked to larger social goals and long-term outcomes" (Bazemore 2006, p.5).

A Risk, But One Worth Taking

Aside from the obstacles described above, Dr. Bazemore pointed out other, perhaps more direct, risks. For example, performance measures will reveal the true purpose of an organization, and there is a possibility that the true purpose does not have widespread public support. Further, performance measures may indicate that performance is poor, they may shine a bright light on the slow rate of progress toward desired outcomes, they may reveal a decline in performance. Positive performance indicators may cause some people to wonder if the mission has been successfully accomplished and if further funding is necessary. However, as Judge William Byers suggested, the political risk that comes with reporting performance outcomes that bring clarity to agency missions—or what may be perceived as bad news, or even premature indicators of mission accomplishment—may be offset by the trust and respect that come with honesty in sharing with the public problems in achieving desired outcomes and the current effort to begin to improve and carefully and honestly track and report future system and agency performance.

> We just need to get out in front of these problems. We didn't create this system, and we have no obligation to defend it... However, we are obligated to try to improve it. This Report Card can be an important tool for making things better. (Bazemore 2006, p.6)

Three Rationales for Performance Measurement

Bazemore presented a vigorous defense of each of the BARJ performance outcome categories and measurement domains. He offered three fundamental reasons for measuring performance of juvenile justice system activities based on normative, pragmatic, and empirical and theoretical principles:

1. **Normative—it is the right thing to do.** Juvenile justice activities are paid for with public funds and carried out for the public good. In a democratic society, the public should know about publicly funded activities. In short, the juvenile justice system owes it to taxpayers to tell them what they are getting for their money.

2. **Pragmatic—there are practical considerations to measuring juvenile justice system performance.** Taxpayers are more likely to support and participate in juvenile justice system processes if they are kept informed. Performance measures help organizations run efficiently and effectively: they inform staff about what is important, establish practical priorities, and reinforce the mission, goals, and objectives of the juvenile justice system or agency. Performance measures may also direct practice, establish priorities, track progress, and prioritize and realign resources.

3. **Empirical and Theoretical—measuring performance provides empirical evidence of effectiveness and supports theoretical explanations of cause and effect.** Specific performance measures make it possible to describe the successes or failures of the juvenile justice system in quantifiable terms. They also make it possible to relate those successes or failures to other theoretically linked outcomes in terms of predicting or explaining outcomes.

Standards for Choosing Specific Measures: Practical Limits and Considerations

Like other large-scale measurement efforts in criminal justice such as the Uniform Crime Reports system, performance measurement at the juvenile justice agency or system level must make use of indicators that sacrifice depth of measurement for breadth, uniformity, and practicality. Elaborating on, and adding to, the criteria considered in the project overview by Harp et al. (2006), benchmark performance measures must, therefore, be:

- **Measurable and accessible.** With few exceptions such as victim satisfaction surveys, performance outcomes will rely on concrete quantifiable indicators based on data already collected as standard requirements of court orders or of the supervision or intervention process (e.g., completion and amount of restitution agreements as part of the court order).

- **Concise, limited in number, and easily understood by community members.** Both outcome domains and ways of measuring outcomes must be straightforward and tied to *mission-based* community needs and expectations.

- **Valid and reliable.** Outcome indicators must convincingly measure what we think we are measuring (validity) and must repeatedly, over time and place, yield similar results (reliability). For example, a measure of an educational competency must accurately/validly measure change (improvement or decline) in that skill over time and should reliably measure the same competency at different times and in different contexts; completing restitution obligations may be a valid and reliable measure of accountability at the behavioral level, while another measure may be needed at the cognitive level.

- **Capable of employing a common unit of analysis, standard of comparison, and "baseline."** The question "How are we doing?" on any outcome raises another vital question: "Compared to what?" A performance indicator must be clear about the unit of analysis (e.g., all cases closed in the past year) and about the baseline for comparison (e.g., pre vs. post intervention). Measures of aggregate amounts of restitution collected may be interesting but are relatively useless as a performance indicator because they lack a baseline (amount of restitution ordered) and a unit of analysis (e.g., for cases closed last year). The standard of comparison must allow for a reasonable contrast between similar units of analysis to avoid comparing apples and oranges (programs with widely varying inputs or resources).

- **Strengths-based rather than deficit-focused.** Based on the assumption that delinquent youth, families, victims, and communities have assets that can be built upon, and the assumption that doing so is more likely to lead to successful outcomes, a "strengths-based" (Saalebey 1992) approach to the greatest extent possible frames outcomes as positive vs. negative performance indicators. Rather than deficit-focused measures (e.g., school failure, recidivism), the emphasis is on support for continuous improvement in such positive attributes as: remaining crime and drug free, improvements in educational status, demonstration of work skills and employment status, completion of community service, and restitution and other reparative obligations as a means of being accountable to victim and community. Strengths-based performance may also be calculated for communities and other collective as well as individual entities.

The Current State of Juvenile Justice Performance Measures

There was a time when one could conduct an internet search and find ample evidence of the ongoing efforts of the original four BARJ Performance Measures sites (Allegheny County, PA; Deschutes County, OR; Cook County, IL; and South Carolina) as well as other jurisdictions that found funding to work with NCJJ to create report cards based on BARJ (Marquette County, MI; Washtenaw County, MI; Lucas County, OH, among others). There were many jurisdictions that took advantage of the *Guide to Developing and Implementing Performance Measures for the Juvenile Justice System* and *Measuring What Really Matters in Juvenile Justice* to independently create and post their juvenile justice report cards.

Twenty years later, the evidence appears to be waning. While Allegheny County and several other Pennsylvania jurisdictions continue to publish report cards on outcome measures driven by BARJ goals it is increasingly difficult to find others. This is not surprising: twenty years is a long time, OJJDP ended its active support for the project after about three years, administrations changed, time moves on. But, as is often the case, there are shadows of past accomplishments that show up in evolving efforts to measure performance. For example, a recent inquiry of an internet-based search engine for "juvenile justice performance measures" revealed that *Measuring What Really Matters in Juvenile Justice* is the first result out of over 1.6 million results.

Allegheny County and other Pennsylvania probation departments continue to publish annual juvenile justice report cards. Allegheny County's 2021 Report Card (Allegheny County Juvenile Justice 2021) provides a recent example of how performance data is used on a routine basis to address the management goal of improved decision-making about more effective use of intervention resources and continuous staff improvements related to these core outcomes. As you can see, Allegheny County has been generating outcome reports related to the BARJ model since 1998. In addition to the public-facing report card, Allegheny County uses these and other mission-driven performance measures to inform budgets, manage caseloads, monitor probation officer performance, and confirm that agency performance is generally in line with expectations for continuous improvement, and if necessary, adjust the focus of probationary supervision. The report card—because it states clearly the Department's mission, goals, and evidence-based practices—provides a very public reminder of the Department's mission-driven purpose, expectations, and outcomes.

The OJJDP continues to invest in improving juvenile justice data and increasing its consistency across states and localities. In 2016, the agency funded the Juvenile Justice Model Data Project (MDP) to develop model measures that monitor trends and assess the efficiency and effectiveness of juvenile justice systems and to develop model data elements with recommended definitions and coding categories. The primary goals of the project were to (1) develop model measures for monitoring trends and assessing the efficiency and effectiveness of juvenile justice systems; (2) identify related model data elements with recommended definitions and coding categories; and (3) develop a comprehensive strategy to disseminate and promote the use of the model data elements and measures. The project resulted in over 100 research-based measures and recommended coding categories.

These fundamental measures, along with recommended coding categories and supporting research, will be published online. A website was established for jurisdictions and agencies wanting to incorporate the measures into their juvenile justice systems (Deal 2018).

A Lasting Legacy

Bazemore left many lasting marks on the canvas of his life. Among all of these, perhaps a single monograph providing a defensible basis for a system of measuring performance of the BARJ model may be easily overlooked. However, like performance measures, every mark in a man's life accumulates to tell a story. Dr. Bazemore understood and embraced the need for and potential of measuring performance in the public sector. He recognized that juvenile justice system processes and practices had gone largely unmeasured for a century or more. He understood the absurd irony memorialized by his longtime friends and colleagues Caren Harp and Dennis Maloney that it is *beyond insane* that people should do the same thing over and over again and have no expectations of results.

In *Measuring What Really Matters in Juvenile Justice*, he took the time to answer the timeless, much-asked, and rarely answered question of "Why measure performance?":

> In a democratic society, the general public and specific constituents of government agencies and systems should receive information about the outcomes of publicly funded activities. More practically, community members are more likely to support and participate in public processes if they are kept informed, and conversely: lack of information often leads to suspicion, distrust, and at times unwarranted criticism. From an agency or system perspective, performance outcome measures also send signals to staff about what is important (i.e., if they are measuring it, it must be important), establish internal priorities for practice, and reinforce mission statements and agency goals and objectives. Indeed, the general conclusion of the "good government" literature of the 1990s, that we "are what we measure" and "what gets measured gets done," suggests that measurement drives practice (e.g., Osborne and Gaebler 1992), improves quality

of services, and helps administrators set priorities for staff and incentives for changing focus; track progress and improvement in achieving goals; prioritize new or previously neglected stakeholders (e.g., crime victims); realign resources toward accomplishment of mission objectives; and fine tune and strengthen practice. In short, you can only manage what you measure. (Bazemore 2006, p.vi)

Dr. Bazemore was instrumental in providing the philosophical and theoretical foundation for BARJ; he developed strategies and programs for implementing BARJ; he educated and trained generations of students and practitioners; and he informed legislators and policymakers on the theory and practice of BARJ. With *Measuring What Really Matters in Juvenile Justice* he helped establish a process for measuring BARJ outcomes and provided us with a theoretical and practical foundation for defending those measures. And, along the way, Gordon Bazemore helped us see what really matters in juvenile justice.

References

Allegheny County Juvenile Justice (2021) Allegheny County Juvenile Probation's 2021 Balanced and Restorative Justice Report Card (April). www.alleghenycourts.us/wp-content/uploads/2022/10/Report-Card-2022.pdf

Bazemore, G. (1997) "Balanced and Restorative Justice for Juveniles: A Framework for Juvenile Justice in the 21st Century." Washington, DC: Office of Juvenile Justice and Delinquency Prevention. www.ojp.gov/pdffiles/framwork.pdf

Bazemore, G. and Walgrave, L.. (1999) *Restorative Juvenile Justice: Repairing Harm of Youth Crime*. Monsey, NY: Criminal Justice Press.

Bazemore, G. (2006) *Measuring What Really Matters in Juvenile Justice*. American Prosecutors Research Institute. www.ojp.gov/pdffiles1/ojjdp/grants/216394.pdf

Berbegal-Mirabent, J., Alegre, I., and Guerrero, A. (2020) "Mission statements and performance: An exploratory study of science parks." *Long Range Planning 53*, 5. doi.org/10.1016/j.lrp.2019.101932

Deal, T. (2018) "Juvenile Justice Model Data Project: Final Technical Report." National Center for Juvenile Justice. www.ojp.gov/pdffiles1/ojjdp/grants/254492.pdf

Feld, B.C. (1991) "The Transformation of the Juvenile Court," 75 Minn. L. Rev. 691, 715.

Freivalds, P. (1996) "Balanced and Restorative Justice Project (BARJ) (Fact Sheet #42)." US Department of Justice, Office of Juvenile Justice and Delinquency Prevention. www.ojp.gov/pdffiles/91415.pdf

Giardino, L.F. (1996) "Statutory rhetoric: The reality behind juvenile justice policies in America." *Journal of Law and Policy 5*, 1, 223–276. https://brooklynworks.

brooklaw.edu/cgi/viewcontent.cgi?referer=&httpsredir=1&article=1442&context=jlp

Harp, C. (2002) "Bringing Balance to Juvenile Justice." Alexandria: American Prosecutors Research Institute. https://web.archive.org/web/20060614065919/http://www.ndaa.org:80/pdf/bringing_balance.pdf

Harp, C., Bell, D., Bazemore, G., and Thomas, D. (2006) "Guide to Developing and Implementing Performance Measures for the Juvenile Justice System." American Prosecutors Research Institute. www.ojp.gov/ncjrs/virtual-library/abstracts/guide-developing-and-implementing-performance-measures-juvenile

Maloney, D., Romig, D., and Armstrong, T. (1988) "The balanced approach to juvenile probation." *Juvenile & Family Court Journal 39*, 3, 1–4. doi.org/10.1111/j.1755-6988.1988.tb00623.x

OJJDP (Office of Juvenile Justice and Delinquency Prevention) (1998) "Guide for Implementing the Balanced and Restorative Justice Model." Washington, DC: US Department of Justice. www.ojp.gov/library/publications/guide-implementing-balanced-and-restorative-justice-model

Pavelka, S. (2016) "Restorative justice in the States: A national assessment of legislation and policy." *Justice Policy Journal 13*, 2, 1–23. www.cjcj.org/media/import/documents/jpj_restorative_justice_in_the_states.pdf

Pavelka, S. and Thomas, D. (2019) "The evolution of balanced and restorative justice." *Juvenile and Family Court Journal 70*, 1, 37–58. doi.org/10.1111/jfcj.12125

Saalebey, D. (1992) *The Strengths Perspective in Social Work Practice.* New York: Longman.

Thomas, D. (2006) "How Does the Juvenile Justice System Measure Up? Applying Performance Measures in Five Jurisdictions." Technical Assistance to the Juvenile Court: Special Project Bulletin. Pittsburgh, PA: National Center for Juvenile Justice. www.ncjj.org/pdf/taspecialbulletinmeasuringjjsperformance.pdf

Van Ness, D. and Strong, K.H. (1997) *Restorative Justice.* Cincinnati, OH: Anderson Publishing.

— Chapter 10 —

Guiding Principles and Restorative Practices for Crime Victims and Survivors

SANDRA PAVELKA, PHD AND ANNE SEYMOUR

This chapter was first published as: Pavelka, S. and Seymour, A. (2019) "Guiding principles and restorative practices for crime victims and survivors." *Corrections Today*, 36–46.

The authors dedicate this chapter to the late, great Dennis Maloney, a pioneer in promoting restorative justice principles and practices within the criminal and juvenile justice systems, crime victim services, and communities across the US.

Restorative justice, which is realized in states and localities as an innovative framework that provides a foundation for fairness in justice policies and practice, views and responds to wrongful occurrences and crime with an alternate and innovative approach. The ultimate goal of restorative justice is to repair the harm caused by a wrongful incident, while addressing the needs of the victim, the offender, and the community (Pavelka and Thomas 2013). Opportunities are provided for those most directly affected by crime to be involved in responding to its impact. This approach ultimately seeks to address the myriad needs of victims and ensure individual and community safety, while the alleged or convicted defendant is held accountable and develops competencies in order to become a better and more productive person.

The principles and practices aligned with restorative justice have been applied to educational settings, prevention, intervention, and diversion initiatives, crime victim and survivor services, juvenile justice, and criminal justice systems. Restorative practices and applications include: victim/offender dialogue (also called victim/offender mediation), circles, reparative and accountability boards, restorative conferencing, "Impact of Crime on Victims" programming, restorative community service, diversion, and apology banks. In addition, restorative justice has been applied in comprehensive facilitative dialogue, capacity building, and community development.

This chapter offers a historical perspective of the United States' crime victim and survivor assistance field, and its role in restorative justice. Six guiding principles for victim- and survivor-focused restorative justice are identified by the authors, as well as restorative legislation, practices, and future perspectives.

The Victim Assistance Field in the United States

While efforts to identify and address the needs of crime victims and survivors began in the 1960s using the "lessons learned" from the women's and civil rights movements, the emergence of the professional field of crime victim services is often cited as occurring in 1972, with the creation of the Aid of Victims of Crime in St. Louis, Missouri, Bay Area Women Against Rape in California, and the Washington D.C. Rape Crisis Center—three organizations that still thrive today. Crime victims had few statutory rights, were viewed primarily as "witnesses" needed to secure convictions, and were often blamed and shamed for their victimization. The nascent days of the field focused on passing victims' rights laws, identifying and addressing the needs of victims across the criminal justice spectrum, as well as providing services for the majority of victims who did not report crimes to authorities.

National leadership that propelled the movement into a professional discipline was provided initially by the National Organization for Victim Assistance and victim-driven organizations founded by grieving survivors, including Mothers Against Drunk Driving (MADD) and the National Organization of Parents of Murdered

Children. The passage of the Victims of Crime Act (VOCA) in 1984 that created a federal fund for victim assistance derived from fines and fees assessed against convicted federal defendants, along with the National "21" Drinking Age Bill promulgated by MADD, set the victim assistance profession on a path to activism that was driven by "the power of the personal story" that is still prevalent today.

The focus then of victim-driven public policy initiatives at the national, state, and local levels was "tough on crime," with collective support from victims and their advocates for longer sentences and more prisons. With victims feeling long-ignored in justice processes, the victim assistance field leaned heavily toward a punitive model of justice.

The Emergence of Restorative Justice

The seminal work of Dr. Howard Zehr, Kay Pranis, and Dr. Mark Umbreit (among others) provided a foundation for restorative justice primarily at the state and local levels as the victim assistance profession was becoming a driving force in criminal and juvenile justice policy (Pranis 1998; Umbreit 1994; Zehr 1990). Compelling arguments were presented for a problem-solving approach, challenging policymakers and stakeholders to develop a justice system that worked more efficiently and fairly with a morally decent alternative (Braithwaite 2002). Empirical evidence found that the restorative alternatives, more often than court-based solutions, have the capacity to satisfy victims' expectations of achieving a meaningful role in the way their cases were processed, as well as delivering restoration, especially emotional restoration, from the harm victims have suffered (Strang 2002). The concept of offender accountability—to their victims, their own families, and their communities—was a stark but interesting contrast to the existing "tough on crime" approach. Two federal initiatives brought this concept to the masses across the United States. Further, these initiatives provided an alternative perspective to potentially have a profoundly positive effect on the justice system by incorporating community participation, victim involvement, and restoration (Pavelka 2016).

In 1996, the US Department of Justice (DOJ) National Institute of

Corrections (NIC) sponsored a teleconference on restorative justice that was attended by over 20,000 people in the US and Canada. The teleconference proposed restorative justice principles that were victim-centered and focused on the need to provide opportunities for offender accountability and community involvement to improve individual and public safety.

A national summit and a series of five regional conferences followed the NIC teleconference in 1997 and 1998 on restorative justice, sponsored by the DOJ Office of Justice Programs. For thousands of justice and victim assistance practitioners and community volunteers, this was their "introduction" to the powerful potential of restorative justice as a foundation for justice and victim assistance policies and practices. Community-level teams returned to their jurisdictions across the nation with a new toolbox of restorative justice research and resources that focused on the harm that crime causes to individuals and to communities; and the need for innovative approaches that engage victims, offenders, and communities in repairing such harm.

Leadership Provided by National Justice Organizations

The "jump-start" provided by the DOJ's restorative justice leadership became the impetus for national criminal justice and corrections organizations to address restorative justice in a meaningful way. By the early 1990s, three leading organizations—the American Correctional Association, the American Probation and Parole Association, and the Association of Paroling Authorities International—had established victim issues committees to promote victim and survivor sensitivity in national policy and program development. The National Association of Victim Assistance in Corrections was founded to promote victims' rights and services in the post-sentencing phases of cases. The dissemination and replication of restorative justice policies and practices became a priority of these leadership organizations, as evidenced by the ongoing and recent work of the ACA Victims and Restorative Justice Committee.

One of the main focal points of this committee has been to include language in ACA's Standards and Policies that acknowledges victim/offender dialogue (VOD) as a viable restorative justice program in corrections. The standards were approved in August 2016, with the following language:

> Where a facilitated victim/offender dialogue program exists, written policy, procedure and practice provide that there is a program initiated and requested only by a victim or victim/survivor that provides an opportunity for such victims or survivors to meet face-to-face or by other means with the inmate responsible for their victimization in a safe, secure and confidential setting after thorough preparation with, and with the assistance of a properly trained facilitator.

The definition submitted for review to the ACA Committee on Performance-Based Standards is as follows:

> Victim Offender Dialogue (VOD) is a post-conviction, victim-initiated process that includes preparation, dialogue and follow-up guided by a trained facilitator. Participation in the VOD program is completely voluntary for the victim/survivor and for the offender. Either party is always at liberty to withdraw from the VOD preparation or dialogue process at any time, and VOD is not intended to directly affect the offender's prison, parole, or community supervision (probation) status.

Criminal justice and correctional organizations that initiate VOD programs should adhere to the "20 Principles of Victim-Centered Victim Offender Dialogue," endorsed by NAVAC, which are available on their website. In addition, VOCA Rule 28 CFR Part 94 includes restorative justice efforts (e.g., Tribal community-led meetings and peace-keeping activities) along with beneficial or therapeutic value suited to meet victim needs.

Guiding Principles of Victim- and Survivor-Centered Restorative Justice

Decades of experience resulting from leadership and commitment from the crime victim and survivor assistance field and allied national justice organizations have helped define six basic principles of victim and survivor-centered restorative justice:

1 Crime is Personal

Everyone has been or knows a victim of crime. Crime has significant and varying effects on individuals, families, friends, and communities. The impact of crime results in physical, financial, psychological, social, and spiritual consequences. A significant amount of crime involves acquaintance or family crime and interpersonal crime. The relationship between victims and offenders has been examined in many contexts, including proximity to the home, duration of stalking, method of homicide, and fear of rape or sexual assault. In addition, the degree of intimacy that exists between victims and offenders has traditionally been a major variable in the outcome in cases of violent crimes in the criminal justice system (McQuade 2014).

2 Restorative Justice Must Be Victim-Centered and Trauma-Informed

Crime victims and survivors often feel removed from services and support that can help them in the immediate, short, and long-term, and from criminal and juvenile justice system processes that should be designed to protect them. In 2015, the DOJ found that only 9.1 percent of victims of serious violent crime sought assistance from a victim services program (Bureau of Justice Statistics 2015). By addressing the victim's trauma and needs, restorative justice can more clearly define the harm caused by crime and its impact on survivors and develop approaches to address such harm.

The US Department of Health and Human Services defines "trauma-informed" to be based upon "three E's"—events, experience of the event, and effect. According to SAMHSA's conceptual framework:

> Individual trauma results from an event, series of events, or set of circumstances that is experienced by an individual as physically or emotionally harmful or life-threatening, and that has lasting adverse effects on the individual's functioning and mental, physical, social, emotional or spiritual well-being. (SAMHSA 2012)

3 The Voices of Victims/Survivors in Restorative Justice Are Integral to Its Effectiveness and Overall Success

The "power of the personal story" from victims and survivors has driven the nation's victim assistance field since its inception nearly half a century ago and has been an important foundation for restorative justice over the past three decades. Nobody understands the devastating impact of crime more than someone who has experienced it. Victims' voices are often a clarion call for survivor services and justice processes that focus on offender accountability and evidence-based practices that have proven to be effective to reduce recidivism.

4 Victim Autonomy Must Be Central to All Restorative Justice Policies and Practices

Every crime victim and survivor is unique. While victimology and justice research offer valuable information about victims' needs and victim impact, restorative justice demands that programs focus on the individual survivor in the individual case. Their feelings and opinions are central to effective restorative justice practices.

Crime victims and survivors often speak about the sense of power and control that their perpetrators exerted over them. A significant component of the healing process is to help victims regain that sense of control over their lives and, if they report crimes, over their participation in justice processes, including diversion. This includes being offered the opportunity to participate in restorative justice programs and, alternatively, the option to decline to participate. It is their decision—no exceptions.

Restorative practices should be made available to victims who report crimes, as well as to those (the majority) who do not. According to the National Crime Victimization Survey, in 2016 only 42 percent of violent crimes and only 26 percent of property crimes were reported to police (Bureau of Justice Statistics 2016). Community-based victim assistance programs that are not affiliated with the criminal or juvenile justice systems—such as domestic violence programs, rape crisis centers, homicide support groups, and MADD chapters—are important partners in restorative justice initiatives, as they provide services and support to all crime survivors, whether they report or not. Victims should also be offered the opportunity to participate in restorative practices, such as community conferencing, within diversion settings.

5 If Restorative Justice Fails to Respect and Reflect Victims' Constitutional and Statutory Rights, It Is Not "Restorative"

Currently, there are over 32,000 state laws and state constitutional amendments that define and protect victims' rights. VictimLaw (n.d.) identifies 12 core rights that crime victims have within the criminal justice system which includes the rights to:

- be treated with fairness, dignity, sensitivity, and respect
- attend and be present at criminal justice proceedings
- be heard in the criminal justice process, including the right to confer with the prosecutor and submit a victim impact statement at sentencing, parole, and other similar proceedings
- be informed of proceedings and events in the criminal justice process, including the release or escape of the offender, legal rights and remedies, available benefits and services, and access to records, referrals, and other information
- protection from intimidation and harassment
- restitution from the offender
- privacy
- apply for crime victim compensation
- restitution from the offender
- the expeditious return of personal property seized as evidence whenever possible
- a speedy trial and other proceedings free from unreasonable delay
- enforcement of these rights and access to other available remedies.

While these core victims' rights validate the victim's experience as someone who was harmed by crime, they also offer unique opportunities for offender accountability—to learn about victim impact; to understand the financial impact of crime on victims that can be addressed through restitution and other legal/financial obligations; and to recognize that defendants' rights in the US Constitution far exceed those of victims.

6 Many Justice-Involved Individuals—Including Youth, Women, and Men—Have Histories of Trauma and Victimization That Can Be Addressed and Validated Within a Restorative Justice Framework

The association between delinquency and victimization is a common focus in juvenile justice research. Some observers have found that victimization and delinquency largely overlap, with most victims engaging in delinquency and most delinquents being victimized at some point in their lives (Cuevas et al. 2013). Women under correctional supervision are more likely to report having experienced physical and sexual abuse as children and adults than their male counterparts (James and Glaze 2006). Further, a number of studies have found that approximately 50 percent of justice-involved women report experiencing some kind of physical or sexual abuse in their lifetime with rates of trauma histories as high as 98 percent (Beck et al. 2013). While victim-centered restorative practices focus on the survivors of the crimes committed by their offenders, such practices often bring up relevant information about their personal experiences witnessing crime in the home, exposure to traumatic events, and/or histories of chronic or acute victimization. Within the context of restorative practices, these factors are not intended to serve as an excuse for decisions to engage in delinquent or criminal activities, but rather as an important and sometimes mitigating factor that can affect the outcome. Anyone who is exposed to or personally victimized by violence can benefit from restorative practices that recognize the often-devastating impact of witnessing or being directly harmed by crime. The survivor-centric philosophy of restorative justice identifies and validates the impact of crime on all victims, including those who end up being justice-involved.

Restorative Justice in Legislation

In 1974, Congress created the Office of Juvenile Justice and Delinquency Prevention (OJJDP) within the DOJ, to provide national leadership, coordination, and supplemental resources to prevent and respond to juvenile delinquency and victimization. The OJJDP further supports states and communities in their efforts to develop and implement effective and coordinated prevention and intervention programs, and to improve the juvenile justice system in order to protect the public, hold justice-involved youth accountable, and provide treatment and rehabilitative services tailored to meet the needs of juveniles and their families (OJJDP n.d.).

Two decades later, the Balanced and Restorative Justice (BARJ) Project, a national demonstration project funded by the OJJDP, worked with a number of state justice systems and stakeholders (i.e., Illinois, Minnesota, New York, Pennsylvania, and others) to provide technical assistance and training to key decision makers and stakeholders in states seeking juvenile justice reform. The BARJ Project facilitated dialogue that was focused on the implementation of restorative principles and practices (Balanced and Restorative Justice Project 1994). Since that time, states across the country have expanded legislation and policy adoption to meet the needs of the significant challenges facing the justice system. State legislatures and local jurisdictions have implemented policies and laws to advance their commitment to restorative justice and justice reform. Implementation expands to include restorative practices, application to schools, and criminal and juvenile justice continua.

Further, national organizations—including the American Bar Association, American Probation and Parole Association, National Association of Community and Restorative Justice, National Council of Juvenile and Family Court Judges, National Council of Crime and Delinquency, and National Organization for Victim Assistance—have endorsed restorative justice and its principles. The United Nations has also encouraged member nations to adopt restorative justice in the wake of crime and violence, and has endorsed the basic principles of restorative justice and the promotion of a culture favorable to the use of restorative justice among law enforcement, judicial, and social authorities, as well as communities across the world (Pavelka 2016).

The articulation of restorative justice varies generally in state statutes and codes; however, common language is pervasive across jurisdictions. A number of laws focus solely on the balanced approach mission, while others discern the restorative justice value context with or without reference to the balanced approach. Restorative language articulated in seven state declarations includes: holding juvenile offenders accountable for their offense; involving victims and the community in the justice process; obligating the offender to pay restitution to the victim and/or a victims' fund; improving the juvenile's ability to live more productively and responsibly in the community; and securing safer communities. Balanced approach terms contained in 11 state statutes or codes denote offender accountability, community protection, and competency development. Balanced and restorative justice language found in 20 state statutes or codes comprehensively addresses principles from each paradigm. It is important to note, however, that the interpretation of the language and extent to which statutes and codes incorporate restorative justice and/or the balanced approach differ across jurisdictions.

Restorative Practices

Restorative practices integrate data and evidence from a number of disciplines and fields—i.e., education, psychology, social work, criminology, victimology, sociology, and organizational development and leadership—in order to build safe communities, increase social capital, decrease crime and antisocial behavior, repair harm, and restore relationships. Restorative practices include: victim/offender dialogue, circles, reparative boards, restorative conferencing, "Impact of Crime on Victims" programs, restorative community service, and apology banks.

Victim/Offender Dialogue

As described earlier, victim/offender dialogue is a process that provides victims with an opportunity to meet with their offender and engage in a discussion of the crime in a safe and structured setting. Facilitated by a trained mediator, the victim is able to share their position about the physical, emotional, and financial impact of the crime with the offender, receive answers to questions about the crime and the offender, and be involved in developing a case plan for the offender that would include restitution in order to pay back their financial debt. Victim/offender dialogue is implemented in all 50 states and in countries worldwide.

Circles

Restorative circles are based in aboriginal justice tradition. Circles were initiated in the mainstream US criminal justice system in Minnesota in the 1990s. The practice is now utilized throughout North America and in other parts of the world for juvenile and adult defendants and for a wide variety of offenses and settings.

As with other restorative practices, circles provide a space for encounter between the victim and the offender, but move beyond this to involve the community in the discussion and decision-making process. Community participants may range from justice system personnel to community members concerned about the crime. All contributors, including the victim, the victim's family, the defendant, the defendant's family, and community representatives, are given a voice. Participants typically speak in turn and pass a "talking piece" around the circle.

Primarily, the circle process is designed to bring healing and understanding to the victim and the offender. Participation in the circle for all participants is voluntary, and the victim must voluntarily agree to attend without any form of coercion. The defendant accepts his/her guilt in the matter and agrees to be referred to the circle. Especially for aboriginal communities, it is important for the defendant to have deep roots in the community. Each circle is led by a "keeper," who directs the movement of the talking piece. Only the person holding the talking piece is allowed to speak, ensuring that each person has an opportunity to be heard.

As the talking piece rounds the circle, the group discusses different topics. In addressing the crime, participants describe how they feel. For the offender, this includes why they committed the crime. For the victim and the community participants, the circle provides an opportunity to explain the impact the crime has economically, physically, and emotionally. Through this process of sharing, participants are able to develop a strategy to address repairing the harm caused by the crime (i.e., restitution, vocational training, letter of apology, and/or community service).

Reparative Boards

Reparative boards, also known as community reparative boards, neighborhood accountability boards, youth panels, and/or community boards, are comprised of four to six community members who are trained to address assigned adult and/or juvenile cases. These cases are usually nonviolent and minor offenses that are diverted from the court system by the prosecutor. Meetings are public, face-to-face meetings with defendants ordered by the court to participate in the process. Victims and community members are able to talk with offenders about their behavior in a constructive manner. Case plans or sanction agreements are developed with the offenders and must be completed within a specified time period. Compliance is monitored with a final report submitted to the court upon completion.

Restorative Conferencing

Restorative conferences are structured meetings among victims, offenders, both parties' family and friends, and other stakeholders, and are increasingly used as a diversion to the juvenile or criminal justice systems. Conferencing involves a larger group of parties impacted by the wrongful occurrence. Trained facilitators guide the discussion on how all were affected, the consequences of the offense, and how best to repair the harm by developing a comprehensive case plan. The goal of the conference is to seek resolution and reparation for the wrongdoing.

"Impact of Crime on Victims" Programs/ Victim Impact Classes

"Impact of Crime on Victims" programs are educational programs designed to teach offenders about the human consequences of crime. Offenders are taught how crime affects the victim and the victim's family, their own family, the community, and themselves. Specific modules address property crimes, sexual assault, domestic violence, child abuse and neglect, elder abuse and neglect, drunk driving, drug-related crimes, gang violence, and homicide. Victim impact classes have been adapted for both adult and juvenile offenders in diversion, probation, prison, pre-release, detention, and parole-supervised settings.

A key element of the classes is the direct involvement of crime victims and victim service providers who share their personal stories of being victimized or of helping victims to reconstruct their lives after a traumatic crime. Parents of incarcerated youth and community representatives, such as insurance adjusters or business owners, may also speak to classes. Offenders are encouraged to enter into a dialogue with the guest speakers.

Some programs integrate victim impact panels, composed of three to four victims of the particular type of crime being examined, into the curriculum. When the panel format is used, the class participants may ask questions at the end of the presentation and, with consent from panelists, can engage in discussion with the victim presenters.

Restorative Community Service

Historically, community service has played an important role in courts and corrections as a sanction to hold offenders accountable for their actions; to "pay back" the community in some way for the harm that is caused by crime; and to establish positive linkages between the offender and the community in which their offense occurred. In the past two decades, the concept of "restorative community service" has taken hold in many jurisdictions. Restorative community service is best described as that which is visible (to the community), viable (meaningful work that helps improve the community), and allows victim input into the types of service that is performed.

Apology Bank/Apology Classes

The concept of an inmate apology bank was created for victims of crime who have an interest in receiving an apology letter from the convicted defendant in their case who is in a state prison or on community supervision. Victims often wonder whether or not their offenders have taken responsibility and/or are sorry for their criminal actions. Likewise, inmates sometimes seek to put into words acceptance of fault, responsibility, and/or pain caused by their actions. They may wish to write a letter of apology to the victim(s) of their crime. However, each state that participates in these programs has strict rules prohibiting inmates from directly contacting their victims. This apology program allows for the letters to be written and received without violating these rules, and the victims' choice to access an apology letter is strictly voluntary.

Justice Reinvestment

Under the Justice Reinvestment Initiative (JRI), sponsored by the DOJ Bureau of Justice Assistance, over 30 states have implemented significant reforms by investing in a data-driven approach to improve public safety. This includes: examining corrections and related criminal justice spending; managing and allocating criminal justice populations in a more cost-effective manner; and reinvesting savings in strategies that can hold offenders accountable, resulting in a decrease of crime and strengthening of neighborhoods. Many of these states have institutionalized restorative practice in their justice systems, legislation, and policy.

Jurisdictions use the justice reinvestment approach to design, enact, and adopt new policies, practices, and programs that reduce recidivism, improve public safety, impact prison and jail populations, and otherwise help generate savings. Jurisdictions then use the justice reinvestment approach to determine how to invest a portion of the generated savings from policy changes such as reducing or averting growth in the jail and prison populations in strategies to increase public safety such as community-based treatment, probation, prevention-oriented policing strategies, and community-based recidivism reduction efforts. In many states, significant reinvestments have supported the implementation of victims' rights, such as automated victim notification and victim restitution programs, and victim services.

Crime survivors and advocates are proactively engaged in all justice reinvestment efforts, and they contributed to the "Sentencing, Corrections and Public Safety Guiding Principles for Crime Victims and Survivors in America," which are restorative in nature (see Appendix 2).

Future Perspectives

The restorative justice movement is transforming communities and criminal and juvenile justice systems while specifically impacting and converging with the crime victims' profession. The authors have presented six guiding principles that include a restorative, survivor-centric approach. In order for restorative justice to be enduring and sustainable, stakeholders and communities must commit to a paradigm shift from traditional responses to wrongdoing. This change occurs collaboratively and comprehensively and includes crime victims and survivors, justice systems, justice-involved persons, schools, and communities. Ultimately, this transition will result in a more responsive, more effective, and more just society.

APPENDIX 1

Resources
Defining Trauma-informed Services
US Department of Health and Human Services

> Substance Abuse and Mental Health Services Administration: www.samhsa.gov/nttac

Victim/Offender Dialogue
Minnesota Department of Corrections

> Victim Offender Dialogue: https://mn.gov/doc/victims/restorative-justice/victim-initiated-restorative-practices/victim-offender-dialogue

Circles
Living Justice Press, "About the Circle Process":

> https://livingjusticepress.org/about-circles

> Impact Justice: https://impactjustice.org/wp-content/uploads/CWW_RJreport.pdf

"Impact of Crime on Victims"

US Department of Justice, Office for Victims of Crime

"Victim Impact: Listen and Learn" free standardized curriculum: www.ovcttac.gov/victimimpact

Restorative Community Service

Justice Solutions: www.justicesolutions.org/art_pub.htm#service

Apology Banks
Pennsylvania Office of the Victim Advocate

Inmate Apology Bank: www.ova.pa.gov/RestorativeJustice/InmateApologyBank/Pages/default.aspx

APPENDIX 2

Sentencing, Corrections, and Public Safety, Guiding Principles for Crime Victims and Survivors in America

Crime victims and survivors have an integral role in America's criminal justice system and efforts to promote individual and public safety. The overall effectiveness of the criminal justice system relies significantly on victims' willingness and ability to participate in justice processes.

Through national criminal justice and public safety reform efforts, victims, survivors, and those who serve them have contributed to the following seven "guiding principles" for sentencing, corrections, and public safety.

1. An ultimate goal of public safety policy is to reduce crime, resulting in fewer people and communities who are harmed.

2. Crime victims and survivors have a significant role in shaping criminal justice policy as individuals who know first-hand the real costs of crime.

3. Crime victims and survivors deserve to be treated with dignity

and validated as persons who have been harmed by crime, with their autonomy and privacy respected at all times.

4. Mandatory supervision of offenders who pose a serious risk to public safety upon their return to the community is essential throughout the offender reentry process in order to promote victim and survivor safety.

5. While it is important for offenders to receive just punishment, the *quantity* of time that convicted offenders serve under any form of correctional supervision must be balanced with the *quality* of evidence-based assessment, treatment, programming, and supervision they receive that can change their criminal behavior and thinking and reduce the likelihood that they will commit future crimes. For many offenses and offenders, shorter prison terms are acceptable if the resulting cost savings are reinvested in evidence-based programs that reduce recidivism.

6. Offenders should pay all court-ordered legal and financial obligations, such as victim restitution and child support. Offender compliance with restitution and support orders is a key measure of offender accountability and the performance of offender supervision agencies.

7. Victims' rights to justice must be enforced in accordance with the law and adequately funded. Survivors and victims have a right to safety, representation, and participation in the legal process. They deserve information and notification about the status of their case and the alleged or convicted offender, access to victim assistance services, as well as restitution in all cases with pecuniary losses, and victim compensation following violent crimes.

These principles offer a foundation for the fair treatment of crime victims and survivors, and for the use of evidence-based practices that hold offenders accountable for their crimes and reduce recidivism.

References

Balanced and Restorative Justice Project (1994) *Balanced and Restorative Justice for Juveniles*. Ft. Lauderdale, FL: Florida Atlantic University, Community Justice Institute.

Beck, A.J., Berzofsky, M., Caspar, R., and Krebs, C. (2013) "Sexual Victimization in Prisons and Jails Reported by Inmates, 2011–12." Washington, DC: Bureau of Justice Statistics.

Braithwaite, J. (2002) *Restorative Justice and Responsive Regulation*. New York: Oxford University Press.

Bureau of Justice Statistics (2016) "Criminal Victimization 2015." Washington, DC: Bureau of Justice Statistics, US Department of Justice.

Cuevas, C.A., Finkelhor, D., Shattuck, A., Turner, H., and Hamby, S. (2013) "Children's Exposure to Violence and the Intersection between Delinquency and Victimization," *OJJDP Bulletin*. Washington, DC: Office of Juvenile Justice Delinquency Prevention.

James, D. and Glaze, L. (2006) "Special Report: Mental Health Problems of Prison and Jail Inmates." Washington, DC: Bureau of Justice Statistics.

McQuade, K.M. (2014) "Victim-offender relationship," *The Encyclopedia of Criminology and Criminal Justice*. Hoboken, NJ: Blackwell Publishing Ltd.

Office of Juvenile Justice and Delinquency Prevention, US Department of Justice (n.d.) https://ojjdp.ojp.gov/about

Pavelka, S. (2016) "Restorative justice in the States: A national assessment of legislation and policy." *Justice Policy Journal 13*, 2, 1–23.

Pavelka, S. and Thomas, D. (2013) "Charting a New Course: Moving Toward Balanced and Restorative Justice in Pennsylvania." In S. Pavelka, A. Seymour, and B. Stuart (eds) *The Legacy of Community Justice*. Kanata, ON: J Charlton Publishing Ltd.

The Pew Charitable Trusts (2012) "Time Served: The High Cost, Low Return of Longer Prison Terms." Washington, DC: The Pew Charitable Trusts. www.pewtrusts.org/~/media/legacy/uploadedfiles/wwwpewtrustsorg/reports/sentencing_and_corrections/prisontimeservedpdf.pdf?_ga=1.87714520.1149243849.1489431524

Pranis, K. (1998) "Promising Practices in Community Justice: Restorative Justice." In *Community Justice: Concepts and Strategies*. Lexington, KY: American Probation and Parole Association.

SAMHSA (Substance Abuse and Mental Health Services Administration) (2012) "SAMHSA's working definition of trauma and principles and guidance for a trauma-informed approach." Rockville, MD: Substance Abuse and Mental Health Services Administration. www.ncbi.nlm.nih.gov/books/NBK207195/

Strang, H. (2002) *Repair or Revenge: Restorative Justice*. New York: Oxford University Press.

Umbreit, M.S. (1994) *Victim Meets Offender: The Impact of Restorative Justice and Mediation*. Monsey, NY: Criminal Justice Press.

US Department of Health and Human Services, National Center for Trauma-informed Care. www.traumainformedcare.chcs.org/resource/samhsas-national-center-for-trauma-informed-care

VictimLaw (n.d.) "About Victims' Rights," US Department of Justice, Office for Victims of Crime. www.victimlaw.org/victimlaw/pages/victimsRight.jsp

Zehr, H. (1990) *Changing Lenses: A New Focus for Crime and Justice.* Scottsdale, PA: Herald Press.

— Chapter 11 —

Are We Serving Harmed People Well?

Assessing Challenges and Opportunities in Restorative Work Regarding Criminal Victimization

TED LEWIS

Like any seashore, the field of victimology continues to shift and change. In the 1980s, major advances were made in the United States with respect to victim rights and protections. Concurrent to this period, early mediation and conference models for harming and harmed parties were developing well before the term "restorative justice" was being used. Growing attention to the needs of people victimized by crime, however, was often matched with more talk and less walk. The promise seemed to outpace the practice. We shall return to that matter soon. More recently, in the last two decades and to a far greater degree in the last decade, trauma-informed approaches and racial justice have both broadened and deepened the restorative impulse to serve harming and harmed people more holistically. Those responsible for criminal activity have come to be re-spected (that is, viewed a second time) for being victimized in their earlier lives. Parallel to this, entire communities that have been historically marginalized or oppressed have also been viewed through larger lenses of victimization. Even victimizing language, in the context of implicit bias, has in some circles moved center-stage.

These broadening tendencies were predictable in the flow of postmodern concerns for all people impacted by harm. At best, they have helped restorative practitioners to re-empower those whom they serve in multiple zones of disempowerment. But one question persists in the midst of the changing seashore of addressing victimization in the United States: as the scope of victimology widens out, are we serving those who have been victimized by crime well? Or to ask this a different way, "As we give greater attention to the prevention of harm, to the holistic treatment of offending persons, and to comprehensive supports for impacted communities, might we be diminishing our capacities to serve people who are traditionally served (or underserved) by victim service agencies?"

The aim of this chapter is to present recent changes in our understanding of victimhood as not only a set of challenges to restorative dialogue work but also as opportunities for growth and holistic services within the North American context. In no way does the author wish to diminish the importance of restorative practitioners going "up stream" to invest more in prevention work, nor to diminish those who are working to change unjust systems through transformative justice. In addition, the author fully supports the deepening of restorative work for offending people that includes their journeys of healing their own past victimization. The primary focus is on the population of people who deserve the best from a restorative community when crime has impacted (or un-peaced) their lives.

Listening to the Gaps of Service for Harmed People

In mapping nearly five decades of restorative work in its modern forms, one can locate an interesting benchmark at the midpoint near the end of the 1990s. Howard Zehr and a team of others (Mika et al. 2004) were prompted to conduct "The Listening Project" to assess how victims were being engaged in the United States through restorative practices. Having already heard some major critiques from victim service workers, the project specifically tuned into those representatives in the criminal justice world who could describe first-hand how restorative justice was both perceived and implemented with respect to victim engagement. After an initial phase of interviewing 120 victims and victim advocates, a two-day meeting allowed victims and victim service personnel to name primary areas of concern.

Overall, participant victims expressed feelings of injustice, disrespect, exclusion, lack of empathy, and irrelevance as a result of the restorative justice process. There was a sense that although victim input and collaboration are touted as central to restorative justice practices, the voices of victims were not heard during the process (Mika et al. 2004).

This qualitative research project confirmed initial speculations that restorative justice practices, after two decades of growth, had migrated toward *offender-centric services*, even when the language of victim-orientation or victim-centeredness was present in program literature. According to the authors of this study, the critiques can be summarized as follows:

- *Lack of inclusion:* restorative justice programs were being implemented without consulting victim service agencies.
- *Lack of supports:* programs had more "talk" than "walk" regarding actual supports and follow-ups for victims.
- *Lack of sensitivity:* language in initial communications to victims lacked sensitivity to the needs and empowerment of victims.
- *Lack of flexibility:* dialogue models and services were too limited to constructively serve all referred victims.

New recommendations to address these deficiencies included a 10-task action plan that promised more responsiveness to the needs of victims and the concerns of victim advocates (Mika et al. 2004). Associated with this plan was the "Ten Signposts for Victim Involvement" which are listed at the end of this chapter. These signposts serve to counterbalance the potential neglect of inclusion, supports, sensitivity, and so on, stressing how victim involvement is optimized (Zehr and Achilles 2000).

Canadian studies have also shown how these same trends have not been unique to the United States, revealing inadequate preparation for victims, pressures for victims to be involved, and insensitivity regarding the timing of a victim's involvement (Wemmers and Canuto 2022). Gaudreault (2005) has described restorative justice as a "disaggregated model" which manifests itself with considerable inconsistency. Consequently, services which have been extended to victims are often difficult to evaluate, given the unevenness of casework. Despite the high level of satisfaction among victims indicated by the research, particularly studies that focused on mediation, we must be cautious still and refrain from overstating the benefits of restorative justice (Gaudreault 2005). She raises a very important question. If there are major limits in restorative justice programming that fail to serve victims well, and perhaps even do occasional harm to them, how are we to understand the substantial documentation of *high rates* of satisfaction among victims who go through restorative dialogue processes? Several studies by Umbreit and his colleagues have shown that more than 90 percent of victims (in victim offender mediation or conferencing) expressed satisfaction with the process of meeting the offender and would do it again (Umbreit et al. 2004).

One way to understand this tension is to identify how victim satisfaction may in fact be directly related to factors involving best practices that take victim sensitivity and preparation very seriously. There is no major contradiction between the negative critiques mentioned above and the positive outcomes for victims who participated in programs that were sensitive to the needs of victims. Most of the studies conducted by Umbreit and colleagues have evaluated victim offender mediation programs which implemented best practices (Umbreit and Armour 2011). Today, many of these practices would be referred to as *trauma-informed restorative practices*, emphasizing the priority of victim safety, victim choice to voluntarily agree to participate or exit at any time, and in-person preparation time before face-to-face meetings with the offending parties. It appears that the primary failures of restorative justice with respect to victim engagement are voiced by the many victims and victim advocates who were *not* included and empowered in potential restorative processes.

But even when this seeming contradiction can be reframed in a way that makes good sense, the anecdotal evidence of North American restorative justice programming, in our current times, persists in showing how victim engagement is lagging in tragic ways. What follows are three examples that came to my attention in 2016. An urban restorative justice program for youth offenders that once invited victims to participate in dialogue has now dropped victim contacts from routine procedures because it is too timely and costly. A restorative conference program, after years of operation, assessed victim participation to fall under 25 percent, and program stakeholders were not able to identify any factors that sustained low participation. A mediation-based program was inviting victims to joint dialogue meetings with minimal preparation, and after mediation meetings with offending parties (which included written reparation agreements), no communications were maintained with victim parties after the dialogue sessions. And so, two decades since The Listening Project was documented, the perennial question continues to ring loudly in restorative programs that appear to be offender-centric: Are we serving people harmed by crimes as well as possible?

While The Listening Project provided a necessary bellwether to reveal the state of victim engagement in the year 2000, we are now at a similar juncture point to assess the state of the restorative justice movement. Indeed, *movement theory* itself is having a new impact on how leaders and practitioners in restorative justice are defining and even redefining the core foundations and practices. Issues of race, social conditions, trauma, historical harm, and community systems are taking center stage in the restorative world. As demonstrated well in the book *Listening to the Movement: Essays on New Growth and New Challenges in Restorative Justice* (Lewis and Stauffer 2021), the field has been shifting from restorative justice as *social service* to restorative justice as an agent of *social transformation*. In other words, are we about helping clients or are we about social change?

What this means is that the older chronic challenge of serving victims within a programmatic context, as described above, is now overlaid with a wider set of questions that stem from viewing restorative justice as a transformative social movement. These questions can certainly be welcomed, as change in the realm of ideas can spur positive growth in the realm of application. But there are also new challenges in our current scene which, when discussed in conjunction with the classic failure to serve victims well, lead us to echo our primary question: Are we serving victims of crimes and harms as well as possible?

Meanwhile, broader applications far beyond the realm of criminal justice are informing new conceptions of restorative justice. This is certainly seen in models that focus on prevention and community-building, hence the popular growth of circle processes in nearly all realms of restorative work. In brief, the shift from simply helping "clients" in need to promoting large-scale transformation in society is raising new opportunities as well as new challenges. This is in addition to the long-standing challenge presented by the dominant offender-centric programming throughout North America. The remainder of this chapter will explore what those opportunities and challenges are with primary attention to the engagement of people victimized by crime.

New Shifts and New Questions

While the restorative justice movement is itself a major paradigmatic shift away from conventional Euro-based forms of addressing conflicts and crimes, there are a number of smaller or sub-paradigmatic shifts that can be observed within the more recent evolution of the restorative movement. In other words (to extend the classic example of shifting paradigms), the Copernican revolution has already been set in motion to offset the Earth-centered view of the cosmos, but in the wake of this revolution, other smaller shifts continue to unfold in more recent years. Here are several that can be identified.

1. Shift from addressing incidents to addressing environments. Fields of conflict transformation and community development have widened the scope of restorative work to address root causes and sustainable solutions in order to effectively *prevent* future harms and crimes. The hybridizing of restorative justice and the field of social work is one example which shows this greater attention to broader social conditions. This also strengthens the future work of building better conditions to improve the social environment.

2. Shift from helping individuals to helping communities. As a restorative view of crime (and the resolution of crime) has highlighted *webs of relationality*, restorative processes have engaged larger circles of participants who play vital roles in sustaining positive outcomes.

Support people are now routine. The rise of "community justice" in neighborhood contexts is one expression of this. Indigenous concepts such as *ubuntu* from the Zulu tradition serve to sharpen this vision. Restorative models have been designed to help entire communities impacted by oppression or violence.

3. Shift from criminal realm to all realms of human relationships. Widening applications of restorative practices in prisons, schools, workplaces, faith communities, race relations, and so on, along with restorative forums and networks for addressing community concerns, have all demonstrated that *justice* applies to *the righting of all relationships in all realms of human interaction*. Consequently, restorative work has broadened out beyond the scope of harm to include the larger scope of conflict.

4. Shift from intervention to intervention and prevention. Concerns for healthy communities and relational networks have expanded dialogue models into the realms of prevention and community-building. Intervention models are increasingly recognized as having preventative merit; at the same time, these models are critiqued when they fail to address root causes and holistic reintegration. Restorative work in prisons and re-entry, for example, combines healing work with prevention of future harms. Non-criminal applications of restorative practices recognize how preventative culture-building requires greater investment in order to reduce interventions.

5. Shift from mediation-based models to circle-based models. Circle processes, moving easily between prevention and intervention contexts, have demonstrated an adaptive capacity to promote the values associated with all of the widening aspects mentioned so far: social environment, community, relationships, and prevention. They also teach skills that allow participants to replicate the model in other life settings. At the same time, mediation and conference models, though having narrower applications, have been recognized for their own distinctive strengths which compensate for the limits of circle processes.

6. Shift from the "narrow present" to the "deep past." Increased awareness regarding trauma issues and historical harm have revised ways in which offenders are held accountable and victims are supported. This includes the recognition of victimization in the lives (and ancestral histories) of offending people, and thus the need for healing. Customized models for addressing sexual assaults and domestic violence also include depth-work. Trans-generational trauma initiatives are opening doors for whole communities to address historical harms and to seek reparations.

7. Shift from professional partnership to people-empowerment. Restorative practitioners, while promoting client-empowerment from the earliest years of practice, have largely depended upon strong partnerships with professionals in government positions. With greater supports to empower the people most involved in a harm or conflict, reliance (and even trust) in professional institutions is diminishing. Restorative stakeholders, especially among people of color in urban settings, are finding new ways to revitalize prevention and intervention work that is increasingly dependent on community-based and grassroots efforts.

8. Shift from limited victim identities to broad victim identities. Whereas restorative language initially reserved victim identification with people who were deemed "victims" in a criminal case referral, victimization language now covers anyone in any harming situation, including offenders, as having either backstories of traumatic victimization or direct impacts from a particular incident. This can extend through an entire community of people who may share a common legacy of historical or intersectional harm. New efforts include the Earth's natural environment as being victimized by human activities.

Altogether, these eight shifts within the past couple of decades in the restorative justice movement demonstrate healthy growth and expansion. It goes without saying that they all share an *intersectionality* whereby they cannot be separated out from each other. At the broadest level, they indicate the larger shift from restorative justice as programming for individuals to restorative justice as *a comprehensive framework for addressing any and all levels of harm and conflict in communal settings*. At the same time, these shifts demonstrate that the primary work of restorative justice has not been co-opted by the main justice system. Indeed, the very expansion of restorative work beyond the realm of criminal justice has allowed the movement to maintain a high degree of autonomy from institutional systems of justice, social work, and education. Its very evolution appears to have gained resiliency from co-optation. But even with this growing autonomy, major sectors of the restorative justice movement are integrating these very systems with ancient wisdom and community ownership.

The Language of Labeling Victims

One ongoing trend that coincides with the shift in victim identities involves a *shift in language*. Attention to terminology and its effects has been a defining feature of the movement; from the earliest years on, there have always been lively discussions about the need to replace old language with improved language. For example, the word "reconciliation" was dropped from most of the original Victim Offender Reconciliation Programs (VORPs) of the 1980s since the concept of reconciliation appeared to be too prescriptive. More recently, the very terms "victim" and "offender" have come under scrutiny. For many in today's restorative world, the fact that this chapter even uses both terms freely is problematic. Not only do these words reflect a carryover from the old paradigm, but they serve to limit a person's identity in ways that could inhibit their journey toward wholeness. At the same time, practitioners have wrestled overusing phrases that are cumbersome for common usage, such as "the one who did the harming" and "the one who was harmed." This topic simply highlights how there is a very real tension that exists between older and newer framings during a time of sub-paradigmatic shifts. While language is not the main focus of this chapter, it does seem right to acknowledge that language matters. Again, this very chapter represents the awkward transition of finding "correct" language, recognizing that language itself is a seashore which is constantly evolving.

As Lewis and Stauffer rightly ask, "How do we find a new language that does not restrict us to the criminal legal labels of 'victim' and 'offender' that present an artificial bifurcation and a political polarization between people who are harmed and who have harmed?" (Lewis and Stauffer 2021, p.3). Judge Carol Perry of the Navajo Nation emphasized the interdependent "fluidity of healing for everyone involved" whereby when offenders are working to repair themselves, everyone helping them is able to get better, too (Lewis and Stauffer 2021, p.12). These examples break down the dichotomy between harming and harmed persons. This is part of the larger shift away from traditional western thinking. But one could still ask, "What are the long-term implications of removing or replacing the term 'victim' for people who have been more severely impacted or traumatized by violent crimes? Will shifts in language eventually strengthen or diminish direct services, say, to individuals whose lives have been *impacted* ('un-peaced' according to the Latin root *pac*) by a major crime?"

A related challenge to the language we use for harming and harmed persons is the rising attention given to offenders and communities as victimized persons or groups. Again, broadening victimized identities has been a positive development during the past decade. The documentary film *Healing Justice* (Butler 2018), for instance, opens the window toward the way incarcerated men and women have a true need to be healed from their own backstories of victimization while taking responsibility for their own harming choices. Call to mind the common adage, "Hurt people hurt people." The deeper question is that as restorative practitioners increasingly innovate language to address these broader dimensions of victimization, how well will those who traditionally have been called "victims" be served? Will they continue to receive services informed by sensitive, best practices that have stood the test of time over the past four decades? Will the increasing attention to social transformation and community wellbeing result in better attention or less attention to restorative services for those directly harmed by conflicts and crimes? This framing, obviously, does not imply that both cannot happen together. Not only can they operate in parallel; the purpose of this chapter is to say they can thrive *interdependently*. At stake, however, is whether recent shifts toward larger, transformative aspects of restorative justice will diminish the traditional commitment of services that are tailored for victims of harm or crime. (One reason the author chose to retain the word "victim" in this chapter is in view of readers who work in victim service capacities. In his own practitioner work with victimized people, however, the label and use of other terms tends to be dropped. The same applies to the word "offender.")

Combining New Perspectives with Old Commitments

Restorative justice practitioners, while embracing opportunities created by new trends toward transformative and liberatory expressions of restorative justice, need to simultaneously reconnect and recommit to the founding principles of the movement from the last century that were so clearly grounded in serving victims well and inviting their active participation in justice processes through various restorative and community initiatives. Let me ground this statement, though, contextually within a modern, North American context, and as a practitioner and trainer of restorative dialogue-based services available to both offending and victimized parties. The positive opportunity, to now draw together both the old and the new, is that the very insights gained within the last decade regarding trauma, historical harm, community supports, root causes, and even prevention can all contribute to a wider, more holistic set of services that are rooted in the original commitment of the restorative justice movement to assist those who have been violated by crime.

This recommitment to original principles, therefore, needs to be anchored in a deep understanding and use of trauma-informed restorative practices. One of the emerging lessons from restorative dialogue practitioners is that in asking both offending and victimized parties to prepare for the benefits of dyadic conversation with each other, both parties share much in common with each other. Both have experienced a type of disorientation and resulting disempowerment, be it from the impactful incident itself or the eventual arrest by law enforcement. Life is no longer normal for either of them. They are both jolted. Both certainly have distrust on many levels, and in this vulnerability, they naturally have their guards up. Trauma stems from the incident itself, but such trauma may very well reverberate more loudly from earlier traumatic experiences. All of this is compounded when someone comes from a community that bears the marks of deeper, historical trauma. The effects of trauma include: (1) estrangement/sense of isolation; (2) feelings of powerlessness or helplessness; (3) changes in one's view of oneself and the world; (4) devastating fear, loss of safety or trust; and (5) feelings of shame, blame, guilt, and stigma (Beyer and Blake 2010). In brief, by looking through the lens of trauma, restorative services will necessarily become more humane and holistic.

This perspective on the commonalities between victim and offender experiences is already an important step in countering the bifurcation that was noted earlier. A sensitive and holistic engagement of offending and victimized persons, in the effort to help them reclaim aspects of their own humanity and see their common humanity in the other person, will help them both take the calculated risk of restorative dyadic encounter. As both parties meet with facilitators in initial sessions, they also experience a similar invitation to *find strength in going down the path of chosen vulnerability*. All of this has to do with the creation of a safe-and-brave container in which difficult, but healing, conversation can happen. Core principles of trauma-informed care with victims of crime help to ensure the safety of this space where re-victimization is safeguarded, and credits of trust are built up to replace debits of trust.

New Recommendations for Engaging Victimized People

Our guiding question can now be modified: *How* can we serve victims of crime well as we move forward in our North American context? On one hand, new measures need to be taken to counterbalance the offender-centric models of restorative dialogue which are mostly rooted in institutional agencies. This issue, as indicated by The Listening Project, is far too perennial if victim service stakeholders (let alone actual victims of crime) continue to feel alienated. On the other hand, a set of shifting trends within the restorative justice movement provide new opportunities for growth, but also some challenges with respect to our capacity to serve victim-survivors in the midst of serving victimized offenders and communities. What follows are some recommendations that can help address both sets of challenges while integrating the learnings of recent trends in the movement. These will be split into two main categories, the first pertaining to victims of crimes, and the second related to other realms of harm and victimization. The latter listing is not meant to be comprehensive but only representative of some areas that could be considered for wider restorative work. These "samplings" are also situated in the intervention realm; however, holistic intervention will always widen into sustainable prevention work.

As Related to Victims of Crime

1. Greater attention to serving victims on their *own* terms, hence:
   - more authentic and sensitive initial communications
   - more flexibility in support and listening services
   - more preparation opportunities that present options
   - more invitation for victims to tell their story in other settings
   - more response to victims of crimes with unidentified offenders.

2. Greater use of *other* victim voices in dialogue processes:
   - victim surrogates (with similar crime experience)
   - victim substitutes (with personal impact story)
   - community members (representing impacted communities)
   - victim-shuttle option (relay of impact statements and reparation requests)
   - use of letters or pre-recorded videos for safer encounter.

3. Greater use of multi-method approaches to cases:
   - conference before broader circle sequence
   - blended circle-conference model

- parallel processes for both victim and offender parties
- support circles for victims only
- post-process communication ongoing supports.

4. Greater collaboration with victim service workers:
   - include them in front-end program design
   - include them in guiding case process and timing factors
   - integrate their volunteerism with restorative options
   - provide brochures on restorative services
   - invite victim-initiated case opportunities.

5. Great attention to conditions and community:
   - effort to address root conditions causing crimes
   - effort to include community members in processes
   - effort to link up victim supports with community
   - effort to address secondary victimization
   - effort to provide meaningful community service.

As Related to Other Realms of Harming and Victimization

1. Bullying and harassment: use of *parallel processes* for serving offending and victimized parties as the default model; inclusion and empowerment of other people (bystanders, friends, family members, etc.); preparation meetings with facilitators are routine; joint-dialogue can sometimes happen *after* signs of improvement and healing; follow-up plans, as in schools, involve a school staff check-in person who oversees progress; ongoing circle processes to build trust and stronger relationships.

2. Large-scale trauma on communities (such as hate crimes, ethical breaches, sudden critical incidents, deaths, etc.): create a team-approach to map out successive, concentric healing

and resolution processes; multi-model approach using both conferencing and circling, moving from smaller groupings to larger groupings; develop strategies for informing wider numbers in the community, including memos and forums; longer-term follow-ups and closure meetings forecasted for people most involved.

3. Incarcerated offenders (both prisons and jails): provide restorative justice learning and dialogue opportunities in both group and individual settings; use of victim surrogates to participate in prison-based circle meetings; open up capacities with state approvals for safe exchange of communications between offenders and victims of similar or same cases; ensure continuity of restorative supports from prison to re-entry settings; re-entry conferencing with family and friends for both amends making and goal-setting with supports.

4. Communities and law enforcement: create frameworks that initially introduce restorative dialogue models for community-building; as pilot groups build up trust and strengthen relationships, then broaden participation to include others; find respected stakeholders in both community and police realms to share facilitator roles; build a citizen-police facilitated dialogue program for complaints; when resolving grievances and building peace, major on finding common ground in everyone's experiences.

5. Marginalized or oppressed communities: provide restorative dialogue models for people with protective-class status who have experienced discrimination of their human rights; support the intersectionality of human and social experiences, also of incidents and past histories; empower leaders representing these groups to facilitate processes; provide community-building strategies through prevention-based dialogue opportunities as a base for having intervention-ready dialogue; consider how reparations and relationship building can strengthen each other.

In closing, the first set of recommendations related to victims of crime add up to a recommitment to the original restorative principles as articulated in the movement's early years and summarized well in the Ten Signposts for Victim Involvement (see the end of the chapter). At the same time these recommendations reflect a wider menu of options that require a flexible and communal approach as informed by more recent trends in the movement. The best of the Old and the best of the New need to hold hands together. Including the second set of recommendations for wider situations of harm and impact reinforces the *communal and relational nature of all restorative work*. Restorative justice is *not* primarily a service-based model for bringing victimized and offending parties together in the same room for dialogue. It is, rather, a holistic approach to justice that helps victimized and offending people to *move forward in life*, whether they come together. In this light, an adaptive and flexible approach to restorative justice can find innovative ways for working with *all* persons who have harmed or been harmed, precisely because there are many other conversation partners who can suitably participate in processes that combine healing and accountability.

A good example of where this broadening impulse can rise up is in a community's commitment to serve victims of crimes where no offender was arrested or apprehended. Many property crimes, for example, occur in situations where offending parties are never caught. Could not a restorative community create specific services and funding to serve people who were victimized, but whose cases never enter the court realm because their information simply went no further than a police or sheriff's department? A caring community would find a way to serve "offenderless" victims no less than other victims who are "in" the system. Why not create a community fund for such victims which can be fed by business and community donors? Community service hours could also release proportional monies from this fund to pay back restitution to victims.

This same community-driven commitment can be applied to victim-survivors of past crimes who truly need greater time in their life journeys before they are ready for healing dialogue. The vast majority of victims of severe and traumatizing crimes will not have the opportunity to ever meet with the offending person(s) in their specific case, either by choice or by circumstances that distance the offender from reachability. Again, other conversation partners, such as surrogate victims, surrogate offenders, and caring community members, can all be called upon for post-incident opportunities for deep healing. The author had the opportunity to facilitate a nine-month process where two people, independent of their respective histories, requested participation in a restorative conference within one month of each other. One was a perpetrator of rape against a young teen girl; the other was a victim-survivor of childhood rape and sexual abuse. After eight months of preparation, they came together, each with a support person, for a conference that lasted six hours. They each experienced a therapeutic breakthrough that had not been possible through individual counseling. This is simply one example of how restorative dialogue, with its adaptive qualities, can honor the profound, dyadic opportunity to help people move forward in life. To view an interview with the female survivor, watch *The Promise of Restorative Dialogue for Surrogates in Sexual Harming Cases* (Lewis 2020).

Concluding Thoughts

The main concern of this chapter, altogether, revolves around victims who do enter a system of justice, be it traditional or restorative, and are not served as well as they deserve to be served. No doubt, limited people-resources among victim service agencies are part of this under-serving pattern. This, in part, was the historical vacuum in which restorative programming could grow over the years since its beginnings in the modern world. Forty years of restorative justice dialogue in North America have certainly established that victims who participate in well-prepared and well-guided conversations with offenders indicate high satisfaction in the justice they experience. Nevertheless, the state of offender-centric frameworks in North America, extending well into restorative programming to this day, has severely limited both the quantity and quality of services to victims of crime. As practitioners attempt to remedy the nature of these services, the newer challenge will be to keep restorative work for victims toward the center of the radar screen as the movement increasingly broadens its vision toward the transformation of social life and institutions. The main goal is not to become either a reformer or a revolutionary. "The focus of the restorative justice movement is to hold in tension both interpersonal and institutional change while at the same time moving towards a cultural shift or societal transformation of how justice is understood and practiced for the future" (Lewis and Stauffer 2021, p.xxvii). It is in this fruitful tension that we, as restorative practitioners, will renew our commitment to serving victims of crime as well as possible.

References

Beyer, L.L. and Blake, M. (2010) "Trauma-informed Care: Building Partnerships and Peer Supports in Supportive Housing Settings" [PowerPoint slides]. Presentation at Services in Supportive Housing Annual Grantee Meeting. Washington, DC.

Butler, S. (dir.) (2018) *Healing Justice*. World Trust film.

Gaudreault, A. (2005) *The Limits of Restorative Justice*. Proceedings of the Symposium of the École Nationale de la Magistrature. Paris: Édition Dalloz.

Lewis, T. (2020) "The Promise of Restorative Dialogue for Surrogates in Sexual Harming Cases" [Video interview]. Center for Restorative Justice & Peacemaking, University of Minnesota, Duluth. https://rjp.d.umn.edu/resources/restorative-justice-and-sexual-harm/surrogate-dialogue-sexual-harm

Lewis, T. and Stauffer, C. (2021) *Listening to the Movement: Essays on New Growth and New Challenges in Restorative Justice*. Oregon: Cascade.

Mika, H., Achilles, M., Halbert, E., Stutzman Amstutz, L., and Zehr, H. (2004) "Listening to victims: A critique of restorative justice policy and practice in the United States." *Federal Probation 68*, 1, 32–38.

Umbreit, M. and Armour, M. (2011) "Restorative justice and dialogue: Impact, opportunities, and challenges in the global community." *Washington University Journal of Law and Policy 36*, 65, 65–90. https://journals.library.wustl.edu/lawpolicy/article/id/1941

Umbreit, M., Coates, R.B., and Vos, B. (2004) "Victim-offender mediation: Three decades of practice and research." *Conflict Resolution Quarterly 22*, 1, 279–304. http://dx.doi.org/10.1002/crq.102

Wemmers, J. and Canuto, M. (2022) "Victims' Experiences with Expectations and Perceptions of Restorative Justice: A Critical Review of the Literature." International Centre for Comparative Criminology, Université de Montréal. rr 2001-9e.

Zehr, H. and Achilles, M. (2000) "Victim Advocate for the Commonwealth of Pennsylvania." *Office of Victim Advocate Newsletter*, State of Pennsylvania, 4 (1).

The Ten Signposts of Victim Involvement (Zehr and Achilles 2000)

We are working toward appropriate victim involvement (in restorative justice) when:

1. Victims and victim advocates are represented on the governing bodies and initial planning committees.

2. Efforts to involve victims originate from a desire to assist in their recovery/reconstruction. Benefits to the offender are not the primary motive of the program for victim involvement. Victims should be free from the burden of rehabilitation or assisting offenders (unless they choose to do so).

3. The safety of the victim is a fundamental element of program design.

4. Victims are presented with clear understandings of their roles, including potential benefits and risks to themselves and offenders.

5. Confidentiality is provided within clear guidelines.

6. Victims are provided as much information as possible about the case, the offense, and the offender.

7. Victims are able to identify and present their needs and are provided options and choices.

8. Victim opportunities for involvement are maximized.

9. Program design provides referrals for additional support and assistance.

10. To the extent possible, program services are made available to victims even when their offender has not been arrested.

― Chapter 12 ―

The Evolution of a Brief Restorative Justice Intervention

DENNIS E. MCCHARGUE, PHD,
SANDRA PAVELKA, PHD AND JAMES JONES

Restorative Justice and Reintegration

Returning citizens, previously incarcerated, in many cases face economic and social challenges to a successful recovery often leading to revocations, rearrests, and reconvictions in the early reentry phase (Jacobs et al. 2022). In response to this revolving door, alternatives to incarceration using restorative justice principles have been tested and made available in both justice and non-justice settings. As has been discussed thoroughly throughout this book, restorative justice aims to mend and diminish damage caused by criminal offending or misconduct. More importantly, traditional forms of reparations (e.g., probation, imprisonment) for criminal behavior are believed to be strengthened through restorative justice approaches by holding the offender accountable while developing a better understanding of the implications of their crime on the victim and survivor, their family, and the community. Restorative justice approaches suggest that this enhanced accountability subsequently decreases the likelihood of recidivism by engaging the person in the reintegration in order to become a productive member of society. While restorative justice is not a new term or practice, and in its evolution, these concepts and applications are continually being refined and adapted (Pavelka 2016; Pavelka and Thomas 2019).

Restorative Justice Interventions

The implementation of restorative justice principles through a variety of interventions, known as restorative justice interventions (RJIs), has been developed by researchers and practitioners over the past three decades. Traditional methods utilize face-to-face meetings between the victim and the offender. These victim-offender dialogue sessions are structured to help the victim repair the harm caused by criminal offending (Marshall 1999). These interventions help the offender recognize the devastating consequences of their transgressions, as well as empathize, make amends, and actively necessitate productive resolutions (Maryfield, Przybylski and Myrent 2020; McChargue, Pavelka and Kennedy 2020). The foundational concept was developed with the intent to generate mutual healing (Dhami, Mantle and Fox 2009), repair harm, and reduce short- and long-term recidivism (Richner, Pavelka and McChargue 2022).

The effectiveness of various RJI methods has been demonstrated in studies with meta-analytic data in both youth and adult offenders (Latimer, Dowden and Muise 2005; Sherman et al. 2015) indicating, on average, a reduction in repeat offending, and victim and offender satisfaction (e.g., Bouffard, Cooper and Bergseth 2017). However, questions remain about the degree to which dialogue and education influence offenders' perspective and future behavior (Roche 2001). Although the mechanism of why offenders' behaviors change is unknown, there is strong evidence to support that the RJIs reduce recidivism over a 12- to 18-month period following the intervention (Bergseth and Bouffard 2012; Forgays and DeMilio 2005). This evidence has led others to begin the process of identifying components of RJIs that are necessary for producing positive changes in offenders and, thereby, reducing recidivism (McChargue et al. 2020; Richner et al. 2022).

Because offenders often do not naturally develop insight into the harms caused by their criminal activity, researchers assert that greater understanding and empathy development by offenders for their victims and the harm they caused will produce emotional and behavioral changes that directly translate to a lower recidivism rate (Marshall and Marshall 2011; Robinson and Rogers 2015). Researchers further imply that empathy enhancement is the key mechanism to enact change among offenders and that it is imperative to engage offenders in activities aimed at increasing empathy. This instruction, in turn, leads to a reduction in criminal recidivism among many within the justice system, but not all. Empathy training for some offenders (i.e., sex offenders) produces adverse effects for they often use empathy to manipulate their victims for personal gain.

In addition to understanding the components of RJIs that produce positive changes in offenders, it is of interest to understand how to implement these interventions in cost-effective ways to reach the greatest number of people. The authors will highlight one agency whose mission was to develop a relatively brief, one-session intervention (b-RJI) that reduced the demand on the staff implementing the intervention, increased the numbers of offenders receiving the intervention, lowered the cost, and, ultimately, reduced recidivism. While research exists on the best procedures for reducing the cost of these programs, finding ways to reach the most individuals while reducing the number of staff necessary to implement these interventions is certainly important for the viability of these programs.

James Jones, a former offender himself, unintentionally created a unique restorative justice program for youthful offenders and at-risk kids called "The Victims First Team." The program Jones created was one of the first in the country to use surrogate crime victims extensively, in absence of the primary affected victim, in a restorative/dialogue framework. These youthful offenders and at-risk youth provide physically restored offenses by others (e.g., vandalism, burglary, robbery, drive by shooting, arson, etc.) and then discussed with the victim the effects of the crime on their lives. Treatment staff recognized anecdotal enhancement of empathy for the victim by the youth offenders because of their work with the victims. These youth would comment on the victims' statements and how the crime that affected their life across multiple domains resonated with them.

The Beginning: The Victims First Team
Following his incarceration, Jones initially worked at the Lincoln Action Program, in the youth after school/tutoring program, in 1995. He noticed many of the youth were at risk, some in gangs and some

justice involved who were on probation. Because of his history, Jones wanted to give back to the community by reducing the likelihood that these youth would go down the same path as he did. He had the idea of showing young people the consequences of their decisions from an individual victim, to a community level.

Youth attended Jones's program several times a week which also included pro-social activities. This program was designed to be graded and sequential. They initially attended a victim awareness session that defined a victim, discussed the impact of crime on a victim, discussed crime's cost to the community, and discussed emotional hygiene techniques (processing the six core feelings). Following the sessions, the youth were then taken to various settings associated with the consequences of criminal behavior (e.g., the jail, morgue, emergency room, and finally prison). They learned about each operation and spoke with individuals associated with the system, including incarcerated individuals, about their experiences and regrets. The youth then attended a process group with facilitators about how to apply their victim impact with their individual experiences. As the youth started to integrate and generalize their knowledge, they were then taught vocational skills that would help them during the six-month or longer community outreach (e.g., victims' services projects) part of the program.

During the community outreach portion, the program partnered with local police and victims' organizations to reach out to victims of crimes (e.g., robbery, domestic violence, vandalism, graffiti, and homicides). After the initial victim's outreach by staff, the youth and frequently off-duty law enforcement would go to homes and businesses afflicted by crime to provide aid to victims by, for example, repairing the physical damage, such as to windows and doors, fixing holes in drywalls, replacing locks, or any other reasonable task the youth could complete within a few hours. The youth would develop their vocational and emotional competencies while completing these victims' service projects in the community. After the victims' service projects, the team would then meet with the victim who served as surrogate to impart their experience being victimized by crime. This meeting was facilitated by staff in a restorative process to discuss how the victims were damaged directly/indirectly and how the community was harmed. The group would discuss the feelings and experiences of the victim, the financial damage to the victim and community, and the long-term damages, while continuing to practice emotional hygiene techniques. Lastly, they would conduct a team-building recreational activity prior to returning home (Jones 1998). These victims' services projects were conducted twice or three times weekly over a long time, exposing youth to victims harmed by crime in their communities.

Bazemore's Involvement

It was not until the mid-1990s that the concept of restorative justice was put into focus for Jones. The US Department of Justice under the leadership of Janet Reno, Attorney General of the United States, held five regional restorative justice symposiums around the country educating and encouraging communities to expand the use of restorative justice (Reno et al. 1996). By chance, Jones was recommended to attend the mid-west symposium where he met Dr. Gordon Bazemore for the first time in the back of the room of the symposium. They were standing against the wall when Bazemore asked Jones, "What do you do?" When Jones described his program about youth offenders and at-risk youth repairing/fixing crime victims' property, but these were not the youth victims, Bazemore responded, "You are doing restorative justice by way of surrogate crime victims." He went on to share, "You are addressing the needs of all three stakeholders at the same time (victims, offenders, and communities)—that is restorative. You ask victims what harm was done and what needs to be done to repair that harm? You are elevating victims to their proper place within the system. You are teaching youthful offenders and at-risk kids how to repair harm and teaching them vocational and their emotional competencies skills. You are also teaching kids how to address negative emotions." Bazemore then recommended that Jones measure the number of youth offenders in his program that recidivate after completion. This was the first time Jones considered that his program may help reduce reoffending. Moreover, research did not evolve in examining restorative justice interventions among youth offenders until the early 2000s (Crawford and Newburn 2002;

O'Mahony and Campbell 2006). Bazemore suggested that Jones was conducting restorative justice in a unique way as compared with the historical victim-offender dialogue. He suggested that Jones's use of surrogate victims was unique and may expand the reach of restorative justice beyond victim-offender dialogues. It was not until years later that the evidence showed the importance of surrogates in restorative justice (e.g., Saulnier and Sivasubramaniam 2015), suggesting Jones's program was more advanced than once thought. From these chance meetings, Jones and Bazemore worked together on various symposia and workgroups associated with restorative justice around the country. This involvement provided Jones with the opportunity to develop and evolve his program beyond the Victims First Team beginnings. Bazemore welcomed Jones back after his incarceration and took him under his wing for many years, and provided him with valuable insight, feedback, and input regarding the work he was doing with youthful offenders and at-risk youth which continues to this day with the justice-involved individuals he works with at the Community Justice Center (CJC) he founded.

Beginnings of the Brief Restorative Justice Interventions (b-RJI)

In the early 2000s, Jones wanted to expand his restorative justice efforts to see if his application of using surrogate victims could work with adult justice-involved individuals. Dr. Bazemore, unknowingly, inspired him to create the CJC in Lincoln, Nebraska in 2001. He developed a brief, eight-hour educational program based on restorative justice concepts while using key components of the Victims First program. As such, the CJC transferred this approach to adult offenders using surrogate victim impact statements posted on the CJC website embedding them into a brief, one-session format. Since then, the CJC has collaborated with several agencies in order to reduce the burden of the criminal justice system, while integrating restorative justice concepts into their programming. The CJC has served almost 15,000 justice-involved individuals through evidence-based programming and forensic peer support in all Nebraska

Correctional Institutions, Douglas and Lancaster County Jails, and all Nebraska Probation Districts across the state, servicing offenders, both in prison and on probation, victims, and impacted families along with other collaborators, within the state and nationally, to implement the restorative practices.

The CJC's mission includes: offering resources and restorative justice (RJ) practices for all harmed by crime, including victims, offenders, and the community; reducing prison and probation populations by advancing their skills in "emotional hygiene," accountability, and responsibility; and returning individuals back into their communities safely. To achieve these goals, the CJC created an eight-hour b-RJI entitled: "Crime Victims Impact/Emotional Hygiene Life Skills Class." This b-RJI teaches inmates about the principles and values of restorative justice via the lenses of surrogate crime victims' perspectives. In each session, 8 to 12 offenders, incarcerated or on probation, work to address the denial and minimization of responsibility often associated with criminal activity. Peer- and other trained facilitators help offenders learn about the "true" impact of their crimes (harms) on their victims, their families, and their community. Finally, offenders are encouraged to learn and apply emotional hygiene skills and to eliminate rationalization and justification for their behaviors to become responsible for their own actions.

The CJC accomplishes these goals through a variety of activities: "My Circle of Victims" (identifying both direct and indirect victims of their criminal activity); "Daily Harm and Damage Reports" (analyzing the harm identified in surrogate victim impact statements); "Harm Letters" (offenders must be able to identify their victims, all the harms and ways to repair that harm, i.e., restitution). The CJC developed Harm Letters as a self-reflection exercise for the offender's own edification and not to go beyond self-reflection. Finally, participants are introduced to a technique called "The Gift—Your Million Dollar Check" whereby they learn how to maintain their emotional hygiene. This technique assists offenders in unlocking their sources of anger as well as how to process the six core emotions guiding them in making better decisions.

Outcomes of the Brief Restorative Justice Intervention
Probation Data

To understand the impact of the b-RJI classes more fully, the CJC has partnered with Dr. Dennis McChargue, an associate psychology professor and substance use expert at the University of Nebraska, Lincoln, and Dr. Sandra Pavelka, a professor and internationally known restorative justice expert at Florida Gulf Coast University. This collaboration with researchers and experts in the field led to the initial mixed-methods investigation that tested the degree to which the CJC's b-RJI delivered within probation would reduce recidivism across six years for those attending the b-RJI as compared with a group of individuals receiving treatment routinely. This peer-reviewed work (McChargue et al. 2020; Richner et al. 2022) showed that probationers receiving treatment as usual ($n = 130$) were twice as likely to recidivate as probationers who attended the b-RJI ($n = 383$). Furthermore, among *those who recidivated*, b-RJI class members had a significantly lower number of subsequent offenses than the treatment-as-usual group. Finally, researchers examined the content of satisfaction surveys that asked open-ended questions about what probationers learned from the class. Qualitative analyses showed that over 50 percent of b-RJI class participants spontaneously reported empathic understanding regarding harm to their victims as well as restorative justice concepts. A majority (60%) also described themselves as engaged and motivated to live a more productive life.

Prison Data

More recently, the research team analyzed data of incarcerated individuals who took the b-RJI from 2001 to 2017 and were subsequently released from prison ($n = 1316$). Results showed that women recidivated far less than men across 13 years. Similarly, older individuals recidivated far less than younger individuals. Among those that recidivated ($n = 283$), taking the b-RJI closer to release from prison significantly delayed recidivism regardless of age, type of crime, gender, and so on (Richner et al. 2022). Conclusions suggest that delaying recidivism rates may implicate the need to have targeted programming post-release to further enhance the effects of the b-RJI.

For the purposes of this chapter and a more nuanced examination of the data, we asked the Nebraska Department of Corrections (NDOC) to provide recidivism data across the years of our examination. We used the years provided by NDOC from 2003 to 2016 of their three-year recidivism rates. Our sample size per year ranged from 28 to 185. As shown in Table 12.1, most years (minus one) produced significantly lower recidivism rates for those that took the class as compared with those released during the same year.

Table 12.1 Three-year recidivism rate comparison

Fiscal year	b-RJI (%)	NDOC (%)
2003	14.3	25.4
2004	9.9	29.7
2005	12.9	31.1
2006	10.4	25.4
2007	5.4	25.6
2008	5.6	25.9
2009	12.7	26.2
2010	27.7	27.7
2011	6.8	27.5
2012	11	30.1
2013	6.1	31.3
2014	10.1	31.8
2015	10.9	27.4
2016	11.2	30.3

Source: Nebraska Department of Corrections (personal communication 2020)

Current Data

The evolution of the CJC's restorative justice mission builds from these beginnings and expands to current grant funding from a Nebraska-based Sherwood Foundation. Funds allow the CJC to reach all Nebraska prisons and to test the effectiveness of the b-RJI among this prison population. These funds also allow the CJC to implement programming in Nebraska jails. The CJC has also begun implementing an online version of the b-RJI classes in order to reach distal populations, to improve cost-effectiveness efforts, to make them available to a greater number of people, and to enhance overall global accessibility. This work has created an opportunity for wider dissemination of the b-RJI classes, the information they provide, and the influence they have on offenders, victims, families, and communities who would otherwise be unable to access these services. Moreover, individuals access the online version at a reduced fee (compared with incarceration costs), which expands coverage to individuals in need.

b-RJI Implications

The use of b-RJIs shows promising effects with offenders in terms of reduced recidivism, increased victim empathy, and improved communities, while offering a direct benefit of being cost-effective on an overburdened criminal justice system. Following its core mission, the CJC will continue to work to affect the community through implementation of b-RJIs with offenders and will seek to substantiate the best practices as they relate to these interventions. Future research must continue to examine and validate the mechanisms associated with offender change in b-RJIs (i.e., reduced recidivism, increased empathy, etc.) while maintaining cost-effectiveness and ease of delivery of these programs. Together, practitioners and researchers can continue to increase the established effectiveness of RJIs within their communities as well as to improve the quality of life for all involved.

References

Bergseth, K. and Bouffard, J. (2012) "Examining the effectiveness of a restorative justice program for various types of juvenile offenders." *International Journal of Offender Therapy and Comparative Criminology 57*, 9, 1054–1075. http://doi.org/10.1177/0306624X12453551

Bouffard, J., Cooper, M., and Bergseth, K. (2017) "The effectiveness of various restorative justice interventions on recidivism outcomes among juvenile offenders." *Youth Violence and Juvenile Justice 15*, 4, 465–480. http://doi.org/10.1177/1541204016647428

Crawford, A. and Newburn, T. (2002) "Recent developments in restorative justice for young people in England and Wales: Community participation and representation." *British Journal of Criminology 42*, 3, 476–495. doi.org/10.1093/bjc/42.3.476

Dhami, M., Mantle, G., and Fox, D. (2009) "Restorative justice in prisons." *Contemporary Justice Review 12*, 4, 433–448. dx.doi.org/10.1080/10282580903343027

Forgays, D. and DeMilio, L. (2005) "Is teen court effective for repeat offenders? A test of the restorative justice approach." *International Journal of Offender Therapy and Comparative Criminology 49*, 1, 107-118. doi.org/10.1177/0306624X04269411

Jacobs, L., Branson, Z., Greeno, C., Skeem, J., and Labrum, T. (2022) "Community behavioral health service use and criminal recidivism of people with mental, substance use and co-occurring disorders." *Psychiatric Services 73*, 12, 1397-1400. doi.org/10.1176/appi.ps.202100530

Jones, J. (1998) "Victims First: A Restorative Justice Program." *The Crime Victim Report*, 22 (May/June).

Latimer, J., Dowden, C., and Muise, D. (2005) "The effectiveness of restorative justice practices: A meta-analysis." *The Prison Journal 85*, 2, 127-144. https://journals.sagepub.com/doi/10.1177/0032885505276969

Maryfield, B., Przybylski, R., and Myrent, M. (2020) "Research on restorative justice practices." *Justice Research and Statistics Association*, December, 1-11.

Marshall, L.E. and Marshall, W.L. (2011) "Empathy and antisocial behavior." *The Journal of Psychiatry & Psychology 22*, 5, 742-759. doi.org/10.1080/14789949.2011.617544

Marshall, T. (1999) "Restorative Justice: An Overview." Occasional Paper. Home Office.

McChargue, D., Pavelka, S., and Kennedy, J. (2020) "Restorative Justice Interventions." *Corrections Today*, November/December, 20-24. www.researchgate.net/publication/348310583_Restorative_Justice_Interventions

O'Mahony, D. and Campbell, C. (2006) "Mainstream Restorative Justice for Young Offenders Through Youth Conferencing: The Experience of Northern Ireland." In J. Junger-Tas and S.H. Decker (eds) *International Handbook of Juvenile Justice*. New York: Springer.

Pavelka, S. (2016) "Restorative justice in the States: A national assessment of legislation and policy." *Justice Policy Journal 13*, 2, 1-23. doi.org/10.1177/0306624X221086555

Pavelka, S. and Thomas, D. (2019) "The evolution of balanced and restorative justice." *Juvenile and Family Court Journal 70*, 1, 37-58. doi.org/10.1111/jfcj.12125

Reno, J., Robinson, L., Price, H.B., and Pranis, K. (1996) "Conferences: Communities, Crime and Justice: Making Community Partnerships Work." *Office of Justice Programs Documentation*, 1-53.

Richner, K.A., Pavelka, S., and McChargue, D. (2022) "A restorative justice intervention in United States prisons: Implications of intervention timing, age, and gender on recidivism." *International Journal of Offender Therapy and Comparative Criminology 67*, 12, 1-18. doi.org/10.1177/0306624X221086555

Robinson, E.V. and Rogers, R. (2015) "Empathy faking in psychopathic offenders: The vulnerability of empathy measures." *Journal of Psychopathology and Behavioral Assessment 37*, 545-552. doi.org/10.1007/s10862-015-9479-9

Roche, D. (2001) "The evolving definition of restorative justice." *Contemporary Justice Review 4*, 3-4, 341-353. http://hdl.handle.net/1885/66189

Saulnier, A. and Sivasubramaniam, D. (2015) "Effects of victim presence and coercion in restorative justice: An experimental paradigm." *Law and Human Behavior 39*, 4, 378-387. https://psycnet.apa.org/doi/10.1037/lhb0000130

Sherman, L.W., Strang, H., Mayo-Wilson, E., Woods, D.J., and Ariel, B. (2015) "Are restorative justice conferences effective in reducing repeat offending? Findings from a Campbell Systematic Review." *Journal of Quantitative Criminology 31*, 1, 1-24. doi.org/10.1007/s10940-014-9222-9

— Chapter 13 —

Dialogue Among Those Committing and Harmed by Crime

Five Decades of Practice and Research

JACOB OTIS AND MARK UMBREIT, PHD

Introduction

The mastery of restorative justice has always been more than lists of ideas and aspirations for a better form of justice. Its true strength resides in the endless hours dedicated by practitioners, researchers, and supporters. Within conversations, and sometimes arguments, the impact of restorative justice on society through fostering humanistic relationships continues to grow. With this growth and influence, however, come newfound questions and challenges.

Supporters of restorative justice have seemingly transitioned from early activists to advocates, and they face a series of different challenges. Public understanding of restorative justice has grown, and more jurisdictions have incorporated restorative justice programming and/or restorative principles. While this increasing attention towards victim-centered approaches is increasing the voice of others, purist and maximalist viewpoints prioritize different aspects of a restorative model. In short, purist models strictly require active, voluntary participation of all parties while maximalist models do not necessitate direct involvement (typically victims) nor the absence of coercion of participation (Bazemore 2000a; McCold 2000). Within these viewpoints, contention arises between practitioners and scholars with different views about the prioritization of participants and coercive engagement.

Within these discussions of restorativeness, restorative justice advocates may find it helpful to look towards the past to inform the future of restorative justice practices. Endless hours of practitioner and researcher participation, millions of dollars, and hundreds of programs are represented in five decades of research. Revisiting this body of literature highlights key aspects of the movement and connects the history of relationships across programs. This chapter offers readers a summary taste of this 50 years of research on the most empirically substantiated form of restorative justice—victim offender mediation (VOM).

This chapter is not meant to be an exhaustive collection of all the practice and research of VOM dialogue in North America, but rather an overview and brief narrative. It is also important to note that this chapter focuses on research conducted in North America and research that is published in academic journals or monographs. Readers are encouraged to discover the many works published in non-academic repositories.

Lastly and most importantly, restorative justice is based on centuries of indigenous wisdom and expertise. The institutionalization and academization of restorative justice often lead us to look towards westernized academics as sources of knowledge, but it is important to honor indigenous knowledge holders as valuable sources. Readers are invited to read *Colorizing Restorative Justice: Voicing Our Realities* (Valandra and Hokšíla 2020) to learn more.

Victim Offender Mediation

When someone is the victim of a crime, the proceeding weeks, months, or sometimes years are often filled with a series of internal and external stressors. If they are involved in the judicial system, they can face a barrage of interviews and fact-finding meetings. Sometimes, victims can face an inquisition from prosecutors and be further victimized through victim blaming and oftentimes endure retraumatization. Internally, victims may question themselves and face mental health challenges. In court, opportunities to express the true impacts of crime are scarce.

Victim offender mediation is the most common descriptor, but it is sometimes referred to as victim offender conferencing, dialogue, reconciliation, or encounters. VOM is a person-centered process that enables victims, offenders, and other stakeholders to have humanizing dialogue in an intimate but safe space. Often occurring after the traditional legal process has ended, VOM's goals often include holding the offender accountable towards their behavior and providing creative forms of assistance to victims (Umbreit 2001). Alongside a trained mediator, victims and offenders are provided a space where victims can have their questions addressed directly by the offender and offenders can contribute towards a personalized restitution plan.

These gatherings typically include three focused perspectives including the victim's party, offender's party, and the mediator/community. In some cases, victims are invited to ask family members, friends, or another advocate to participate and serve as a source of support. Offenders are similarly invited to include family members, friends, or other advocates in the mediation. Lastly, the mediator serves as a representative, not of the criminal justice system, but as a stakeholder of the community invested in healing a harm within their community network. In addition to these three typical perspectives found in VOM, other community members, such as criminal justice system employees (e.g., probation officers, social workers, court staff, etc.), may also be present to encourage accountability, provide contextual information on the case, or serve as a delegate of a system when appropriate. Research has found that the inclusion of these support persons is common in the majority of VOM meetings (Umbreit and Greenwood 1999).

Confidentiality is also a core aspect of VOM and integral to a successful mediation. While these meetings are often referred to by the criminal justice system, specific details of the mediation are not shared with outside parties. It is commonplace to see nondisclosure agreements or similar documents signed by all parties prior to its start. These agreements have multiple purposes, not just the standard legal intent to prevent their participation from having what said used against them in the future. These agreements ensure that victims, offenders, and others feel safe to share as much as they feel comfortable sharing. The integrity of the conversation also is dependent upon these mutual agreements of confidentiality. Additionally, confidentiality further strengthens the impartiality of the facilitator and fosters a non-judgmental atmosphere. However, some exceptions from confidentiality are possible, such as the content of agreements that are cosigned at the end of the mediation, evaluation data gathered by researchers, the possibility of a subpoena, and mandating reporting.

Facilitators of VOM typically have completed training prior to hosting mediations. Different programs and different jurisdictions have different requirements but will typically require an educational background in a social sciences field, such as sociology, social work, psychology, or criminology. Alongside this educational background, training hours vary and typically include classroom instruction and supervised practice. While certificates and degrees in VOM mediation are scarce, a growing number of programs are offering specific credentialing for mediators. Within the restorative justice field, this credentialing has been critiqued as a form of capitalization of indigenous practices and will inevitably be at the center of this "professionalization of restorative justice" future (Braithwaite 2004; Takagi and Shank 2004). Great care and deference must be taken by future programs to culturally appropriate these practices.

The role of the facilitator within these meetings is also meant to instill a deeper connection between participants and represent a sense of mindfulness. Representing the core aspects of mindfulness, remaining present, and radical acceptance, a grounded facilitator enables an authentic and meaningful experience for all present (Hansen and Umbreit 2018; Lewis and Umbreit 2015).

A close kin to VOM is family group conferencing (FGC), which has many of the same components of VOM, but typically includes juveniles and members of relevant family members. The key distinction between VOM and FGC, other than the focus of FGC on juveniles, is the different focuses on the role of community, with VOM focusing on the specific relationship between the offender and victim and finding a mutually satisfying resolution, whereas FGC is primarily focused on community involvement in addressing systemic issues which may have led to the harm (Umbreit and Armour 2010). Notably, these restorative processes are sometimes used in a blended fashion and sometimes used in conjunction with problem solving and/or community-building circles.

Victim offender mediation is among the oldest and most empirically validated models of restorative justice dialogue and continues to be widely used throughout the United States (Bazemore and Umbreit 1995; Van Ness *et al.* 2022; Zehr 1990). As an evidence-based practice, VOM has been used in cases ranging from simple vandalism to serious violent crimes such as homicide. Historically, VOM evolved out of a number of community-based programs which worked to rethink traditional criminal justice system programs. The following sections will detail some of the historical development of VOM over the past 50 years and offer selected research from each decade.

A survey of VOM programs in 2011 found over 300 in the United States alone, but it is unclear exactly how many VOM programs exist now (Umbreit and Armour 2010). While there are likely many more today, programs vary widely in size, funding, their adherence to a purist, maximalist, or restorative justice model, and many other methods.

With dozens of studies evaluating outcomes such as satisfaction of the process, financial impacts on parties, recidivism, and others all showing consistent findings, tracing VOM's evolution allows us to understand its impacts on society but also some areas of drift away from the original intent (Umbreit and Armour 2010). Readers should also note that there are many other studies and scholars which focus on the impacts of the criminal justice system and restorative justice on specific demographic groups. Contextual lived experiences matter, and different groups experience different sets of advantages and challenges. The selected studies have a variety of limitations in terms of externalizability and generalizability across groups, and readers are encouraged to expand their understanding to tailor and individualize VOM to their communities.

VOM in the 1970s

In the mid-1970s, prototypes of restorative justice across the United States brought victims, offenders, and community members together. Victim Offender Reconciliation Programs (VORPs) began to be implemented for relatively minor property crimes across the country (Umbreit, Coates and Vos 2004). These programs stood separate from similar mediation initiatives because of their uncoupling from settlement-driven meditation and towards a dialogue focus.

The first among these programs in North America was established in Kitchener, Ontario in 1974. Developed by the Mennonite Central Community in Canada, this program brought victims, offenders, and community members into facilitated meetings to initially address property offenses, such as vandalism, but this quickly expanded its use into more serious, violent cases (Bender [1986]2019).

In 1977, community panels were established under the goal to further include the community in the resolution of crimes in Minneapolis, Minnesota (Bazemore 2000b). A year later in 1978 in Elkhart, Indiana the first VORP was established under the perspective of a humanistic approach and combined with PACT (Prisoner and Community Together) in 1979 (Umbreit [1978]2006; Weingart 2017). However, some practitioners and criminal justice stakeholders initially pushed back against VORP for its perceived intention to reconcile the victim and the offender (Umbreit [1978]2006).

These VOM pilot programs in North America positioned early prototypes of restorative justice as plausible alternatives to the criminal justice system and led to heightened attention towards challenging the justice status quo. It must also be noted that reports and research in the 1970s are scarcely digitized and published in formal academic journals. Future efforts to digitize and upload these documents and provide ready access are needed.

Research in the 1970s

There were several research studies conducted on what we now refer to as restorative justice in the 1970s, which established some of the earliest validations of effectiveness as an alternative to the traditional criminal justice system.

In the mid-1970s, Howard Zehr evaluated the effectiveness of the first VOM program initiated in 1974 in Kitchener, Ontario in Canada through the Mennonite Central Committee's VORP. The program was found to be successful in promoting reparation and reducing recidivism for juvenile property crimes.

Mark Yantzi and David Worth from the Mennonite Central Committee examined the concept of restorative justice and its potential as an alternative to the traditional criminal justice system in 1974. The case study showed that restorative justice could be a more effective and efficient way to address crime and its impact on victims and communities. Additionally, it set a precedent for judicial authority to order VOM (Bender [1986]2019; IIRP 2012; Leung 1999).

Following these initial seeds of promise, the 1980s led to the first roots into the concrete pillars of the criminal justice system. However, restorative justice was not yet restorative justice, and convincing jurisdictions to incrementally relinquish their power and control over justice was still a far-fetched hope for these early activists.

VOM in the 1980s

The 1980s saw further expansion of VOM programs, primarily in the area of juvenile justice systems and focused on minor property crimes. Furthermore, the 1980s saw more attention and focus on including community voices in these meetings. Focus on assessing offender and victim satisfaction in the process shifted the balance towards intentionally looking at the impacts on victims, not just recidivism of offenders. While the 1970s hosted some of the initial, exploratory studies on VOM, the 1980s hosted the majority of earliest empirical studies.

Patterns in the findings of studies during this time found that variables such as the time and place of the mediation, the training and experience of facilitators, and support of victims and offenders impacted VOM outcomes. First, the timing of mediation was found to be an important factor in success or failure. Research from the 1980s found that the most effective time for VOM was as early in the prosecution process as possible, such as pre-conviction or pre-sentencing. Additionally, the location of where the VOM took place affected outcomes, for example at a government building, a nonprofit office, or other locations. Second, the qualifications and quality of facilitators directly impacted victim and offender satisfaction with VOM. Third, providing the opportunity for victims and offenders to invite friends, family members, or other advocates influenced the effectiveness of programs.

Critically, research during the 1980s was crucial to highlighting both risks and benefits of this alternative approach. This decade was still a time of strong skepticism, namely whether VOM was actually an effective complement to, or substitute for, the traditional criminal justice system. One key concern from VOM was regarding some possible risks to victims. Revictimization was among these chief concerns, which were fears of coercing victims to meet with their offender, possibly causing anything from discomfort to retraumatization. In addition to revictimization, skeptics of VOM were concerned at the extant shortage of victim support and felt that resources may better be spent elsewhere. Lastly, on the offender's side, some feared that offenders would simply capitalize on VOM as a means to mitigate their consequences or become defensive, or outright aggressive, towards victims and/or their families.

Research in VOM in the 1980s also helped establish a framework and understanding of the potential of this model of problem solving. The effectiveness of VOM in resolving conflicts and feeling harms between victims, offenders, and the community was consistently proven from this decade of research.

Research in the 1980s

The 1980s saw a number of research studies which evaluated and validated some of the earliest VOM programs in North America. Again, as mentioned above, there are simply too many studies to include in this short chapter. It is also important to note that in the 1980s specific statutes for VOM within the restorative justice approach were not yet signed into law. Research during this time was still based on small-scale pilot studies and community initiatives.

- "Victim offender reconciliation: An incarceration substitute" (1982) by Howard Zehr and Mark Umbreit found that victim offender reconciliation programs served as an effective substitute to incarceration and are enhanced when integrated with other services like counseling and group therapy.

- "Victim Offender Mediation – Conflict Resolution and Restitution" (1985) by Mark Umbreit explored the impacts of VOM in Indiana and found that VOM was effective in incurring offenders to take accountability and allow victims to voice the impacts on their lives.

- *Victim Meets Offender: An Evaluation of Victim-Offender Reconciliation Programs* (1985) by Robert Coates and John Gehm assesses three Indiana VORP and finds the impacts of social pressures on changing behavior.

- "Victim offender mediation: A national survey" (1986) by Mark Umbreit measured the number of VORP-style mediation programs throughout the United States. Survey results indicated over 50 programs which used different titles from VORP but used similar methods.

- "Mediation of victim offender conflict" (1988) by Mark Umbreit reviewed the literature on victim offender mediation and identified key issues and concerns related to the practice. The study reviewed that while mediation can be effective in resolving conflicts and reducing recidivism, it is important to carefully screen participants and provide appropriate support services alongside VOM.

- "Crime victims seek fairness, not revenge: Towards restorative justice" (1989) by Mark Umbreit counters the public narrative of victims as wanting retributive sanctions for offenders and highlights victims' desires to have the opportunity to talk with their offender(s).

VOM in the 1990s

The 1990s led to a number of policy changes throughout the United States and Canada including the Oregon Youth Accountability Act of 1995, the New Jersey Community Justice Act of 1999, and others and led to the further establishment of a legal framework and funding for restorative justice programs (Pavelka 2016). In Canada in 1997, Saskatchewan also passed a law which allowed victims and offenders to participate in a VOM (Pavelka forthcoming).

With 20 years of momentum pushing restorative practices into public discourse from works such as Howard Zehr's pivotal book *Changing Lenses*, the American Bar Association endorsed VOM. A year later in 1995, the National Organization for Victim Assistance further legitimized restorative justice and established a second foothold in the legal landscape (Young 1995).

Alongside the increase in public legitimacy of restorative justice, the quantity and diversity of research programs exponentially rose based on studies conducted during this time. These firmly entrenched restorative justice as an alternative form of punishment and as an appropriate way to include victims and the community in the justice process.

The 1990s were also a time where restorative justice programs began entering new settings, such as schools. VOM notably is the most evidence-based practice of restorative justice, but the importance of the circle process in these settings must also be acknowledged. While this chapter does not focus on circles specifically, circle processes during the 1990s are often thought of as one of the core restorative justice methods.

Lastly, the sheer number of restorative justice practitioners and programs exponentially grew during the 1990s. Programs and restorative justice practitioners found support from both offender and victim advocates who often felt frustrated by the limitations of the criminal justice system. Alongside the growth of research on VOM programs, this desire for a better way to do justice greatly increased restorative justice's profile as a possible and relevant alternative.

Research in the 1990s

The 1990s had a number of key restorative justice studies, which primarily focused on the use of VOM. Many empirical studies completed during the 1990s laid the basis for many programs and organizations that continue to work today, including the Center for Restorative Justice and Peacemaking (1994), the Center for Justice and Peacebuilding (1999), and the National Association of Community and Restorative Justice (NACRJ 1999).

Notably, *Changing Lenses: A New Focus for Crime and Justice* (1990) by Howard Zehr was published and provided one of the first comprehensive explorations of restorative justice as a different form of justice. This work was pivotal in bringing restorative justice into public discourse as a means of shifting away from retribution justice and towards healing harms caused by crime.

- "Mediated Victim-Offender Restitution Agreements: An Exploratory Analysis of Factors Related to Victim Participation" (1990) by John Gehm found that victims were more likely to participate in VOM for misdemeanors over felonies.

- "Minnesota mediation center produces positive results" (1991) by Mark Umbreit found that the victims and offenders were pleased with the quality of the program and the ability to meet and discuss the harm.

- "The Impact of Mediating Victim Offender Conflict: An Analysis of Programs in Four States of the U.S." (1992) by Mark Umbreit and Robert Coates reported data on 868 crime victims and offenders and found that offenders and victims were satisfied with the program and had lower recidivism and restitution completion rates for VOM participants.

- *Public Opinion Research Challenges Perception of Widespread Public Demand for Harsher Punishment* (1992) by Kay Pranis and Mark Umbreit found that 82 percent of citizens in Minnesota would consider participating in a VOM program for property crimes.

- "Crime victims and offenders in mediation: An emerging area of social work practice" (1993) by Mark Umbreit highlighted the importance of considering restorative justice within areas of social work practice.

- *Victim Meets Offender: The Impact of Restorative Justice and Mediation* (1994) by Mark Umbreit, Robert Coates, and Boris Kalanj found in four states that VOM was effective for victims and offenders and specifically helped victims get answers to their questions with less fear of retaliation.

- "The effect of victim-offender mediation on severity of reoffense" (1995) by William Nugent and Jeffery Paddock found that VORP juvenile participants were less likely to offend within one year and recidivism offenses were less severe.
- "Rethinking the sanctioning function in juvenile court: Retributive or restorative responses to youth crime" (1995) by Gordon Bazemore and Mark Umbreit highlighted sanction shortcomings and argued for changes within juvenile courts.
- "Restorative family group conferences: Differing models and guidelines for practice" (1996) by Mark Umbreit and Howard Zehr highlighted some similarities and differences of VOM and FGC.
- "Restorative justice through victim-offender mediation: A multi-site assessment" (1998) by Mark Umbreit found general reductions in recidivism and increases in victim satisfaction and offender accountability from multiple sites.
- "Restorative Justice: An Evaluation of the Restorative Resolutions Project" (1998) by James Bonta, Jennifer Rooney, and Susanne Wallace-Capretta in Canada found lower recidivism and increased payments or restitution.
- "National survey of victim-offender mediation programs in the United States" (1999) by Mark Umbreit and Daniel Greenwood found 45 percent of VOM programs in the US offered services strictly to juveniles and 46 percent to juveniles and adults, while only 9 percent were strictly for adults. They also found that 43 percent were hosted in non-profit organizations and 33 percent in justice systems. Seventy-eight percent of cases had preparatory meetings.
- "Participation in victim-offender mediation and reoffense: Successful replications?" (2001) by William Nugent, Mark Umbreit, Lizabeth Wiinamaki, and Jeff Paddock found a 32

percent reduction in recidivism of those who participated in VOM.

VOM in the 2000s

Alongside the continued growth of restorative justice programs, organizations, research, and conceptual development, VOM also increased its involvement within different criminal justice systems. Being used both in the juvenile and adult criminal justice systems, VOM and restorative justice principles further entered into school, workplaces, and other settings.

Generally, during this time VOM was still primarily focused on lower-level property offenses and generally programs were not well funded. For juvenile cases, VOM continued to be increasingly used and research consistently found promising results for recidivism and process satisfaction. However, some research during this time period found VOM to not be effective, such as in some cases of intimate partner violence and cases of severe violence.

Research in the 2000s

Research during the 2000s continued to focus on understanding why victims choose to participate, the use of VOM in cases of severe violence in multiple contexts, and the increased codification of restorative justice into policy and law in states across the US (Pavelka 2016).

- "Homicide survivors meet the offender prior to execution" (2000) by Mark Umbreit and Betty Vos interviewed victim family members about their mediations with death row inmates and found the dialogue surpassed victim family member expectations and aided their healing journeys.

- "The Effectiveness of Restorative Practice: A Meta Analysis" (2001) by Jeff Latimer, Craig Dowden, and Danielle Muise reviewed existing research and found a pattern of restorative justice as a more effective approach. It also highlighted self-selection bias that is inherent in a restorative justice voluntary process and offered motivation measures as a means to mitigate.

- "Juvenile Victim Offender Mediation in Six Oregon Counties" (2001) by Mark Umbreit, Robert Coates, and Barbara Vos found that 91 percent of victims felt their participation was voluntary and offenders felt less so. These findings suggest that programs may have been inadvertently coercing participation.

- "Participation in victim offender mediation and reoffense: Successful replications?" (2001) by William Nugent, Mark Umbreit, Lizabeth Wiinamaki, and Jeff Paddock reviewed research including 1,298 juveniles and calculated a 32 percent lower recidivism rate for VOM juvenile participants.

- "Offender conferencing: Washington County, Minnesota Community Justice Program" (2003) by Robert Coates, Heather Burns, and Mark Umbreit found that individuals representing businesses harmed by crime were more likely to participate than the individually impacted victims. It also found that victims chose not to participate because of safety, pressure from family or friends, and not wanting to help the offender. Additionally, individual jurisdiction pressures may also impact victims' decisions to participate.

- *Facing Violence: The Path of Restorative Justice and Dialogue* (2003) by Mark Umbreit, Betty Vos, Robert Coates, and Katherine Brown chronicled the earliest correctional VOM programs in the United States in Ohio and Texas. Enabling victims and offenders of serious violent cases to meet face to face, this research validated the ability of VOM to foster emotional healing and increased accountability of offenders.

- "An analysis of state statutory provisions for victim offender mediation" (2004) by Elizabeth Lightfoot and Mark Umbreit measured statutory provisions in the US in the early 2000s and found 29 states with VOM statutes of varying degrees of comprehensiveness.

- "Restorative justice at work: Examining the impact of restorative justice resolutions on juvenile recidivism" (2007) by Nancy

Rodriguez found that juveniles who participated in restorative justice programs were less likely to recidivate.

VOM from the 2010s to today

Over the past decade, VOM and restorative justice have continued to steadily grow with some areas receiving newfound attention. COVID-19, for example, greatly increased the familiarity and utility of video conferencing's role in VOM. Originally used out of necessity to prevent the spread of disease, video conferencing also enables greater accessibility and inclusion within the VOM process.

Video conferencing, such as Zoom, enabled VOM facilitators more flexibility and greater opportunities for preparatory sessions with individual offenders and victims. However, conducting VOM individual sessions and the joint dialogue virtually can be considered less personal. On the other hand, allowing individuals to connect from their personal space in their own homes may increase their comfort.

Research from the 2010s to today

Researchers continue their relevant and impactful work as part of the evolution of VOM and restorative justice dialogue in the present day, including the following examples:

- *Restorative Justice Dialogue: An Essential Guide for Research and Practice* (2010) by Mark Umbreit and Marilyn Armour is a comprehensive summary of research and practice considerations.

- "Exploring communities of facilitators: Orientations toward restorative justice" (2013) by Gregory Paul and Ian Borton found that facilitators seemed to orient towards four types of facilitation: (1) facilitation as advocacy; (2) facilitation as counseling; (3) facilitation as healing; and (4) facilitation as community peacemaking.

- "Patterns of victim marginalization in victim-offender mediation: Some lessons learned" (2013) by Jung Choi, Michael Gilbert, and Diane Green found several patterns of victim marginalization including not being prepared thoroughly, behavioral pressure from facilitators, and feelings of intimidation by offenders and/or offender support persons.

- "Restorative justice in the States: A national assessment of legislation and policy" (2016) by Sandra Pavelka found that 38 states articulate restorative justice in statute or code. Common language is pervasive across jurisdictions. The state of Colorado, examined as a case study in this research, has been on a progressive path to implement systematic reform by integrating restorative justice in law, policies, and practices. Pavelka's career research in restorative justice law and policy is noteworthy.

- "Beliefs about victim-offender conferences: Factors influencing victim-offender engagement" (2017) by Gregory Paul and William Schenck-Hamlin explored expectations of victims who participated in VOM and how perceptions about the criminal justice system, anticipated emotions, supports, and desire foreclosure impacted their participation.

- *Violence, Restorative Justice, and Forgiveness* (2018) by Marilyn Armour and Mark Umbreit explored the role of forgiveness within VOM through intensive interviews with victims and victim family members of severe violence. The authors detailed the benefits and challenges of using restorative justice as a process to elicit the energy of forgiveness.

- "The effect of school conditions on the use of restorative justice in schools" (2018) by Allison Payne and Kelly Welch examined school conditions' influences on the use of restorative justice. They found that larger schools, and schools with predominantly Black, Hispanic, or socially disadvantaged students, were more likely to use peer mediation, and predominantly white schools were less likely to use restorative justice.

Conclusion

Victim offender mediation and restorative justice research over the past five decades has ebbed and flowed. The 1980s to 2000s saw an increase of empirical research being published and reviewed, while in the last decade, the restorative justice movement has seen considerably less empirical publications on the effectiveness of the VOM. Restorative justice practitioners and researchers have benefited for decades from this initial research, but the context of today's criminal justice zeitgeist has changed with new technologies, policies, and realities facing the next generations of restorative justice advocates.

The development of research approaches and methods of VOM and other restorative justice practices, such as circles, must keep pace with new demands from criminal justice partners and communities. Every year the foundational research of the 1980s to 2000s becomes more and more dated and subject to relevance critiques. Today, there is no shortage of meta-analysis, scoping reviews, and other literature reviews. Again, while these allow for new insights into patterns from older studies, continued development is needed.

Restorative justice scholars established in their fields must extend and expand their thinking beyond their immediate circles. Initiating mentorships and coalitions and looking beyond our borders will help to continue the evolution of VOM and restorative justice. Readers are encouraged to look to the past to understand some of the origins of restorative justice, but at the same time they must look towards the future of the next decade of restorative justice research.

References

Armour, M. and Umbreit, M. (2018) *Violence, Restorative Justice, and Forgiveness: Dyadic Forgiveness and Energy Shifts in Restorative Justice Dialogue*. London: Jessica Kingsley Publishers.

Bazemore, G.S. (2000a) "Rock and roll, restorative justice, and the continuum of the real world: A response to 'purism' in operationalizing restorative justice." *Contemporary Justice Review 3*, 4, 459–477.

Bazemore, G. (2000b) "Community justice and a vision of collective efficacy: The case of restorative conferencing." *Criminal Justice 3*, 225–297. www.ojp.gov/criminal_justice2000/vol_3/03f.pdf

Bazemore, G. and Umbreit, M. (1995) "Rethinking the sanctioning function in juvenile court: Retributive or restorative responses to youth crime." *Crime and Delinquency 41*, 3, 296–316. doi.org/10.1177/0011128795041003002

Bender, J. ([1986]2019) "The Birthplace of Restorative Justice." *Mennonite Central Committee Peace Section Newsletter* 16, no. 1.

Bonta, J., Rooney, J., and Wallace-Capretta, S. (1998) "Restorative Justice: An Evaluation of the Restorative Resolutions Project." Ottawa: Canada Solicitor General.

Braithwaite, J. (2004) "Restorative justice and de-professionalization." *The Good Society 13*, 1, 28–31. doi.org/10.1353/gso.2004.0023

Center for Justice and Peacebuilding (1999) "What we do." https://emu.edu/cjp/about

Center for Restorative Justice and Peacemaking (1994) "About." https://rjp.d.umn.edu/about-0

Choi, J.J., Gilbert, M.J., and Green, D.L. (2013) "Patterns of victim marginalization in victim-offender mediation: Some lessons learned." *Crime, Law and Social Change 59*, 113–132. doi.org/10.1007/s10611-012-9382-1

Coates, R.B., Burns, H., and Umbreit, M.S. (2003) "Offender conferencing: Washington County, Minnesota Community Justice Program." Minneapolis, MN: Center for Restorative Justice and Peacemaking. www.researchgate.net/publication/237517890_Victim_Participation_in_Victim_Offender_Conferencing_Washington_County_Minnesota_Community_Justice_Program

Coates, R.B. and Gehm, J. (1985) *Victim Meets Offender: An Evaluation of Victim-offender Reconciliation Programs*. Valparaiso, IN: PACT Institute of Justice.

Gehm, J. (1990) "Mediated Victim-Offender Restitution Agreements: An Exploratory Analysis of Factors Related to Victim Participation." In B. Galaway and J. Hudson (eds) *Criminal Justice, Restitution, and Reconciliation*. Monsey, NY: Criminal Justice Press.

Hansen, T. and Umbreit, M. (2018) "State of knowledge: Four decades of victim offender mediation research and practice: The evidence." *Conflict Resolution Quarterly 36*, 2, 99–113. doi.org/10.1002/crq.21234

IIRP (International Institute for Restorative Practices) (2012) "Mark Yantzi Talks About First Case Where Offenders Met Victims." www.iirp.edu/news/mark-yantzi-talks-about-first-case-where-offenders-met-victims

Latimer, J., Dowden, C., and Muise, D. (2001) "The Effectiveness of Restorative Practice: A Meta-Analysis." Department of Justice, Canada: Research and Statistics Division Methodological Series.

Leung, M. (1999) "The Origins of Restorative Justice." www.cfcj-fcjc.org/sites/default/files/docs/hosted/17445-restorative_justice.pdf

Lewis, T. and Umbreit, M. (2015) "A humanistic approach to mediation and dialogue: An evolving transformative practice." *Conflict Resolution Quarterly 33*, 1, 3–17. doi.org/10.1002/crq.21130

Lightfoot, E. and Umbreit, M. (2004) "An analysis of state statutory provisions for victim offender mediation." *Criminal Justice Policy Review 15*, 4, 418–436. doi.org/10.1177/0887403403260953

McCold, P. (2000) "Toward a holistic vision of restorative juvenile justice: A reply to the maximalist model." *Contemporary Justice Review 3*, 4, 357–414. www.researchgate.net/publication/292733753_Toward_a_holistic_vision_of_restorative_juvenile_justice_A_reply_to_the_maximalist_model

NACRJ (National Association of Community and Restorative Justice) (1999) "About." https://nacrj.org

Nugent, W. and Paddock, J. (1995) "The effect of victim-offender mediation on severity of reoffense." *Mediation Quarterly 12*, 4, 353–367. doi.org/10.1002/crq.3900120408

Nugent, W., Umbreit, M., Wiinamaki, L., and Paddock, J. (2001) "Participation in victim offender mediation and reoffense: Successful replications?" *Research on Social Work Practice 11*, 1, 5-23. doi.org/10.1177/104973150101100101

Paul, G.D. and Borton, I.M. (2013) "Exploring communities of facilitators: Orientations toward restorative justice." *Conflict Resolution Quarterly 31*, 2, 189-218. doi.org/10.1002/crq.21073

Paul, G.D. and Schenck-Hamlin, W.J. (2017) "Beliefs about victim-offender conferences: Factors influencing victim-offender engagement." *Conflict Resolution Quarterly 35*, 1, 47-72. doi.org/10.1002/crq.21190

Pavelka, S. (forthcoming) "Public Policy and Legislation: International Comparisons." *Encyclopedia of Social Justice in Education.*

Pavelka, S. (2016) "Restorative justice in the States: A national assessment of legislation and policy." *Justice Policy Journal 13*, 2, 1-26.

Payne, A. and Welch, K. (2018) "The effect of school conditions on the use of restorative justice in schools." *Youth Violence and Juvenile Justice 16*, 2, 224-240. doi.org/10.1177/1541204016681414

Pranis, K. and Umbreit, M. (1992) *Public Opinion Research Challenges Perception of Widespread Public Demand for Harsher Punishment.* Minneapolis, MN: Citizens Council.

Rodriguez, N. (2007) "Restorative justice at work: Examining the impact of restorative justice resolutions on juvenile recidivism." *Crime & Delinquency 53*, 3, 355-379. https://doi.org/10.1177/0011128705285983

Takagi, P. and Shank, G. (2004) "Critique of restorative justice." *Social Justice 31*, 3, 97, 147-163. www.jstor.org/stable/29768262

Umbreit, M. ([1978]2006) "Community Based Corrections in Indiana – A Humanistic Perspective." www.ojp.gov/ncjrs/virtual-library/abstracts/community-based-corrections-indiana-humanistic-perspective

Umbreit, M.S. (1985) "Victim Offender Mediation – Conflict Resolution and Restitution." www.ojp.gov/ncjrs/virtual-library/abstracts/victim-offender-mediation-conflict-resolution-and-restitution

Umbreit, M.S. (1986) "Victim offender mediation: A national survey." *Federal Probation 50*, 4, 53-56. https://heinonline.org/HOL/P?h=hein.journals/fedpro50&i=355

Umbreit, M.S. (1988) "Mediation of victim offender conflict." *Journal of Dispute Resolution 5.* https://heinonline.org/HOL/P?h=hein.journals/jdisres1988&i=91

Umbreit, M.S. (1989) "Crime victims seeking fairness, not revenge: Toward restorative justice." *Federal Probation 53*, 3, 52-57. https://heinonline.org/HOL/P?h=hein.journals/fedpro53&i=250

Umbreit, M.S. (1991) "Minnesota mediation center produces positive results." *Corrections Today 53*, 5, 194-196.

Umbreit, M.S. (1993) "Crime victims and offenders in mediation: An emerging area of social work practice." *Social Work 38*, 1 (January), 69-73.

Umbreit, M.S. (1998) "Restorative justice through victim-offender mediation: A multi-site assessment." *Western Criminology Review 1*, 1 (June), 1-28.

Umbreit, M.S. (2001) *The Handbook of Victim Offender Mediation: An Essential Guide to Practice and Research.* San Francisco, CA: Jossey-Bass.

Umbreit, M.S. and Armour, M.P. (2010) *Restorative Justice Dialogue: An Essential Guide for Research and Practice.* New York: Springer Publishing Company.

Umbreit, M.S. and Coates, R.B. (1992) "The Impact of Mediating Victim Offender Conflict: An Analysis of Programs in Four States of the US." Minnesota Citizens Council on Crime and Justice. www.ojp.gov/pdffiles1/Photocopy/140289NCJRS.pdf

Umbreit, M.S., Coates, R.B., and Kalanj, B. (1994) *Victim Meets Offender: The Impact of Restorative Justice and Mediation.* Monsey, NY: Criminal Justice Press.

Umbreit, M.S., Coates, R.B., and Vos, B. (2001) "Juvenile Victim Offender Mediation in Six Oregon Counties. Final Report." Minneapolis, MN: Center for Restorative Justice and Peacemaking. https://drive.google.com/file/d/1zF_8zJNQsn8V0R6 cXYNvhohDILpE3-fS/view

Umbreit, M.S., Coates, R.B., and Vos, B. (2004) "Victim offender mediation: Three decades of practice and research." *Conflict Resolution Quarterly 22*, 1-2, 279-303. dx.doi.org/10.1002/crq.102

Umbreit, M.S. and Greenwood, J. (1999) "National survey of victim-offender mediation programs in the United States." *Mediation Quarterly 16*, 3, 235-251. doi.org/10.1002/crq.3890160304

Umbreit, M.S. and Vos, B. (2000) "Homicide survivors meet the offender prior to execution: Restorative justice through dialogue." *Homicide Studies 4*, 1, 63-87. doi.org/10.1177/1088767900004001004

Umbreit, M.S., Vos, B., Coates, R.B., and Brown, K.A. (2003) *Facing Violence: The Path of Restorative Justice and Dialogue.* Monsey, NY: Criminal Justice Press.

Umbreit, M.S. and Zehr, H. (1996) "Restorative family group conferences: Differing models and guidelines for practice." *Federal Probation 60*, 3, 24-29.

Valandra, E. and Hokšíla, W. (2020) *Colorizing Restorative Justice: Voicing Our Realities.* St. Paul, MN: Living Justice Press.

VanNess, D., Strong, K., Derby, J. and Parker, L. (2022) *Restoring Justice: An Introduction to Restorative Justice* 6th ed. New York, NY: Taylor Francis Publishing. DOI 10.4324/9781003159773

Weingart, J. (2017) "First US Victim Offender Reconciliation Program Funding at Risk." www.wfyi.org/news/articles/first-us-victim-offender-reconciliation-program-funding-at-risk

Young, M.A. (1995) *Restorative Community Justice: A Call to Action.* Washington, DC: National Organization for Victim Assistance.

Zehr, H. (1990) *Changing Lenses: A New Focus for Crime and Justice.* Scottsdale, PA: Herald Press.

Zehr, H. and Umbreit, M.S. (1982) "Victim offender reconciliation: An incarceration substitute." *Federal Probation 46*, 4, 56-63. www.ojp.gov/pdffiles1/Digitization/87801NCJRS.pdf

— Chapter 14 —

Restorative Justice and Gender-Responsive Programming

A Blended Approach for Girls and Young Women in Diversion

AGGIE PAPPAS

My first memory of Dr. Gordon Bazemore was in the early 2000s during a Juvenile Justice Advisory Board meeting, where he presented a compelling case for integrating restorative justice practices with the Children's Services Council (CSC) Broward County's Juvenile Justice Diversion Funded Programming—New Day (New Alternatives for Youth). Dr. Bazemore's passion and belief in implementing restorative justice practices to prevent and reduce juvenile delinquency were intriguing. His presentation made sense to anyone dedicated to diverting young people from the juvenile delinquency system. At the time, I was the Executive Director of Pace Center for Girls (Pace) in Broward County, Florida. I was immediately hooked and excited to see the benefits of integrating restorative justice programming into our work with girls and young women.

My subsequent encounter with Dr. Bazemore was during a restorative justice training that he and his team conducted for our new Pace Center for Girls New Day Reach diversion/civil citation counselors. In 2010, with the support of the CSC, Pace was awarded the opportunity to develop a gender-responsive diversion/civil citation program for girls to include restorative practice interventions. Through his work with Pace, Dr. Bazemore began to understand Pace's mission, program model, and impact; he was intrigued by the agency's successful history of providing gender-responsive, trauma-informed, and strength-based work to prevent and divert girls from the juvenile delinquency system. For Dr. Bazemore, the theory and practice of juvenile justice reform and restorative justice aligned with the concepts and methods supported by the advocates and researchers of gender-responsive theory. As collaboration efforts grew, Dr. Bazemore became even more supportive of our juvenile justice prevention and intervention work with girls. Eventually, he invited me as a guest lecturer to his restorative justice classes to share how Pace facilitated restorative justice principles into our programming with girls.

A few years later, I received an unexpected call from Dr. Bazemore. It was the summer of 2010. He needed an adjunct professor for the Women and Criminal Justice elective course at Florida Atlantic University. In his positive, "glass is always full" kind of way, Dr. Bazemore was pleasantly compelling and encouraging and not a bit concerned that classes were starting in a few weeks and that there was no prepping, syllabus, or time. Likewise, he was not worried that I had not lectured before (only as a guest speaker) and that I was a social worker, not a criminologist. His belief in my work and his subtle yet unyielding encouragement made it impossible for me to say "No."

In the end, and after many hours of prep work for the course, it all worked out, and I was better having had the experience. Dr. Bazemore's encouragement and belief in me helped me expand my skills, knowledge, and mindset; as someone educated and trained in psychology and social work, I came to acquire profound respect and interest in the science of criminology, and women, social justice, and restorative justice work—all thanks to Gordon and his strong belief in me and the mission of Pace. I will forever be grateful for his encouragement, friendship, and passion for wanting to make the world a better place through restorative justice and healing circles.

Introduction

Pace Center for Girls (Pace), established in 1985, serves as the premier provider of gender-responsive prevention, intervention, and diversion services to at-risk girls throughout Florida. Pace academic and social services are designed for girls and young women, recognizing their unique needs and how they interact in their communities. With 21 centers in Florida and 19 Reach Counseling programs in Florida, Georgia, and South Carolina, Pace understands that, for girls to change their lives, they and their families must have a voice in shaping their present and future. Thus, to achieve Pace's vision—to create a world where all girls and young women have power in a just and equitable society—Pace applies gender-responsive, trauma-informed, and strength-based individualized practices to improve girls' self-efficacy and advocacy skills and their relationships with peers, family members, and adults in their communities (Pace 2020). Restorative justice programming is one practice that Pace strongly believes allows girls and women to find their voices and improve their lives. Thus, since 2009, Pace has successfully integrated restorative justice into its Reach Counseling program to divert girls from the juvenile justice system in Broward County, Florida.

Restorative justice programming logically made sense as a critical element in designing a diversion program for girls. Restorative justice's foundational theory and practice are grounded in repairing, strengthening, and healing relationships (Zehr 2014). Grounded in relational theory, gender-responsive theory is the belief that women develop a sense of self and self-worth when their actions arise from and lead back to connections with others. Gender responsiveness means paying attention to the unique needs of females, valuing their perspectives, respecting their experiences, understanding developmental differences between girls and boys and women and men, and ultimately empowering girls and women (United Nations Children's Fund 2017). From a humanistic perspective, these two theories and practices are rooted in building, improving, and restoring relationships and are valuable and necessary tools for designing effective juvenile justice prevention and intervention programming for adolescent girls and young women.

This chapter will use a practical lens to describe how Pace has blended restorative justice and gender-responsive approaches by developing a girl-focused, gender-specific juvenile diversion and civil citation program in Broward County, Florida. It will also explore the connections between restorative justice practices and gender-responsive programming to reduce recidivism while improving girls' lives, supporting long-term positive outcomes and a healing experience benefiting the community.

Aligning Restorative Justice with Gender-Responsive Approaches

Working to divert marginalized girls and young women faced with intersectional factors related to race, gender, sexual orientation, and poverty, and personal, familial, and societal challenges, can often make building healthy and trusting relationships difficult. As part of this relationship-building process, girls need time to feel safe and free of shame, judgment, and trauma. As a result, the journey toward healing and empowerment can be arduous and challenging. Unfortunately, without proper support from trained professionals, guidance, and reliant systems of care, girls are often relegated to navigating systems designed for their adolescent male counterparts. Furthermore, girls identified as at risk for entering the juvenile justice system or those who may already be at the onset of juvenile delinquency involvement, including first-time or low-end offenders, often struggle in systems that do not offer gender-responsive, trauma-responsive, and strength-based approaches. Girls, in short, experience childhood and adolescence trauma heavily influenced by their gender. Therefore, it is impossible to discuss their problems, criminal behavior, and what they encounter in the juvenile justice system without regard to gender in all its aspects (Chesney-Lind and Shelden 2014).

Women and girls need to experience an environment of growth-fostering relationships based on respect, mutuality, and empowerment (Covington 2008). When exploring girls and their relational nature, sadly, the focus often turns to "aggression," whereby girls are depicted as "mean, manipulative and angry." These labels lead most adults in authority to judge and criticize their behaviors when they should instead be working to understand the underlying trauma that creates these tendencies—acknowledging that girls in the juvenile justice system are more likely than boys to have experienced sexual violence, extreme family conflict, and child maltreatment (Bright and Jonson-Reid 2008). Fostering safe spaces where girls are coached and guided by peers and adults who can role model trusting relationships built on mutual regard and respect helps to create positive experiences and transferable skills for healthier relationships in the future. At Pace, team members described their relationships with girls as central to implementing a gender-responsive approach, and their answer aligned with gender-responsive theory about the relational needs of girls (Treskon, Millensky and Freedman 2017). These team members agree that "girls are relational," and without trust, there is no relationship. This theory holds that relationships are central to girls' lives and self-esteem (Gilligan 1982).

To support a girl's relational domain, Pace creates a culture that is sensitive to the needs of girls as a framework for providing safety with a relationship-focused environment. Program staff members emphasize fostering girls' strengths while understanding how the effects of trauma may influence the girls' responses and behavior (Treskon et al. 2017). Understanding each girl's circumstances, past experiences, and triggers is critical to forming trusting relationships that encourage opportunities for growth and change.

Establishing spaces and programs where girls can feel safe is paramount in creating an atmosphere for positive change. Gender responsiveness means creating an environment through site selection, staff selection, program development, content, and material that reflects an understanding of the realities of the lives of women and girls while addressing their strengths and challenges (Covington and Bloom 2003). Fostering an environment devoted to helping marginalized girls grow and develop allows them to find their inner strength, voice, and power. With proper timing and a safe space to test and re-test the trust of professionals, a slow gravitational pull toward healthier relationships allows girls to take chances, build confidence, explore their inner voice, to gain control of their circumstances and destiny. The foundational principles of gender responsivity include: (1) acknowledging that gender matters; (2) creating an environment based on safety, respect, and dignity; (3) developing policies, practices, and programs that are relational and promote healthy connections; (4) addressing substance abuse, trauma, and mental health (utilizing a comprehensive/integrated approach); (5) providing opportunities to improve socioeconomic conditions; and (6) emphasizing community supervision (when possible) utilizing collaborative reintegration services (Bloom, Owen and Covington 2003). This level of empowerment also develops a girl's social and emotional growth, strengthening a positive internal-value system where she can contemplate and take ownership and accountability for her actions. Typically, girls are better able than boys to accept responsibility for their harmful actions towards others and confront the difficulties they have experienced in their interpersonal relationships when they are allowed to connect with service providers (Zavlek and Maniglia 2007).

The benefits associated with restorative justice programming for girls facing entry into the juvenile justice system are numerous. A restorative approach promotes pro-social behaviors through the development of social and emotional skills (e.g., responsibility), listening skills, peaceful conflict resolution, positive interpersonal relationships, and trust, and greater collaboration between schools, police, justice system, and families (Lodi et al. 2022). These tools work to develop long-lasting transferable skills whereby girls can better navigate relationships and conflict while building self-efficacy, independence, and wellness. Decision-making, resiliency skills, and the bolstering of protective factors help reduce risks associated with juvenile delinquency. Other restorative justice benefits for youth in the early onset of delinquency involvement include the reduction of future offenses, understanding how their actions have affected other people, taking responsibility for the harm inflicted on others, and outcomes to help to repair harm while gaining closure for all (Zehr 2014).

Integrating restorative justice intervention programs for girls as a core element in a voluntary diversion program allows accountability and repair of relationships through empathy and healing for all involved parties. Restorative justice provides social justice through healing encounters between victims and offenders within a community context (Presser and Gaarder 2003). Thus, restorative justice programming for girls who have experienced both the role of victim and offender can help create pro-social communication, empathy, healing, and acceptance. Because of the importance of intimacy and relationships to the growing adolescent girl, restorative strategies offer an ideal gendered form of conflict resolution (Van Wormer and Bartollas 2014). These opportunities for girls not only divert their juvenile delinquency charges but provide the benefits of restorative justice programming and address their challenges and trauma. It is both a plausible and a straightforward means to lower recidivism rates by reducing a girl's propensity to reoffend.

The alignment of gender-responsive approaches with restorative justice principles would create even better chances for girls and young women to repair the harm done and restore relationships with their peers, family, and community while developing empathy and healing strained and broken relationships.

For these reasons, it was necessary to build a diversionary program with a restorative justice component where girls can address their traumatic experiences, abuse, and neglect with trained professionals who offer unconditional regard, trust-building, and acceptance in a safe and accepting environment.

The Pace Center for Girls Model

The Pace Center for Girls logic model recognizes that girls have a unique way of relating to the world and champions services promoting the development of girls and young women as capable, strong, self-directed, and critical contributors to the wellbeing of their communities. The model supports systems of care geared towards the healthy development of each girl by strengthening protective factors and cultivating positive life skills. From its inception, Pace has adopted a holistic approach and acknowledges a unique combination of risk and protective factors that informs the developmental path for each girl.

The Pace model provides an effective alternative for girls pulled into the delinquency and dependency systems by helping them decrease high-risk behaviors and find pathways to success at home, in school, and in their communities. With the mission of providing girls and young women with an opportunity for a better future through education, counseling, training, and advocacy, Pace values all girls by believing each one deserves an opportunity to find her voice, achieve her potential, and celebrate a life defined by responsibility, dignity, serenity, and grace. By strengthening protective factors, girls can empower themselves and improve future generations. Pace's approach is guided by a strong organizational culture that adheres to its mission, values, and guiding principles. Combining these practices improves a girl's self-efficacy and advocacy skills, and relationships with peers, family members/caregivers, and their communities (Benítez 2021).

Pace incorporates gender-responsive programming into all services with a focus on safety and relationships, an emphasis on recognizing and building on girls' strengths, and an awareness of the effects of trauma. Girls served by Pace likely have experienced high levels of risk factors associated with delinquency and Adverse Childhood Experiences (ACEs). For these reasons, Pace focuses on the intersection of socio-emotional health and education. These practices improve girls' self-efficacy and advocacy skills and their relationships with peers, family members, and adults in their communities.

Girls who attend Pace tend to come from low-income families, often struggle with school, and have a range of other health, safety, and delinquency related risk factors. Therefore, Pace's prevention and intervention model intentionally meet girls' unique academic, behavioral, and mental health needs by providing social-emotional learning, life-skills coaching, career readiness training, and behavioral, therapeutic, and cognitive behavioral health services.

The use of multi-dimensional gender-responsive approaches, the Friedman Trans-Theoretical Model Theory of Change, and the Pace Values and Principles offers interventions to address the unique needs of girls (Treskon et al. 2017). In addition, the five behavioral change levels—including Pre-Contemplation, Contemplation, Planning, Action, and Maintenance—are integrated into individual sessions and treatment plan reviews. By using these behavioral change levels, counselors discuss and explore the progress of the care plan and personal goal objectives with each girl.

Pace's long-established values and principles include: (1) Honor the female spirit; (2) Focus on strengths; (3) Act with integrity and positive intent; (4) Embrace growth and change; (5) Value the wisdom of time; (6) Exhibit courage; (7) Seek excellence; (8) Create partnerships; and (9) Invest in the future, and are all utilized as a theoretical framework to improve girls' decision-making skills. The primary interventions—improving girls' social skills, emotional skills, and social support—are grounded in promoting healthy adolescent girl development within six domains (i.e., physical, emotional, intellectual, relational, sexual, and spiritual).

The focus of care planning and intervention strategies is to reduce risk factors, bolster protective factors, address trauma, and improve behavioral health and resilience, thus safeguarding the girls and restoring public health and safety. Intervention includes wrap-around case management services, including monitoring school attendance/performance and re-offending charges to ensure supervision is built into the program. To keep girls and their families motivated and engaged, the program also offers enrichment activities to foster healthy family functioning and educate prevention; intervention presentations from community partners addressing risk factors and current trends in the community are provided in group sessions.

For services to effectively fit into local systems of care, Pace understands the need to adopt participatory approaches and use "real-time" data to generate insights about our programs. Therefore, Pace engages girls and their families in activities and services that allow them, in developmentally appropriate ways, to learn about and tackle challenges impacting their lives and communities. While at Pace, girls and families engage in surveys, interviews, focus groups, town halls, and councils that provide opportunities for self-advocacy. Girls also provide input about our data collection methods. Their experiences and insights help us learn what works and what could be improved in implementing our programs and identify the local, state, and federal policies and practices that might need reform (Benítez 2021).

As a result of their work with girls, Pace is recognized as a national model for reducing recidivism and improving school success, employment, and self-sufficiency amongst girls by the Annie

E. Casey Foundation, Children's Defense Fund, National Mental Health Association, National Council on Crime and Delinquency, and the Office of Juvenile Justice and Delinquency Prevention, US Department of Justice. Through a proven, evidence-based model, Pace has changed the life trajectory of more than 40,000 girls and is recognized as one of the nation's leading advocates for girls (Pace Center for Girls 2008).

Designing a Girl-Focused Diversionary Programming with the Integration of Restorative Justice Interventions

In 2009, Pace Center for Girls in Broward County established the Pace Reach Counseling program, a community-based program offering gender-responsive, trauma-informed, and strength-based counseling and therapeutic services to girls aged 11 to 18 seeking individual, family, and group therapy, in addition to its academic and counseling day programs. Adolescent girls eligible for services exhibit multiple health, safety, and delinquency risk factors, such as poor academic performance, exposure to abuse or violence, truancy, risky sexual behavior, juvenile justice involvement, domestic violence, human trafficking, and substance abuse. The core services of Pace's Reach Counseling program include individual, family, and group counseling and therapy. In addition, Reach therapists, counselors, and care managers focus on delivering support services to address behaviors, feelings, and thoughts contributing to problems and challenges, and increasing pro-social behaviors, problem-solving abilities, and personal responsibility to achieve overall wellness. Soon after the inception of the Pace Reach Counseling program in 2009, the State Attorney's Office of Broward County adolescent division recognized the program's success as a viable option to refer adolescent girls in need of therapy, counseling, and care management support services while engaged in a voluntary judicially supported diversionary program. This started Pace's journey of offering structured, gender-responsive diversionary programming tailored for girls identified as first-time or low-end offenders.

As a result of the successful diversionary pilot program, in October

2010, the Children's Services Council (CSC) of Broward County funded the New Day Alternatives for Youth (New Day) diversionary programming to reduce deep-end involvement in the juvenile delinquency system by providing structurally prescribed services that divert low-risk girl offenders from adjudication while reducing recidivism rates of low-risk juvenile offenders, thus preventing the escalation of juvenile crime. The program service components include a comprehensive bio-psychosocial assessment; pre/post resiliency scale surveying; care goal (treatment) planning; individual, family, and group counseling sessions; case management; service learning/community services projects; parent/caregiver educational sessions; and restorative justice conferencing/circles. In addition, since domestic violence-related charges are prevalent with justice-involved adolescent girls, interventions focusing on anger management, building healthy family relationships, conflict resolution, and family communication techniques are program requirements. The top frequent charges presented for girls referred to diversion and civil citation programming include petty theft, loitering, domestic violence, and battery.

Pace Reach New Day diversion/civil citation services were modeled after Pace's evidence-proven continuum of care service model. To establish a positive working relationship with the girl and her family/caregiver, and depending on need, diversion counselors would need to access emergency services, including medical, food, clothing, and transportation assistance (e.g., bus passes at no cost and gift cards for gas). The overall desired outcome was for cases/charges to be closed successfully, for girls to desist from future juvenile justice involvement, to expunge records when plausible, and for the girls not to re-offend after program completion.

It is important to note that the Reach New Day diversionary program was structured to provide services and outcomes like the other community-based programs funded by the Broward County Children's Services Council; however, to be successful, the method, approach, and strategy require the program to deliver services with a gender-responsive approach, tailored to the unique and holistic needs of girls. As such, the milieu would need to be safe, positive, inviting, and conducive to girls feeling accepted and welcomed.

The intent was that blending restorative practice interventions into Pace's methodology would divert girls from juvenile delinquency and thus reduce recidivism while positively impacting their wellbeing, life trajectory, communities, and society. In addition, restorative justice would help to resolve conflict, restore human connections, and build partnerships for a vulnerable sub-group of girls facing the possibility of long-term involvement with the juvenile justice system.

The expected outcomes for girls enrolled in this diversionary program include the following: complete all diversion program requirements and services, increase protective factors associated with delinquency, decrease risk factors associated with delinquency, experience no new violations during program participation, and commit no new law violations within 3, 6, and 12 months post-program check-ins. As part of the enrollment into the diversionary program, girls and their parents/caregivers are provided with a comprehensive orientation of the program, including information on how and why restorative justice conferencing would be an integral part of the experience. Once enrolled, through the support and encouragement of a diversion counselor, girls discuss their charges or citations, explore the motive, reflect on the experience, and consider their feelings and those of their victims. Analyzing the tangible loss, fear, and possible trauma experienced by the victim and the community helps foster empathy and connectedness for the offender. This healing process requires time for all parties to prepare and be comfortable with the conferencing process and outcome. Here the goal is to move all stakeholder participants (i.e., victim, offender, parents/caregiver, and community representative) to the moment where amends, repair, and resolve can be attained for all parties. The process is not intended to be transactional but transformational for the parties involved.

Once enrolled, the girl and parent/caretaker, and a diversion counselor, complete a comprehensive orientation that provides a girl (offender) the opportunity to explore, through verbal and written narratives, what led to her committing the offense. This helps start the process of accountability. Once she is acknowledged and heard, she can then be encouraged to explore the victim's perspective. Next, the diversion counselor discusses what a genuine apology encompasses and offers support and guidance. Finally, the girl writes her apology letter, which consists of an explanation of what caused her to offend, actions for which she will accept responsibility, what she learned from this incident, and how she will make better choices when facing similar situations. The agreed-upon case plan specifically indicates how restoration would be achieved, including community service, restitution, return or repair of property, reflective essay, and so on.

Upon completing the apology letter, the diversion counselor then prepares and coordinates the restorative justice conference by communicating with all parties involved. Participants may include the victim, offender, parents, law enforcement, support person for the offender, support person for the victim, the counselor, therapist, and mediator. The facilitator is typically not the participant's assigned diversion counselor but another program counselor. This allows the facilitating counselor to remain objective throughout the conference. This is vital for all conference attendees to feel validated and understood and that the environment remains impartial.

The diversion counselor prepares attending participants through pre-conferencing efforts by reviewing the goals for the conference and what will be achieved for closure and healing. In preparing for a restorative justice conferencing session, a girl processes and practices with her diversion counselor to ensure she is ready to meet with the victim without the attachment of shame, guilt, or judgment. Instead, the experience is designed to be strength-based and supportive so that the girls take responsibility and accountability for their actions. This allows internal reflection and acceptance before the restorative justice conferencing session occurs. In addition, counseling and trauma response support is also provided, thus mitigating triggers and the re-traumatization of the girl who may have experienced trauma in the past.

The diversion counselors also conduct a preliminary, separate restorative justice pre-conference with the victim to explain the program, process, and purpose. This ensures that they, too, are open, willing, and ready to participate in the conferencing session without fear of retaliation or further victimization. From the victim's vantage point, the goal is healing and finding resolve, and regaining control, a sense of security, and safety. In cases where the victim is uncomfortable participating in the process, victims are encouraged to write a letter that can be read out loud during the restorative justice conferencing session. This helps to bring the voice of the victim to the table. Sometimes, surrogates or trained volunteers, including law enforcement officers, step in to represent the victim's side when victims cannot be reached or contacted. In these cases, the diversion counselor shares a letter of apology and restoration plan with the offender.

When victims, offenders, and community members meet to repair the harm caused by the crime or wrongdoing, the results can be transformational. The diversion counselor does not ask what law or rule was broken, who is responsible, and what punishment should be given. Instead, the concern is with those hurt, their needs, and determining responsibility for making things right. Based on the restoration of the community and the relationships of those residing there, the restorative justice conference is consistently aligned with the values and principles of Pace. During the conference, the diversion counselor establishes a strength-based tone by emphasizing who is responsible for making things right. The girl who has committed the offense reads her apology letter to the victim, and the dialogue focuses on how the victim feels about the incident. The girl, along with the other attendees of the restorative justice conference, explores how she will make things right and creates a restorative justice agreed-upon contract that she will follow to ensure these items are accomplished before successful program completion. Additionally, the girl discusses what she learned from this experience and how she plans to make better choices in the future. Law enforcement helps educate the offender about the law and provides an opportunity for the girl to interact with law enforcement positively. A deputy or officer attends each conference through a partnership with local law enforcement.

Following the restorative justice conference, the offender can write down what she learned from the experience. Reflection questions may include:

- Who did my actions affect?

- How would I feel if I was mistreated in this way?

- What can I do to make things right/better?
- What will I do to prevent this offense from occurring again?
- How do my actions set an example for other youth in our community?

Another critical element in designing the Reach New Day diversionary program is that a girl's decision to enroll is strictly voluntary. Here, a girl and her family decide to either go through the juvenile court process and handle the charges judicially or select the diversionary/civil citation option. In this case, her charges and court processing would be on hold until the girl completes the diversionary program requirements. If the girl does not fulfill the obligation of the diversionary program, she returns to court for her charges to be processed judicially. In the case of a civil citation, a girl's case could be elevated, and charges may be initiated, whereby court sanctions may need to be fulfilled. Although volunteering to enter a diversionary program is offered to all youth, in the case of girls, the ability to choose is directly aligned with Pace's methodology that encourages the ability to regain control, increase self-efficacy, and achieve personal responsibility for their behavior. These are the first steps toward empowerment, growth, and positive decision-making leading to independence.

Girls enrolled in this diversionary program can also utilize the continuum of care services offered by Pace's Academic Day and Reach Therapy programs, including mental health assessments, therapeutic counseling, academic assessments, middle school/high school education, substance abuse intervention therapy, health and wellness services, and referrals for employment and college/work readiness assistance. Maximizing their success by utilizing the "no wrong door" entry option, a girl either choosing not to attend her assigned school, or, if not attending school at all, could elect to enroll in the Pace Day program while simultaneously participating in the Reach New Day diversionary program. Additionally, a girl could enroll in the Day program any time after enrollment in the diversion program or after completing the diversion program to pursue her education and receive additional support services. If a girl needs therapeutic support while in the diversion program, a Reach therapist is also assigned to her care. This holistic and easy-to-access approach ensures the delivery of timely wrap-around services and individual care planning afforded to all girls. The process is designed to meet girls where they currently are and to eliminate all possible barriers. Because circumstances vary for each girl and her family/caregiver, flexibility is necessary, especially when the goal is to gain trust and relationships.

A significant barrier in electing to participate is sometimes the fear of the unknown, a lack of understanding of the diversion process, and possible embarrassment by the girl and her family/caretaker in having been arrested, charged, detained, and diverted which can cause apprehension and mistrust. In addition, shame, anxiety, failure, and self-consciousness impact a girl's self-esteem and create thoughts of hopelessness and helplessness. For these reasons, presenting the program and all its services in a strength-based, unconditional, and supportive manner is fundamental to a girl's success. Furthermore, engaging "girls as girls" and not "juvenile delinquents" creates an atmosphere conducive to growth and development that also decreases risky behaviors.

Experiences, Outcomes, and Lessons Learned

Providing opportunities for adolescent girls and young women to experience restorative justice intervention programming as part of a structurally designed girls' gender-responsive program, like the Pace Reach New Day diversionary program, proved to be highly successful at several levels. First, this program design created an added level of intervention to divert the girls from the justice system while allowing them to be accountable for their actions and safeguard their freedom, youth, and independence. To date, this very successful diversionary program has been operating for over a decade, providing over 800 girls with a life-changing opportunity whereby the trajectory of their lives took a path away from not only juvenile delinquency but, most likely, adult criminal involvement, victimization, substance use, human trafficking, and homelessness.

When designing a diversionary program for girls, acknowledging past trauma, childhood experiences, and other mitigating circumstances related to their charges is critical to ensuring their unique needs are addressed. As Van Wormer and Bartollas (2014) described, to prepare them for this process, the girls often need to get in touch with their own earlier victimization and feelings that were aroused at the time and possibly regressed and transformed into anger. Considering the multiple factors impacting girls who enroll in this diversionary program, team members worked to provide them with the time and support needed to address their circumstances and trauma. "Valuing the wisdom of time" allows for trust and relationships to be built so that healing can take place. Through counseling, goal planning, skill building, and care management, girls are given the time and tools necessary to begin exploring and understanding the relevance of their behavior and learn how to navigate the juvenile justice system to divert their charges while gaining a better understanding of restorative justice processes. Developing decision-making, coping, and accountability skills become life-long tools that girls can access when faced with challenges and new opportunities. In 2021, of the 124 girls served in the Broward New Day program, 89 percent of girls successfully completed the program and had resolution of their cases; 98 percent of these girls did not obtain any new law violations while enrolled in the program, and 97 percent of girls who completed the program did not obtain any further law violations within one-year post completion.

Since its inception, the Pace New Day diversionary program continues to experience great success in helping girls to divert from the juvenile justice system. Through a supportive, nonpunitive, honoring, and restorative practice experience, girls, families, and communities have come to find better ways to resolve conflict. In 2022, 93 percent of the girls who completed the program, including restorative justice conferencing sessions, were engaged in school, employment, or post-secondary education. Moreover, only seven percent of those served recidivated while in the program.

Girls Experiencing Restorative Justice through a Gender-Responsive Lens

CARLA, 17

The State Attorney's Office referred Carla to the Reach diversionary program for a battery charge. Having participated in several months of diversion counseling, group sessions, and service-learning projects, Carla was ready for her restorative justice conferencing. The restorative justice session included her mother, several diversion counselors, and a law enforcement officer, there to represent the victim and the community. Although apprehensive initially, Carla took full responsibility and shared her actions openly, honestly, and remorsefully. She revealed that this experience showed her how she could have done things differently. Carla apologized to everyone and explained how she now had gained better coping strategies and techniques and how these tools would assist her in the future. Carla then listened intently as the law enforcement officer shared her impressions from the victim's perspective and how her actions impacted the community. Because her identified victim did not wish to be present, the Officer read the victim's letter to Carla, explaining her feelings, experience, and how the incident impacted her trust and feeling of security. Carla was able to write a letter of apology that was then mailed to her victim. After completing the program, Carla's charges were expunged, and she graduated in 2022 with a 4.0 GPA. Later that year, Carla was accepted to join the US Army.

MARY, 16

Mary and her mother entered the meeting room and were met by a diversion counselor, community representative—Law Enforcement Officer Brown—and the victim, Ms. Smith. Following a brief introduction, the counselor explained the process of the restorative justice conferencing session. Mary was then asked to share the story that led to her arrest and entry into the diversion program. Mary prepared a letter of apology that she read to all the circle members. In the letter, she shared details about her life, her current circumstances, and what led her and her friend to break into Ms.

Smith's car and steal personal items. Mary also shared that through counseling and group sessions, she now understands how her actions affected herself, the victim, her mother, her siblings, and the community. The girl also explained that she would make better choices in the future. Mary shared that she now sees herself as a leader who knows right from wrong and will use her voice to speak up if peers encourage her to go against her values. Ms. Smith, in turn, shared her experience the night her car was burglarized. Ms. Smith had just come from the nursing home to visit her gravely ill mother; she was so heartbroken and preoccupied that she forgot to take her belongings into the house. She shared that the incident made her feel violated and bewildered. Mary and her mother were tearful as they listened intently to Ms. Smith's every word. Ms. Smith also explained that she appreciated Mary's sincerity and willingness to set things right.

Next, Officer Brown expressed his viewpoint on the incident and how it impacted law enforcement and the community he strives to protect. He encouraged Mary to keep making better choices and continue her path to becoming a leader. He also praised Mary for her participation in his weekly restorative justice healing circle. Mary agreed to pay restitution to Ms. Smith to repair the harm and make things right. All parties signed a contract. Mary paid the restitution as promised. The diversion counselor mailed a money order along with a letter from Mary to Ms. Smith, thanking her and letting her know she successfully completed the program in four months. Mary's charges were expunged a few months later, and after a year of completing the program has not incurred any new charges.

Opportunities Gained and Lessons Learned

There are numerous opportunities and lessons learned from this venture:

1. During the initiation of the program, all team members, program managers, and directors received comprehensive restorative justice training from Dr. Gordon Bazemore and

his team. The training included understanding the historical perspective of restorative justice, establishing program components, and strategies to prepare offenders, victims, and community stakeholders for restorative justice conferencing. Because of their dedication and belief in restorative justice practices, the CSC continues to cover the cost of training team members for all their diversionary funded programs.

2. Since its inception in 2010, Pace has successfully utilized restorative justice with all eligible participants. Over the years, Pace has had the opportunity to attend numerous restorative justice training sessions offered by the CSC. For example, in June 2015, Pace participated in the three-day National Association of Community and Restorative Justice Conference held in Ft. Lauderdale. Moreover, in 2016, Pace representatives attended the three-day restorative justice training facilitated by the River Phoenix Center for Peacebuilding. Additionally, Pace has attended a restorative justice refresher course annually or as offered. The success of restorative justice in the Reach New Day program has fostered the implementation of restorative justice in Pace's Academic Day program to promote collaboration and resolve conflict effectively with long-term positive impact for all participants.

3. As part of the CSC-funded programming, Pace Center for Girls joined the Broward County Diversion Coalition, made up of key community stakeholders responsible for leading efforts to support diversionary and civil citation programming. Monthly meetings focused on increasing diversionary opportunities for youth and leveraging support from the State Attorney's Office, Public Defender Law Enforcement, and private non-profit agencies. Collaboration, best practices, and leveraging stakeholder support to ensure the diversionary programs maximize their impact on the youth they serve is a crucial focus of this group.

4. The evolution of diversionary and restorative justice programming for girls worked to strengthen partnerships with

Juvenile Judges, as well as members of the State Attorney's Office and Public Defenders Office adolescent division. These partnerships help to divert low-end offending girls to alternative services where their needs could be better met while decreasing court processing, recidivism, and costs related to operating these systems.

5. Creating partnerships with local law enforcement departments and officers to gain support for diversionary and civil citation as a viable alternative to charging youth and encouraging their participation in restorative justice conferencing sessions representing community stakeholders has been incredibly beneficial.

6. Facilitating opportunities for girls to see and interact with law enforcement officers in a positive, non-threatening way improves interpersonal relationships with adolescent girls who often have very negative and fearful opinions toward them. In addition, having law enforcement officers engage in restorative justice conferencing, healing circles, and service-learning projects with the girls has helped to strengthen community relations benefiting all stakeholders.

7. Through their work with juvenile justice-involved girls, one of Pace's successful community campaigns lobbied for misdemeanor and civil citation legislation so that law enforcement could censure girls for petty crimes without arresting them. Florida has also funded other prevention measures to keep girls out of the juvenile justice system. As a result, over the past decade, the number of girls arrested annually in Florida has dropped by about 65 percent (Benítez 2021).

8. More recently, Pace was proud to join the Justice Project of South Florida (JPSFL), created in 2015, to facilitate meaningful and positive interactions between law enforcement and marginalized communities, using restorative justice practices as a framework for dialogue. JPSFL is a coalition of law enforcement agencies, social service providers, clergy, businesses, community members at large, academic institutions, and

representatives from the local, state, and federal governments to confront local challenges that mirror the problems surrounding race and police relations across the country. The mission of JPSFL is to reduce arrests and incarceration of youth; increase cultural competency, racial equity, and social justice; and promote positive interactions between law enforcement and communities of color. In addition, JPSFL members hope to eliminate the negative perceptions, stereotypes, and interactions between law enforcement and communities of color. JPSFL has found much success in the practices of police-youth dialogues, restorative justice practices training, cultural sensitivity workshops, restorative justice peace circles, and promoting undoing/dismantling racism initiatives.

Conclusion

According to Zehr (2014), restorative justice is more focused on needs: the needs of those harmed, those causing harm, and the communities in which these situations arise. As such, better outcomes for everyone can be achieved when taking steps to blend restorative justice in programming that offers alternative solutions and support, particularly for marginalized girls.

Reviewing Pace's practical experience of blending restorative justice with gender-responsive programming services for at-risk girls has shown great potential in successfully reducing recidivism while improving girls' lives by developing empathy, pro-social skills, decision-making, resilience, and accountability. The blending of relational theory and gender-responsive programming with restorative justice practices greatly expanded Pace's effort to reduce juvenile crime while helping offenders and victims heal and move toward a restorative outcome. In addition, restorative justice practices blended into a gender-responsive diversionary program for girls have shown tremendous benefits, including economic, by reducing costs associated with detaining and processing youth in the juvenile justice system, yielding negative results.

It is encouraging to see that this innovative program designed by

Pace, with the dedicated support of the Children's Services Council, the late Dr. Bazemore, and community stakeholders, will continue to evolve and create ongoing positive change for the girls, their families, victims, and communities. As noted by Bazemore and Schiff (2006), as more restorative justice conferences occur and the word spreads about the value of these events for informal sanctioning and support of young people and their families and for resolving conflict and harm as an alternative to court, more community members would hopefully participate and thereby expand the pool of efficacious citizens and community groups.

In the end, the blending of gender-responsive and restorative justice does hold great potential in reducing recidivism while improving girls' lives, supporting long-term positive outcomes, and creating a healing experience benefiting the community and its members.

References

Bazemore, G. and Schiff, M. (2006) *Juvenile Justice Reform and Restorative Justice.* London: Routledge.

Benítez, L. (2021) "How Youth Participate in Building Evidence at Pace Center for Girls." Project Evident. https://projectevident.org/wp-content/uploads/2022/08/PaceCenterActionableEvidenceCaseStudyOct2021.pdf

Bloom, B., Owen, B., and Covington, S. (2003) "Gender Responsive Strategies: Research, Practice, and Guiding Principles for Women Offenders." USDOJ, National Institute of Corrections. https://s3.amazonaws.com/static.nicic.gov/Library/018017.pdf

Bright, C.L. and Jonson-Reid, M. (2008) "Onset of juvenile court involvement: Exploring gender specific associations with maltreatment and poverty." *Children and Youth Services Review 30*, 8, 914–927. https://doi.org/10.1016/j.childyouth.2007.11.015

Chesney-Lind, M. and Shelden, R.G. (2014) *Girls, Delinquency, and Juvenile Justice*, 4th edn. Chichester: John Wiley & Sons, Inc.

Covington, S. (2008) "The Relational Theory of Women's Psychological Development: Implications for Criminal Justice Systems." In R.T. Zaplin (ed.) *Female Offenders: Critical Perspectives and Effective Interventions*, 2nd edn. Sudbury, MA: Jones and Bartlett Publishers.

Covington, S. and Bloom, B. (2003) "Gendered Justice: Women in the Criminal Justice System in Gendered Justice." In B. Bloom (ed.) *Gendered Justice: Addressing Female Offenders.* Durham, NC: Carolina Academic Press.

Gilligan, C. (1982) *In a Different Voice: Psychological Theory and Women's Development.* Cambridge, MA: Harvard University Press.

Lodi, E., Perrella, L., Lepri, G.L., Scarpa, M.L., and Patrizi, P. (2022) "Use of restorative justice and restorative practices at school: A systematic literature review."

International Journal of Environmental Research and Public Health 19, 1, 96. doi. org/10.3390/ijerph19010096

Pace Center for Girls (2008) "Faces of Pace: 2008 Annual Report." www.pacecenter. org/media/5qxiadxd/anlrpto8.pdf

Pace Center for Girls (2020) "Our Approach." www.pacecenter.org/about/ our-approach

Presser, L. and Gaarder, E. (2003) "Can Restorative Justice Reduce Battering?" In B. Price and N. Sokoloff (eds) *The Criminal Justice System and Women: Offenders, Prisoners, Victims, and Workers*, 3rd edn. Boston, MA: McGraw Hill.

Treskon, L., Millensky, M., and Freedman, L. (2017) "Helping Girls get Back on Track: An Implementation Study of the Pace Center for Girls." MDRC. www.mdrc.org/ sites/default/files/PACE_Interim_Report_2017-Web.pdf

United Nations Children's Fund (2017) "Gender Equality: Glossary of Terms and Concepts." UNICEF. www.unicef.org/rosa/media/1761/file/ Genderglossarytermsandconcepts.pdf

Van Wormer, K. and Bartollas, C. (2014) *Women and the Criminal Justice System*, 4th edn. Boston, MA: Pearson.

Zavlek, S. and Maniglia, R. (2007) "Developing correctional facilities for female juvenile offenders: Design and programmatic considerations." *Corrections Today* 69, 4, 58–63.

Zehr, H. (2015) *The Little Book of Restorative Justice*. Intercourse, PA: Good Books.

Reflections

The opportunities for restorative justice and continued dialogue to build learnings and construct foundations for the implementation of this work worldwide is inspiring. The distinguished collective of international experts who contributed to this collection with their research, perspectives, and experiences are impactful and thought-provoking in their approach. Reflections of these international restorative justice perspectives in the focus areas of legal systems, education, and community in this volume are far-reaching. The "maximalist agenda of restorative justice" offered by Walgrave in this volume contends the opportunity to divert the system from its retributive and/or treatment focus towards a steadfast priority for restorative responses with an emphasis to be more constructive, provide more standing and support for crime victims, and offer (at a minimum) no fewer opportunities for offender reintegration and rehabilitation than systems grounded in individual treatment assumptions. Further, as examined by Pavelka and Erbe, restorative justice has emerged as a standard in law and policy, incorporating restorative principles and practices to varying degrees, while being considered a contemporary justice solution by countries internationally. Blackburn discussed Pennsylvania's progress towards advancing the statutory mission and the related operational goals through policy, practice, and programmatic enhancements that transformed the state's juvenile justice system.

The importance of readiness assessments to determine their capacity and motivation for change and to decide whether they have the structure and strengths needed to successfully implement a complex initiative, data collection and measurement, and evaluation in its applications in educational settings, community-based non-profits, legal systems, and other organizations is discussed (see chapters by Brown, Teske, Thomas, and Pappas in this volume). The use of restorative practices and interventions and their applications—as discussed in chapters by Pranis, Pappas, McChargue, Pavelka, and Jones, and Pidgeon and Karp—support long-term positive outcomes and address harm with healing experiences and restoration benefiting the affected parties, including victims and survivors (see chapters by Pavelka and Seymour, Otis and Umbreit, and Lewis), and the community. Landry explored the community justice model which provides a means for the community to take an active role in identifying the issues that contribute to criminal and harmful behaviors, to respond to crime, and to provide the necessary community resources to help those impacted by crime and harmful behavior.

For restorative justice to be enduring and sustainable, stakeholders and communities must commit to a paradigm shift from traditional responses to wrongdoing and crime. This change occurs collaboratively and comprehensively and includes crime victims and survivors, legal systems, justice-involved persons, educational settings, and communities. Ultimately, this transition toward restorative justice will result in a more responsive, more effective, and more just world.

Subject Index

ACA Victims and
    Restorative Justice
    Committee 202-3
accountability 55, 67, 131-2
active responsibility 26
apology bank/apology
    classes 212-3
apology letter 283, 284

Balanced and Restorative
    Justice (BARJ)
    adopted in Pennsylvania
        73-8, 81
    competency
        development
        goal 83, 88
    conception of 10
    Court and Community
        Collaboration
        Committee 81
    education about 81
    goal definitions
        83-4, 185-6
    Introduction of
        180, 208-9
    Justice Committee 81
    juvenile justice report
        cards in 187-9, 195
    measuring performance
        185-94
    mission of 182-6
    overview 179-81
    policy and program
        alignment 86-92
    publications about 82-6
    White Papers 82-5
bottom-up approach 28
brief restorative justice
    interventions (b-RJI)
    origins of 244-5

outcomes 246-8
bullying 232

campus police
    distrust for 123-4, 124-6
    firearm presence 123
    student perceptions
        of 122-4
    see also policing;
        restorative policing
        (on campus)
Canada
    implementation in 35-8
    Indigenous people
        34, 35-8
    justice system 35
    legislative mandate
        38-40
    machinery of restorative
        justice 43
    mode of restorative
        justice 44-5
    multiculturalism
        and restorative
        justice 46-7
    R. v Gladue 39
    unicultural perspective
        34-8, 37-8, 47
    Youth Criminal
        Justice Act 39, 41
Carey guides 91
change
    Friedman trans-
        theoretical
        model of 278
    only in an
        uncondemned
        space 66-7, 68
    organizational change
        theories 146-7

circle practices
    in Canada's criminal
        justice system 40, 41
    circle sentencing 36, 41
    the gifts of 68-9
    and listening skills 71
    overview 210-1
    peace circle 115-9
    restorative policing
        132-4
    shift towards 225
    talking piece 71, 210
Clayton County
    Collaborative
        Child Study Team
        (Quad C-ST) 108
coercion, possibility of 20
Community Intensive
    Supervision
    Project (CISP) 74
community justice
    51-4, 56
    see also Village Model of
        community justice
Community Justice
    Center (CJC)
    Nebraska 244-8
Community Justice
    Council 57
community service
    projects 99, 212
competency
    development 55
condemnation 67
confidentiality 253-4
consequential approach
    includes reparative
        sanctions 23
    and the law 25-6
    overview 22-3

consequential
 approach *cont.*
 and the transformative
  agenda 26–7
credentialing 254
criminal justice system
 guiding principles
  25–6
 relationship with
  restorative
  justice 18–20
"criminology of
 trust" 27–8
critical incidents 232–3

dialogue *see* victim
 offender mediation
 (VOM); victim/
 offender dialogue
 (VOD)
Diversion Assessment
 Instrument 105
diversion programs
 New Day diversionary
  programming
  281, 286–92
 Reach Counseling
  program 280–6
 school offense
  diversion 103–6
 voluntary participation
  in 285

"earned redemption" 96
education/training
 for VOM 254
Einstein, Albert 177
emancipatory
 movements 27–8
empathy enhancement
 240–1
ethical breaches 232–3

family group conferencing
 (FGC) 254–5
felony offenses 108, 109
Friedman trans-
 theoretical model
 of change 278

gaps between intention
 and impact 69–71

gender-responsive
 programming
 aligning restorative
  justice with 274–7
 case studies 288–9
 designing 280–6
 foundational
  principles 275–6
 New Day diversionary
  programming
  281, 286–92
 relational needs
  of girls 275
 restorative practice
  interventions 282
 understanding
  underlying
  trauma 274–5
 see also Pace Center
  for Girls
gender-responsive
 theory 273
Georgia Juvenile State
 Advisory Group 114
girls *see* gender-responsive
 programming
graduation rates
 improvement in 113
 relationship with
  crime rates 102

harassment 232
harmed people *see* victim
hate crimes 232–3
holistic approach 8,
 96, 111–3, 234

imitator paradox 18
implementation
 fidelity 144
implementation
 science 148–9
Indigenous people
 knowledge 252
 restorative justice in
  Canada 34, 35–8

judges
 detention decision-
  making of 99
 perception of role
  with victims 98

Justice Reinvestment
 Initiative (JRI) 213
Juvenile Court Procedural
 Rules Project 82
Juvenile Detention
 Alternatives Initiative
 (JDAI) 105
juvenile justice
 absence of a mission
  178–9
 performance measures
  in 176–9, 181, 194–6
 report cards 187–9, 195
 statements of mission
  in 182–3
Juvenile Justice and
 Child Welfare
 Collaborative 105–6
Juvenile Justice Model
 Data Project 195–6

language 227–9
learned behavior 64
"Listening Project,
 The" 220–3

marginalized
 communities 233
"Massachusetts
 Experiment" 103
maximalist approach
 17–8, 21–2
*Measuring What Really
 Matters in Juvenile
 Justice* 176–7, 196–7
mediation *see* victim
 offender mediation
 (VOM)
Miller, Jerome 103
mindfulness 254
misdemeanor crimes 53
misimplementation
 models 169
Models for Change
 juvenile justice
 reform initiative 89
Mothers Against
 Drunk Driving
 (MADD) 200–1
motivational
 interviewing 90
movement theory 223

Subject Index

multiculturalism (in US and Canada) 45-7

National Association of Victim Assistance in Corrections 202
National Organization for Victim Assistance 200, 260
nondisclosure agreements 253-4

objective vs. process-focused view 19-20
offender-centric services 221
"offenderless" victims 234-5
Office of Victim Advocate (OVA) 78
organizational change theories 146-7

Pace Center for Girls
  intervention strategies 279
  logic model of 277-80
  opportunities and lessons from 289-92
  overview 272-4
  Reach Counseling program 280-6
  therapeutic support 285-6
  values and principles 278-9
  see also gender-responsive programming
past crimes 234-5
peace circle 115-9
  see also circle practices
Pennsylvania
  Act 86 (Bill of Rights for Victims of Juvenile Crime) 86-7
  Balanced and Restorative Justice (BARJ) adopted in 73-8, 81
  BARJ policy and program alignment 86-92
  BARJ White Papers 82-5
  Center for Juvenile Justice Training and Research (CJJT&R) 86
  Commission on Crime and Delinquency (PCCD) 79
  community service projects 99
  Council of Chief Juvenile Probation Officers (PCCJPO) 80
  Crime Victims Act 86-7
  decentralized juvenile justice system in 78-9
  goals for juvenile justice in 76-7
  Juvenile Act (42 PaCS Section 6301) 75-7
  Juvenile Court Judges' Commission (JCJC) 79
  Juvenile Justice and Delinquency Prevention Committee (JJDPC) 80
  Juvenile Justice Outcome Measures 85-6
  Juvenile Justice System Enhancement Strategy (JJSES) 89-91
  key state agencies in 79-80
  mission statement for juvenile justice 77-8
  National Center for Juvenile Justice (NCJJ) 80, 85
  Office of Victim Advocate (OVA) 78, 80
  Victim of Juvenile Offender (VOJO) advocates 87
  Victim Services Advisory Committee (VSAC) 80, 81
performance measurement in Balanced and Restorative Justice (BARJ) 185-94
  current state of 194-6
  data collection 186-7
  defensible basis for 189-91
  definition of measures 190
  Juvenile Justice Model Data Project (MDP) 195-6
  lack of in juvenile justice system 178-9
  Measuring What Really Matters in Juvenile Justice 176-7, 196-7
  rationales for 191-2
  standards for choosing measures 192-4
  traditional efforts 176-8
personal nature of crime 204
policing
  national conversation about (2020) 127
  trust 109
  see also campus police; restorative policing (on campus)
policy, emergence of restorative justice in 34-5
process vs. objectives-focused view 19-20
punishment 24

R. v Gladue 39
Reach Counseling program 280-6
readiness assessments
  definition of "not ready" 150-1
  definition of "ready" 149-50
  done over time 151
  general capacity 152, 158

— 299 —

readiness assessments
cont.
  implementation
    science 148-9
  innovation (RJE)-
    specific capacity
    152-3
  motivation 153-4
  not dichotomous 150
  organizational change
    theories 146-7
  purpose of 143
  R=MC² assessment
    process 154-5
  R=MC² case study: high
    school 156-65
  R=MC² case study:
    middle school 165-9
  R=MC² overview 151-4
  *Restorative Justice
    Practices Tiered
    Fidelity Inventory
    for School-Wide
    Implementation* 145
  school leaders 146-7
  see also restorative
    justice in
    education (RJE)
recidivism rates 91-2,
  109-10, 240-1, 246-7
"reconciliation" (term
  dropped) 227
reintegration, restorative
  justice and 239
reparative boards 211
reparative sanctions 23-4
report cards (juvenile
  justice) 187-9, 195
reporting rates
  (crimes) 205
restorative censuring 25-6
restorative
  conferencing 211
restorative justice
  and active
    responsibility 26
  balanced approach in 55
  definition 17, 55-6
  emergence in law and
    policy 34-5, 201-2
  inconsistency of 222
  in legislation 208-9
  limits to 22, 23

normative theory of 184
purist vs. maximalist
  approach 18-20
recent shifts in 224-7
recommitment to
  original principles
  of 229-30
relationship with justice
  system 18-20
values of 18-20
Restorative Justice
  Division (RJD) 109
restorative justice in
  education (RJE)
  misimplementation
    models 169
  overview 142-3
  process evaluation
    role 170
  purpose of 143
  sustainability of 143-6
  see also readiness
    assessments
restorative justice
  interventions
  overview 240-1
  Victims First Team
    241-4
  see also brief restorative
    justice interventions
    (b-RJI)
*Restorative Justice
  Practices Tiered
  Fidelity Inventory
  for School-Wide
  Implementation* 145
*Restorative Juvenile Justice:
  Repairing the Harm of
  Youth Crime* (1999) 29
restorative policing
  (on campus)
  accountability 131-2
  benefits of 124-6
  case study: University of
    San Diego 126-37
  commitments 135-7
  compassion 130
  engagement outside
    of incident
    response 130
  improved
    communication 129
  mutuality 129

overview 121-2
partnership 132-5
sustainable change
  through 137
trust 130
understanding
  needs 127-30
restorative practices
  apology bank/apology
    classes 212-3
  reparative boards 211
  restorative community
    service 212
  restorative
    conferencing 211
  victim impact
    classes 211-2
  victim/offender
    dialogue 209-10
  see also circle practices
retraumatization 258
retributivism 25, 26
revictimization 258
*Road Less Traveled,
  The* 96-7

"School Reduction Referral
  Protocol" 107-8
School-Justice
  Partnership 107-10
schools
  arrests in 100-2, 111
  conditions and use
    of restorative
    justice 266
  in loco parentis duty 100
  leaders in 146-7
  offense diversion 103-6
  see also readiness
    assessments;
    restorative justice
    in education (RJE)
shame 70
shifts in restorative justice
  (recent) 224-7
Standardized Program
  Evaluation Protocol
  (SPEP) 91
structural inequality 26-8
Supervised Track and
  Phase Supervision
  (STAPS) 97-8

Subject Index

surrogate offenders 235
surrogate victims 231, 235, 241, 242–3, 244

talking piece 71, 115–6, 210
Ten Signposts for Victim Involvement 221, 237
terminology 227–9
top-down approach 18
training/education for VOM 254
transformative agenda 26–7, 28, 223
trauma history 108, 207, 274–5, 287
trauma-informed practice 204

uncondemned spaces 66–7, 68
US
  colonial influence 36
  cultural influences in 36
  implementation of restorative justice in 35–8
  justice system 35
  legislative mandate 38–40
  machinery of restorative justice 42–3
  mode of restorative justice 43–4
  multiculturalism and restorative justice 45–7
  overrepresentation of black populations within justice system 36–7
  pluralist perspective 34–8
  research into restorative practice in 37
  restorative justice cited in state laws/codes 35, 39

values
  in restorative justice 18–20
  shared with emancipatory movements 27–8
victim
  ACA Victims and Restorative Justice Committee 202–3
  assistance field in US 200–1
  autonomy of 205–6
  broadening identities of 226, 228
  commonalities with offender 230
  core rights of 206–7
  guiding principles of victim- and survivor-centered restorative justice 203–7
  integral role of 215–6
  language of labeling the 227–9
  listening to gaps of service for 220–4
  mediation satisfaction rates 222
  National Association of Victim Assistance in Corrections 202
  new recommendations for engaging 230–5
  "offenderless" 234–5
  surrogate 231, 235, 241, 242–3, 244
  Ten Signposts for Victim Involvement 221, 237
  trauma history of 207
victim blaming 252
victim impact classes 211–2
victim offender mediation (VOM)
  in the 1970s 256–7
  in the 1980s 257–9
  in the 1990s 259–63
  in the 2000s 263–5
  2010s to today 265–6
  dominant model in US 41
  education/training for 254
  endorsed by American Bar Association 260
  location of 257–8
  overview 252–5
  participants 253
  timing of 257
Victim Offender Reconciliation Program (VORP) 41
victim/offender dialogue (VOD) 203, 209–10
victimology's increased scope 219–20
Victims of Crime Act (1984) 201
Victims First Team 241–4
Village Model of community justice
  Community Justice Council 57
  community role 59
  corrections officials role 61–2
  courts role 61
  creation of 53–4
  goal of 56
  law enforcement role 60
  objectives 56–7
  operations of 58
  programmatic components 59
  prosecutor/state attorney role 61
  roles in 59–62
  schools role 60
  strategic planning process 57–8

women see gender-responsive programming

youth
  circle practice with 68–9
  consistency of adults' behavior with 65–6, 69–71
  control and punishment used with 66–7
  listening to 69–71
  modeling respect and dignity to 64–5
Youth Justice Committees (Canada) 41

— 301 —

Author Index

Abolitionist University 123
Achilles, M. 221, 237
Aiello, M.F. 123
Alegre, I. 182
Allegheny County
   Juvenile Justice 195
Allen, A. 123
Amstutz, L. 147
Anderson Hooker, D. 18
Armour, M. 222,
   255, 265, 266
Armstrong, T. 73, 180
Attrill, S. 143, 144, 145,
   146, 150, 154

Baehler, K. 25
Balanced Restorative
   Justice Project 208
Bartollas, C. 277, 287
Bazemore, G. 14, 17, 19,
   37, 43, 54, 96, 98, 121,
   122, 127, 128, 131, 132,
   176, 178, 179, 183, 184,
   188, 190, 191, 197, 251,
   255, 256, 262, 293
Beck, A.J. 207
Beckman, K. 170
Bender, J. 256, 257
Benítez, L. 278, 279, 291
Berbegal-Mirabent, J. 182
Bergseth, K. 240
Berkowitz, K. 145
Beyer, L.L. 230
Blake, M. 230
Blood, P. 146
Bloom, B. 275, 276
Bonta, J. 262
Borton, I.M. 265
Bouffard, J. 240

Boyes-Watson, C. 146
Braithwaite, J. 18, 23,
   26, 201, 254
Bralley, J. 98
Breslin, B. 147
Bright, C.L. 275
Bromley, M. 125
Brown, M.A. 144, 146, 147,
   148, 149, 153, 162, 164,
   167, 168, 169, 170, 171
Bureau of Justice
   Statistics 204, 205
Burns, H. 264
Butler, S. 228

Campbell, C. 244
Canto, A.I. 125
Canuto, M. 221
Center for Justice and
   Peacebuilding 261
Center for Restorative
   Justice and
   Peacemaking 260
Chesney-Lind, M. 274
Childress, C. 122, 127
Choi, J.J. 265
Christie, N. 18
Claessen, J. 23, 24
Coates, R.B. 256,
   259, 261, 264
Cooper, M. 240
Correctional Services
   Canada 40
Covington, S. 274, 275, 276
Crawford, A. 243
Crifasi, C. 125
Cuevas, C.A. 207

Daly, K. 23

Dary, T. 113
Davidson, M. 122, 127
Deal, N. 98
Deal, T. 196
Deane, M.H. 125
DeMilio, L. 240
Dhami, M. 240
Di Lallo, S. 170
Dignan, J. 23
Dowden, C. 240, 263
Draper, L. 125
Duff, A. 23, 144
Dzur, A. 28

Elias, M.J. 146
Ernest, K. 37
Evans, K. 142, 146, 147,
   162, 164, 169

Farolan, C. 122
Federal-Provincial-
   Territorial Working
   Group on Restorative
   Justice 37
Feld, B.C. 179
Forgays, D. 240
Fox, D. 240
Frampton, M.L. 146
Freedman, L. 275
Freivalds, P. 180
Fullan, M. 143, 162, 170

Gaarder, E. 276
Gaudreault, A. 221, 222
Gehm, J. 259, 261
Gelpi, A. 125
Giardino, L.F. 179
Gilbert, M.J. 265

Author Index

Gilligan, C. 275
Glaze, L. 207
Glynn, T. 144
Goldring, E. 146
Gougelet, K. 123
Gravelle, J. 122, 127
Green, D.L. 265
Greenwood, J. 253, 262
Gregory, A. 162, 164, 169
Griffith, J.D. 125
Griffiths, C. 121, 128
Guerrero, A. 182

Hall, G.E. 146
Hancock, K. 125
Hansen, T. 37, 254
Harp, C. 176, 177, 180, 182, 193
Harris, N. 23
Hart, H.L.A. 24
Heetderks Strong, K. 18
Herlitz, L. 144
Hernández, L. 123
Herting, J.R. 105
Hines, D. 121, 122, 131, 132
Hokšíla, W. 37, 252
Hopkins, B. 146, 147
Hoppey, D. 146
Hord, S.M. 146
Hoyle, C. 18
Huff, J. 146

IIRP (International Institute for Restorative Practices) 257
Inoue, M. 123

Jacobs, L. 239
Jacques, S. 123
James, D. 207
James, V. 123
Johnson, M.E. 124, 125
Johnson, R.P. 125
Jones, J. 243
Jonson-Reid, M. 275
Juvenile Court Judges' Commission 78, 79, 82, 85, 86, 90

Kalanj, B. 261
Karp, D.R. 122, 123, 147

Kennedy, J. 240
Kingkade, T. 123
Kingston, B. 149, 150
Kirkwood, S. 18

Latimer, J. 240, 263
Laub, J.H. 105, 106
Lawton, B.A. 123
Leung, M. 257
Lewicki, R.J. 125, 254
Lewis, T. 223, 227, 228, 235
Lieberman, M.G. 156, 159
Lightfoot, E. 264
Lipsey, M.W. 91
Llewellyn, J. 18, 21, 26
Lochner, L. 102
Lodi, E. 276
London, R. 24

McChargue, D. 240, 246
McCluskey, G. 143, 147
McCold, P. 18, 20, 23, 251
McKinney, R. 144
McLeskey, J. 146
McQuade, K.M. 204
Maloney, D. 73, 75, 180
Maniglia, R. 276
Mantle, G. 240
Margolis, G. 123
Marshall, L.E. 240
Marshall, T. 18, 240
Marshall, W.L. 240
Maryfield, B. 240
May, H. 146, 167
Mazzucato, C. 23
Mika, H. 220, 221
Millensky, M. 275
Miller, J. 103
Moore, M. 144
Morris, J.D. 156, 158
Morrison 168, 170
Morrison, B. 146, 147
Muise, D. 240, 263
Mullet, J.H. 147
Myrent, M. 240

NACRJ (National Association of Community and Restorative Justice) 42, 261
Newburn, T. 243

Nor, S.M. 126
Norton, B. 125
Nugent, W. 262, 264
Nussbaum, M. 24

O'Brien, S. 13, 54, 56, 58
Office of Juvenile Justice and Delinquency Prevention 73, 75, 176
O'Mahony, D. 244
Owen, B. 276

Pace Center for Girls 280
Paddock, J. 262
Paul, G.D. 265, 266
Pavelka, S. 35, 36, 39, 40, 47, 179, 180, 181, 199, 201, 208, 239, 240, 260, 263, 266
Pavlich, G. 18
Payne, A. 266
Pemberton, A. 19
Pennsylvania Commission on Crime and Delinquency 89, 90
Pennsylvania Juvenile Court Judges' Commission 92
Pew Charitable Trusts 216
Pickeral, T. 113
Piggot, E. 37
Pointer, L. 125
Pranis, K. 18, 127, 132, 201, 261
Presser, L. 276
Prevost, J. 98
Przybylski, R. 240

Ravani, S. 123
Reaves, B. 122, 123, 126
Reimer, K. 149
Reno, J. 243
Reuland, M. 125
Richner, K.A. 240, 246
Riestenberg, N. 143, 147
Robinson, E.V. 240
Roche, D. 240
Rodriguez, N. 123, 265
Rogers, C. 122, 127
Rogers, R. 240
Romig, D. 73, 180
Rooney, J. 262

Roslan, S. 126
Rossner, M. 23

Saleebey, D. 194
SAMHSA (Substance Abuse Mental Health Services Administration) 150, 204
Sammons, P. 146
Sampson, R.J. 105, 106
Sanchez, R. 121
Saulnier, A. 244
Savasta, M. 123
Sayers, D. 121
Scaccia, J.P. 145, 146, 149, 150, 151, 152, 153
Schachter, M. 122, 123
Schenck-Hamlin, W.J. 266
Schiff, M. 18, 37, 43, 54, 293
Schiraldi, V. 103
Scott Peck, M. 96
Segal, E. 125
Shank, G. 254
Shelden, R.G. 274
Sherman, L.W. 240
Shtull, P. 123
Sickmund, M. 75
Silverman, C.J. 146
Sivasubramaniam, D. 244
Snyder, H. 75
Splett, J.W. 143, 149
Statistics Canada 46
Stauffer, C. 223, 227, 228
Stein, A. 122
Strang, H. 201
Strong, K.H. 55, 62, 127, 185
Stuart, B. 36
Sullivan, D. 21, 26
Summers, L. 123
Sumner, M.D. 146, 147
Suzuki, M. 23
Sweeten, G. 101

Takagi, P. 254
Teske, S. 102
Thacker, P. 123
Thomas, D. 47, 178, 181, 182, 186, 187, 188, 189, 199, 239
Thorsborne, M. 143, 146
Tifft, L. 21, 26
Tomlinson, E.C. 125
Torbet, P. 75

Treskon, L. 275, 278
Turner, B. 143
Tyler, T. 23

Umbreit, M. 37, 41, 201, 222, 253, 254, 255, 26, 258, 259, 261, 262, 263, 264, 265, 266
United Nations Children's Fund 273
University of San Diego 126
University of San Diego Department of Public Safety 126
University of San Diego Department of Residential Administration 126
UW Implementation Science Resource Hub 148

Vaandering, D. 142, 146, 147, 168
Valandra, E. 37, 252
Van Ness, D. 18, 55, 62, 127, 185, 255
Van Wormer, K. 277, 287
VictimLaw 206
von Hirsch, A. 24
Vos, B. 256, 263, 264

Walgrave, L. 17, 19, 22, 23, 25, 27, 28, 127, 184
Walker, S.C. 105
Wallace-Capretta, S. 262
Watson, A.K. 151
Wearmouth, J. 144, 147
Weingart, J. 256
Weisburg, J. 124, 125
Welch, K. 266
Wemmers, J. 19, 221
Williams, R. 125
Wood, W. 37
Wright, J.C. 125

Xiaoyu, Y. 23

Young, M.A. 260
Young, R. 121
Youth Justice Board for England and Wales 144, 146

Zavlek, S. 276
Zehr, H. 25, 36, 131, 201, 221, 237, 255, 258, 261, 262, 273, 276, 292
Zins, J.E. 146